Public Sector
Accounting and
Financial Control

Public Sector Accounting and Financial Control

SECOND EDITION

Douglas Henley

Formerly Comptroller and Auditor General
Adviser, Deloitte, Haskins and Sells

Clive Holtham

Director of Finance
London Borough of Hammersmith and Fulham

Andrew Likierman

London Business School

John Perrin

Emeritus Professor of the University of Warwick
Honorary Fellow of the University of Exeter

Published in cooperation with CIPFA

 Van Nostrand Reinhold (UK) Co. Ltd

First published in 1983
Reprinted 1983, 1985
Second edition 1986

Van Nostrand Reinhold (UK) Co. Ltd
Molly Millars Lane, Wokingham, Berkshire, England

Typeset in 10 on 11pt Palatino by
Columns Ltd, Reading

Printed in Great Britain by
Billing & Sons Ltd, Worcester

British Library Cataloguing in Publication Data

Public sector accounting and financial control.—
    2nd ed.— (The VNR series in accounting and
    finance)
    1. Finance, Public — Great Britain — Accounting
    I. Henley, *Sir* Douglas   II. Chartered Institute
    of Public Finance and Accountancy
    657'.835'00941   HJ9925.G6

    ISBN 0–442–31751–4

Contents

Contents

Preface

Since the first edition of this book was written in 1982, there have been notable advances in recognizing the importance of the financial disciplines which it covers. In the field of central government, the early tentative steps to implement the financial management initiative have been taken much further, and managerial improvements have been made an important part of the government's strategy for the civil service. In local government, pressures arising from economic restraint have accelerated the need for improved financial planning and control and better accountability for spending and assets. A number of nationalized industries have been privatized since the last edition and when the new one was being prepared a further attempt was being made to establish an acceptable framework for accountability. The water industry, formerly treated on a quasi-commercial public utility basis, has become subject to nationalized industry disciplines. In the Health field there has been yet another reorganization, with radical initiatives to involve hospital doctors for the first time as budget holders accountable for the volume and cost of their services for patients. In the external audit field, major institutional change has been achieved with the creation of the National Audit Office and the establishment of the Audit Commission, in both cases giving statutory recognition to important advances in approach and technique.

These and other developments have reinforced the need for a well-informed group of professionally trained people at all levels of seniority and experience, who understand the financial structures of the public sector and can apply their specialist skills and informed judgement in the operation of existing policies and in advising on new ones.

The main aim of this book remains what it was three years ago – to help to improve financial management and control in the public sector by these practitioners and those who are studying to join them. A new edition is necessary to ensure up-to-date treatment of the subject. It recognizes that what was until recently the somewhat slow-moving world of financial control is now in the forefront of managerial thinking throughout the public sector.

Douglas Henley, Clive Holtham,
Andrew Likierman, John Perrin

Foreword

Noel Hepworth, OBE, IPFA, DPA
Director, Chartered Institute of Public Finance and Accounting

Accountancy in the public sector is about financial management. Those accountants who define their role either implicitly or explicitly in traditional terms as a keeper or inspector of accounts are not able to provide the style of accountancy expertise which public sector financial management now requires. Therefore accountants, if they are to be successful, while they need an accounting technical background, also require a thorough understanding of the political and economic climate in which the public sector in general, and their part in particular, has to operate. But they also need to recognize that politics is as much about relationships between institutions as between political parties.

The public sector, though, is not a uniform organization. Parts of it are very similar to and are subject to the same influences as commercial organizations, yet because they are part of the public sector, the final sanction of bankruptcy does not exist. Other parts operate as commercial organizations but in practice are in their own field monopolies and are consequently subject to constraints other than those of the market place to prevent exploitation of the consumer or to promote value for money. Other parts of the public sector could in no way be described as running commercial services, hence trading and profit and loss accounts are entirely inappropriate ideas, but the problems remain of how to contain costs, measure performance, and promote value for money.

Value for money is of underlying concern throughout the whole of the public sector. It surfaces in the need for consistent planning; for clarity in the statement of institutional or policy objectives; for the adequate recording of events; and for review of achieved performance against objectives. Value for money is an expression of the economy, the efficiency and the effectiveness with which the institutions of the public sector operate.

The different parties involved in the management of public sector institutions have different interests. Perhaps the most important difference of interest is between the politician and the professional manager or administrator. The politician has a relatively short time horizon, often no more distant than the date of the next election; the professional manager is concerned with the long-run success of his service or activity but he has to discharge his responsibilities under whichever political party controls the government or local authority. The difference is most marked over attitudes towards capital investment where consistency of decision and long lead times may be required but are not always forthcoming, for example investment in nuclear power generation. Again, political success in terms of potential electoral gain may be regarded from the professional manager's point of view as a failure. An example of this is a decision to manipulate the prices of the products of the nationalizeed industries for reasons which are unrelated to the interests of those industries, to optimal resource use, or even in the longer term to the interests of their customers. Divergence of interest may sometimes emerge between different parts of the public sector – for example, between the Treasury and other central government departments; between both and the nationalized industries; between central and local government; between the Department of Health and Social Security and the regional health authorities. These differences of interest may lead to a concentration by one party on a definition of success which the other may not subscribe to. The Treasury may define success as causing spending departments and local authorities to keep within defined public expenditure plans and the nationalized industries to keep within their external financing limits. Their paramount concern is the management of the economy and the control of total public spending. But the central government also has a concern about the efficiency with which the public sector operates, and cash limits and external financing limits can be used in a crude generalized way to impose a resource squeeze upon the affected organization in an attempt to force out greater efficiency. In a sense this does create the opportunity for a coincidence of interest with the manager of the industry or local authority service. He has a direct interest in maximizing value for money in order to enable him to provide the most efficient and effective service in response to demand. But in practice this coincidence of interest may not emerge and in the face of constant pressure on public sector resources the relationship between the central government and the other institutions of the public sector has tended to be one of greater or less friction.

A complicating factor in all of these relationships is inflation. The economist is well used intellectually to the problems which inflation brings. But the accountant has only latterly sought to find ways of showing the impact in accounting terms of inflation upon the performance of any organization. The accounting standard which has been devised to allow for the effects of inflation has as its objective the informing of shareholders of the effects of inflation upon the operation of their business and the consequences for themselves as shareholders. This is clearly an inappropriate standard to apply to the non-commercial public sector where capital expenditure is met either from the proceeds of borrowing on public credit or from public revenues, as in central government and the health service.

Yet what is clear is that the accountant in the public sector must recognize that inflation has important effects. These can distort the management of the undertaking unless properly recognized, can make day-to-day budgetary control and cash flow control difficult, can distort pricing policies whether or not attempts are made to recover full costs, can change the relative value of assets employed, and can lead to an unplanned switch of economic resources into the public sector where private sector pricing responds to inflation and public sector pricing does not.

The nationalized industries have adopted current cost accounting using the principles set out in the relevant accounting standard. The trading undertakings, run directly as part of central government, prepare their accounts using the same principles. The accounts of local authority direct labour organizations follow this pattern as well.

But outside these parts of the public sector the implications of price movement have not been fully recognized. For example, with local authorities, annual budgets are usually fixed on a November price base, with central reserves or contingencies being set aside to finance inflation as it occurs. The service manager's weekly or monthly statement of costs incurred includes inflation and throughout the financial year the actual price level is moving away from the November date. The service manager's problem is then how to identify the element of cost associated with the underlying level of service and the element caused by price change.

The role of the accountant in the public sector should be to organize accounting systems so that the redistributive effects of inflation upon the equity interests of the different parties is properly recognized. Management's responsibility (probably the political management's) is then to make decisions about how and when the different equity interests should in fact be redistributed or restored to their original position.

For example, basing council rents upon historic costs gives a benefit to the tenant in an unplanned way because the extent of the benefit depends entirely upon the incidence of inflation. The use of current cost accounting would identify that benefit (at least to a degree) and a political managerial decision could then be made about what was the proper benefit for the tenant to get.

Current cost accounting as at present conceived may not be the ideal system for controlling the distribution of equity but it is a workable system capable of adaptation and evolution. The problem of managing the public sector and of maintaining the efficiency of public sector operations has become more difficult with inflation. The accountant needs to recognize first that that has occurred and consequently what ought to be done to respond to the circumstances created by inflation.

Finance permeates most organizations because it is the measure of resource use and of priorities, but to provide a sensible message to management, finance needs to be related to work done or performance. The traditional attitude towards budget preparation and the provision of information to management has been a concern with cash. Obviously this is important because of the significance of cash flow management. In the private sector the developing position of the company treasurer (a post which exists also in some nationalized industries) recognizes this. But the accountant's role, particularly in the public sector, goes beyond that. The emphasis of central government controls upon the institutions of the public sector is certainly upon cash and the accountant needs to have the expertise to understand how far in the interests of his organization the rules governing the cash controls can be developed and defined. The accountant, though, needs to strive to establish a workable relationship between cash and organization performance because only the two combined give any real understanding of the efficiency with which the organization is operating. And that relationship needs to be established on a systematic basis, not limited to the result of ad hoc enquiries about which management may occasionally think.

In the trading part of the public sector, target rates of return can be established and performance compared with the target. But elsewhere the problem is more difficult to solve. In theory output measures should be developed as indicators of performance, but in practice such measures are difficult, indeed frequently impossible, to devise. The main source of information available to the accountant and manager is therefore about inputs – the number of employees, their pay levels, expenditure on textbooks and class materials, the number of hospital beds maintained; or at best 'intermediate outputs' – miles of motorway constructed, usage of vehicles, occupancy of hospital beds and so on. The financial manager in these circumstances needs a comparative yardstick to evaluate performance. That yardstick may be the performance of the same organization in a previous period or the performance of another organization.

Local authorities are particularly good at publishing comparative information at the most detailed level. Within the health service comparative information is also available, but not easily accessible to the public. The nationalized industries have developed a wide range of performance measures individually but there is no way of systematically comparing the discharge of similar functions between industries. To make comparative information more widely available for analysis would be particularly helpful to the public sector accountant in providing management with better performance indicators.

While the public sector accountant has the responsibility of developing systematic arrangements to assist management in comparing and improving the performance of the service or institution, the public sector auditor has, among other duties, the complementary role of examining whether management actually performs that task efficiently. In this way, the responsibility of the public sector auditor, apart from the auditor of the nationalized industries which are subject to the same type of audit as private companies, goes beyond the responsibility of auditors to companies in the private sector. Like them, the public sector auditor has to satisfy himself that the accounts have been prepared in accordance with statutory and constitutional requirements and regulations, and that proper accounting practices have been observed in their compilation. But in addition to this he has other responsibilities, including those which in the local authority context take the form of satisfying himself that the accounts 'do not disclose any significant loss arising from waste, extravagance, inefficient financial administration, poor value for money, mistake or other cause'. That is a fairly wide, not to say daunting, remit.

The Chartered Institute of Public Finance and Accountancy has recognized these special responsibilities in its training arrangements for accountants in the public sector. It not only aims to provide basic technical skills, but emphasizes within its training scheme the need to develop financial management and audit skills, including analytical skills, within the context of the special requirements of the public sector including a knowledge of public sector finance, economics and institutional relationships.

This book is written for this style of accountant and auditor, and for others engaged in financial management in the public sector. The authors have examined the financial control mechanisms that affect the different institutions within the public sector at various levels, including those of policy formulation, policy control and intra public sector institutional relationships.

Critics of the public sector tend to adopt a simplistic approach to the management of its institutions. They frequently fail to recognize the political element in management and to detach their own political judgements in making criticisms of the non-political managers in the public sector. The skill of the successful professional manager in the public sector is to be able to cooperate fully with the political policy maker but to retain that degree of independence which enables him to work just as closely with the present political policy maker's opponent should that prove necessary in the future, and to retain the confidence of both. But to do that the manager has to have a thorough understanding of the environment in which he operates as well as the appropriate techniques. This is an authoritative book which fills a significant gap and will help him gain that understanding.

1

Introduction

Financial management and control issues in the public sector have become the focus of increasing attention in recent years. Cuts in public expenditure have been one cause. These have put pressure on public authorities to maintain services with less money (in real terms) and to do so they have had to improve their financial analysis so that action can be taken to improve efficiency and value for money. Another cause has been the call for improved measures of performance, as part of pressure for stronger accountability. This has brought accounting practices in public services under scrutiny. A third cause has been pressure within the accountancy profession to standardize accounting practices and to examine whether public sector practices should not be brought more into line with those in the private sector. Finally, on the heels of government interest in cutting expenditure and trying to improve performance and accountability in the public services, all the professional accountancy institutes have become more interested in public sector practice. No doubt this is because they feel that their members have marketable skills to help improve accounting and performance information.

At the same time, many accountants in the public services have become more conscious of, and more concerned about, the differences of methodology and of philosophy which have separated their work from that of the other branches of the accountancy profession. This may have been the result of interests widened by the various (aborted) attempts to integrate the profession. It may stem also from cross-fertilization of thinking resulting from the increased mobility of accountants from different backgrounds. There were certainly moves into new branches of public service employment following the reorganization in the 1970s and 1980s of, for example, local authorities, the National Health Service and water authorities. The moves to encourage the public sector to behave more like the private sector and privatization in the 1980s also helped to break a number of barriers. But these pressures have become more insistent and more political in recent years, as those who believe that the public sector is chronically inefficient have moved to the centre of the political stage. Such people have maintained with increasing vehemence that the only way to remedy the position is to transfer the provision of services where at all possible to the private sector, and that what remains in the public sector should follow private sector financial and management practices.

In general the public sector has not succeeded in mobilizing support for its own ways of doing things, and the political attacks at national level have been reinforced by calls at the local elected level for improved efficiency. All this has undoubtedly led to lower morale in many public sector bodies, even though there are considerable misgivings about whether much of what is done in the private sector is in practice transferable. Accountants have not been immune to this fall in morale, though their status within the public sector may well have risen because of the increased importance attached to financial skills.

As a result of all these pressures and influences, there has been a growing self-consciousness among accountants in the public sector about following practices which are markedly different from those in the private sector or which do not receive the understanding and approval of fellow accountants and financial managers in other sectors. There has also been a good deal of questioning, not only in the public sector but throughout the accounting profession, about whether or not some public sector accounting practices are anyway conceptually sound. The attempts in recent years to establish the authority of the Accounting Standards Committee (ASC), and to improve the degree of cooperation between separate professional institutes in the quest for improvement and greater standardization of accounting and financial practices, have served to intensify this self-questioning. A more visible sign of the need for action in the public sector was the establishment, early in 1982, of an ASC standing sub-committee – the Public Sector Liaison Group – to explore how far the scope of present accounting standards, or other new standards or guidelines, might appropriately be extended within the public sector.

1.1 THE ISSUES

Some of the financial and accounting issues which have been the subject of public debate, for example external reporting and monitoring, are common to several parts of the public sector, and these are dealt with in this book. Some of these are conceptual issues, some practical. Some are related to external reporting and monitoring, others to internal financial control. But two general questions arise.

The first concerns how specific accounting and control problems should be tackled in a public sector context. Such problems arise because of the distinctive constitutional, economic and financial features of public sector bodies. These are bound to affect the way in which their operations are accounted for and controlled. Areas of special concern include, for example, the implications of financing through public funds, the treatment of capital equipment and capital financing and the need to provide non-financial indicators to supplement financial data because of the non-profit basis of most parts of the public sector.

The second question, following naturally from the first, is how far should public sector practice relate to practice in the private sector and in what respects, if any, should it diverge? This question has been asked about most aspects of financial reporting, including the form of financial statements and the treatment of individual items in the accounts, such as capital asset valuation and depreciation. The question is also asked about internal financial and economic issues, such as the use of investment appraisal techniques and monitoring.

The fact that issues cannot be taken in isolation applies to almost all the main issues covered in this book. For example, questions about the form of external financial statements clearly cannot be separated from the nature and objectives of particular public sector operations and the fact that there is a different set of users for financial statements in the public sector, with different kinds of needs. Similarly, the relationship between auditing practices in the public and private sectors cannot be examined without looking at the different ways in which accountability is exercised for the various public sector institutions as compared with the purposes and forms of accountability of private concerns.

A number of other issues span the main chapters. In the area of financial reporting, for example, there is the question of how far there should be uniformity, and how much flexibility ought to be allowed, between similar types of institutions. Another recurrent theme is the issue of how accounting rules should be developed, while on the use of external financial information the nature and rights of different user groups are not always clear. As for internal financial control, the pressure on resources has in most cases given rise to a call for improved systems for monitoring, both internally and for external disclosure and for performance reviews. Finally, on a more personal level, the role of accountants within their organizations and in relation to the accountancy profession as a whole continues to be a matter of concern to many public sector accountants.

1.2 PUBLIC SECTOR DIVERSITY

The public sector is both extremely diverse and extremely large. Even ignoring the large sums expended on transfer payments (such as pensions, welfare benefits and subsidies), the total expenditure of the public sector on employing people, goods and services in carrying out both trading and public service activities is enormous – about 40% of the gross national product. Table 1.1 gives an idea of the relative size of net public sector expenditure for the main sectors covered in this book. It can be seen that local authority expenditure amounts to a quarter of all public expenditure, and expenditure on health rather more than 10%. The nationalized industries, by contrast, make little overall demand on the public purse because, although the amounts they spend are large, they are trading entities and as such recoup their costs in whole or part from their customers. In the case of local authorities, expenditure is spread across no less than 12 of the 18 programmes. Table 1.2 puts the figures for public expenditure as a whole in the context of changes and plans for change in the period 1982/3 to 1987/8. Note that the first column of Table 1.1 has the same figures as the fourth column of Table 1.2.

While the scale of the public sector is essentially a matter of political choice, the financing of whatever size is chosen through a variety of combinations of taxes, rates, charges and prices is a matter of both politics and economics. In this book the financing of the public sector as a whole is taken as given. The concern is rather with the financial management and control of public sector activities, and with the accounting, financial control and audit practices whose underlying aims are to provide satisfactory accountability and promote the best service and value for money.

The private sector has managed to achieve a higher degree of standardization of financial, accounting and audit practices than has so far been achieved in the public sector. This is not

Table 1.1
Public expenditure – the relative magnitudes[1] (£ billion)

Programmes (ranked by size)	Public expenditure	of which		NHS
		Local authorities[3]	Nationalized industries[4]	
Social security	40.1	2.5		
Defence	18.1			
Health and personal social services	16.5	2.5		14.0
Education and science	13.6	11.2		
Scotland[2]	7.2	3.9		
Law, order and protective services	5.2	3.5		
Industry, energy, trade and employment	4.7	0.1		
Transport	4.5	2.2		
Northern Ireland[2]	4.3			
Other environmental services	3.5	2.9		
Wales[2]	2.7	1.8		
Overseas aid/other overseas services	2.6			
Housing	2.3	1.0		
Agriculture, fisheries, food and forestry	2.1	0.1		
Other public services	1.9			
Common services	1.1			
Arts and libraries	0.6	0.4		
Local authorities not allocated (England)	0.6			
Adjustments	0.6	0.6		
	132.1	32.7	1.3	14.0

1. Planned for 1985-86. Rounded to nearest £ hundred million.
2. Scottish, Welsh and Northern Irish programmes cover a variety of services covered in other programmes for England.
3. Does not include Northern Ireland, which is treated separately.
4. Cannot be divided exactly between programmes.
Source: Public Expenditure White Paper. Reproduced by permission of the Controller, Her Majesty's Stationery Office. Crown copyright.

surprising. There are some differences in accounting practices between, for example, industrial firms, retail firms and banks, but their common basic objectives relate to profitability, and managers, shareholders and employees of all three types of private-sector organization have broadly the same financial information needs. They relate in particular to information on current profits and the stability and trend of profits (for guidance

Table 1.2
Public expenditure in cash terms by programme[1] (£ billion)

	1982-83 outturn	1983-84 outturn	1984-85 estimated outturn	1985-86 plans	1986-87 plans	1987-88 plans
Defence	14.4	15.5	17.2	18.1	18.6	18.9
Overseas aid and other overseas services	2.1	2.6	2.5	2.6	2.5	2.8
Agriculture, fisheries, food and forestry	1.8	2.1	2.1	2.1	1.9	1.9
Industry, energy, trade and employment	5.8	5.9	7.2	4.7	3.7	3.5
Arts and libraries	0.6	0.6	0.7	0.6	0.7	0.7
Transport	4.4	4.4	4.8	4.5	4.8	4.8
Housing	2.7	3.1	3.1	2.3	2.5	2.6
Other environmental services	3.5	3.7	3.8	3.5	3.6	3.5
Law, order and protective services	4.2	4.6	5.1	5.2	5.5	5.6
Education and science	12.8	13.4	13.7	13.6	14.0	14.2
Health and personal social services	13.8	14.8	15.8	16.5	17.4	18.1
Social security	32.5	35.2	37.9	40.1	41.9	44.0
Other public services	1.7	1.7	1.9	1.9	2.0	2.0
Common services	1.6	0.9	1.0	1.1	1.1	1.2
Scotland	6.2	6.7	7.1	7.2	7.3	7.3
Wales	2.4	2.6	2.6	2.7	2.9	2.9
Northern Ireland	3.5	3.7	4.1	4.3	4.5	4.6
Local authority current expenditure not allocated to programmes (England)				0.6		
Adjustments						
Special sales of assets	-0.5	-1.1	-2.0	-2.5	-2.2	-2.2
Reserve				3.0	4.0	5.0
General allowance for shortfall			-0.5			
Planning total[2]	113.4	120.3	128.1	132.1	136.7	141.5

1. Figures rounded to £0.1 billion.
2. Programmes may not sum to totals due to rounding.

Source: Public Expenditure White Paper, 1985. Reproduced by permission of the Controller, Her Majesty's Stationery Office. Crown copyright.

on valuation and risk) and, for lenders, further details on assets, liabilities and capital structures.

In contrast, the public sector has a considerable diversity of activities and aims. While nationalized industries operate commercially as trading entities, government departments, local authorities and health authorities do not exist to produce goods or services for sale, do not have shareholders, and are funded by compulsory levies – rates and taxes – or by borrowing on public credit. It is not therefore surprising that the results are presented in a different way. Another factor in explaining the diversity even within the public services sector is the factor of history. As an example, whereas local government has a long history of relatively autonomous development of its own distinctive accounting practices, the history of the National Health Service is much briefer and its accounting methods have been more closely influenced by the direct and explicit monitoring and control requirements of central government.

For the future therefore it is still questionable how far and how fast it will be desirable and feasible to effect greater standardization of financial, accounting and reporting practices between the private and public sectors, and between different types of non-trading public sector bodies. Agreement on change between a number of interest groups would be needed. Many of these interest groups have their own reasons to oppose change and that change would then have to be reflected in extensive amendment to government regulations and perhaps legislation. For anyone seeking to understand the pros and cons of change, a clear understanding of the differences between public sector bodies and in their financial practices is essential. This book sets out those differences in some detail.

1.3 THE AUTHORS' APPROACH

The diversity in financial, accounting and control practices in the various parts of the public sector is reflected in the use of authors who are experts in their own areas. Accordingly the main chapters, apart from that on external auditing, cover individual branches of the public sector rather than particular aspects of financial management and control, although the final chapter of the book considers in more detail some of the general issues raised in this introduction.

Each author of this book takes responsibility for the coverage and views expressed in his own chapters. The authors claim no consensus on the detail of any standardized model of public sector accounting and finance in the future. They are deeply grateful to numerous contacts – too numerous to mention individually – within the several branches of the public sector, who have given much time to the reading of drafts and the framing of advice.

2

Central government framework

This chapter summarizes how public expenditure is planned, controlled and monitored by the central government, and the role of Parliament. It indicates the relationship between public expenditure and the government's economic and financial policies, and it describes the system of central government accounts. Certain issues in the field of central government accounting are dealt with in the appendix.

2.1 PARLIAMENTARY CONTROL OF EXPENDITURE

Parliament exercises full constitutional control over the annual expenditure of government departments and certain closely related bodies, for example the research councils and national museums, by what is known as 'Supply' procedure. Every department prepares its Estimates for expenditure in the coming financial year and is required to agree them with the Treasury. The Treasury submits the approved Estimates to the House of Commons, thus meeting the long-established constitutional practice by which the Crown (the government) demands money from Parliament. In recent years the main Estimates have been presented on Budget day. Three 'Estimates Days' are allotted in the House of Commons timetable each session for debating the Estimates. Statutory authority for the supply of funds to meet the expenditure set out in the Estimates, or Votes, is given in the Consolidated Fund (Appropriation) Act, passed before the summer recess.

The Supply procedure also has to meet further requirements. Government departments need authority to start spending money from the first day of the financial year, whereas the Appropriation

Act will not be passed until some months later. Parliament is therefore asked to provide it by a system of 'Votes on Account', usually presented in December and amounting to about 45% of the amounts authorized to date in the current financial year. Statutory authority for these advances is given in a winter Consolidated Fund Act. Second, departments are permitted to present Revised Estimates before the Appropriation Act is passed, but this normally occurs only where *reduced* financial provision is sought, or to take account of transfers of departmental functions. Third, the government may need to ask Parliament for additional money during the year, necessitating the presentation of Supplementary Estimates at various times, and authorization in a Consolidated Fund Act. Fourth, it is sometimes essential, in Ministers' judgement, for urgent additional expenditure to be incurred in advance of provision by Parliament. The Contingencies Fund, established by Parliament, exists for this purpose, but money advanced from it on strict criteria applied by the Treasury must be repaid when the sums have been subsequently voted.

In 1984-85 the separate Estimates or Votes totalled 183, grouped into 18 classes closely aligned with the functional programmes set out in the Public Expenditure White Paper (see below). Table 2.1, reproduced from the government's note of guidance to the Supply Estimates, shows this classification.

Each Vote contains the following main information about the services for which it provides.

(a) An introductory note describes the expenditure, indicates whether the Vote is treated as a cash limit (see below), and compares the provision sought with the provision and/or likely outturn in the previous year.

(b) Part I gives a brief formal description of the services to be financed (known as the 'ambit' of the Vote), the net sum required, the department which will account for the Vote, and the amount allocated in the Vote on Account.

(c) Part II analyses the provision by functional public expenditure programme and subdivides it into subheads and sometimes further into items. The provision sought is compared with actual expenditure in the last completed year and total provision in the current year (actuals will not be known at this stage); and for the Vote as a whole the forecast outturn for the current year is also shown. Expenditure must be accounted for by subheads: savings on one subhead may be applied, with Treasury sanction, to meet excesses on another – a process known as

Table 2.1

Class number	Title	Number of votes
I	Defence	5
II	Overseas aid and other overseas services	9
III	Agriculture, fisheries, food and forestry	6
IV	Industry, energy, trade and employment	24
V	Arts and libraries	12
VI	Transport	5
VII	Housing	1
VIII	Other environmental services	7
IX	Law, order and protective services	11
X	Education and science	11
XI	Health and personal social services	2
XII	Society security	5
XIII	Other public services	23
XIV	Common services	7
XV	Scotland	24
XVI	Wales	8
XVII	Northern Ireland	2
XVIII	Rate support grant, financial transactions, etc	19
	Total	181
XIII	A House of Commons: administration	1
XIII	B National Audit Office	1
	Total votes	183

Reproduced from the *Memorandum by the Chief Secretary to the Treasury on the Supply Estimates 1984-85*. Reproduced by permission of the Controller, Her Majesty's Stationery Office. Crown copyright.

'virement'. Part II also shows those receipts which may be 'appropriated in aid' of the Vote, i.e. used to meet some of the gross expenditure. Any receipts above the amounts so specified must be surrendered to the Exchequer (Consolidated Fund) as 'extra receipts'.

(d) Part III shows particulars of receipts which are expected to be received but will be paid into the Consolidated Fund.

(e) Part IV analyses the total by functional programme, distinguishes between 'public expenditure' (see below) and other expenditure and within the former between capital and current.

(f) Additional information about the expenditure by the Vote is sometimes given in appended tables, e.g. details of works services.

The Estimates are based entirely on a cash accounting system.

The sums authorized to be spent are those which 'come in course of payment' during the year, i.e. where the liability to pay has matured and the instrument of payment has been issued. Any money not so spent must be surrendered to the Exchequer: no carry forward into the next financial year is permitted.

The price basis of the Estimates has important implications for control of expenditure. Until recently the goods and services on which departments expected to spend their Estimates provision in a given financial year were priced at the prices ruling, broadly, in the prceding autumn. With high inflation they inevitably required substantial extra funds in the succeeding year, which Parliament had no option but to provide in large and extensive Supplementary Estimates. In 1979-80 the price basis was changed to the 'expected outturn prices' for the coming financial year, based on the government's own assumption about inflation and their intentions for public service pay. This assimilated the price basis of the Supply Estimates with that of cash limits (see Section 2.8), introduced greater realism into departmental estimating, and reduced the extent of the Supplementary Estimates, thus opening the way for Parliament to pay more attention to those which were still necessary. This opportunity does not yet seem to have been grasped.

While the Appropriation Act gives annual authority for expenditure which conforms to the scope and structure of the votes, Parliament expects government to seek specific statutory powers for continuing services. For example, the extensive system of social security benefits and the various forms of agricultural and industrial assistance are authorized by special legislation, which governs the preparation of the relevant annual Estimates.

Moreover the fact that money has been made available in the Estimates and the Appropriation Act does not necessarily give departments the right to spend within those limits: they must also seek Treasury approval for individual projects not covered by their own delegated powers, though in the case of major departments such delegations will be large and extensive. Any new policy proposals or developments which involve expenditure, and there are few which do not, must be discussed with the Treasury before any necessary Ministerial approval is sought. The Treasury's views on such proposals will take full account of their likely cost, current and future, in relation to the forward planning and control of public expenditure as a whole (see below).

2.2 ROLE OF PARLIAMENTARY SELECT COMMITTEES

The traditional, somewhat complex arrangements whereby Parliament, assisted by the Comptroller and Auditor General (see Chapter 7) controls departmental spending and its allocation to particular services are constitutionally important but have little substantive impact on the government's plans. The enormous growth in the size and range of governmental expenditure since the main features of these procedures were instituted in the 19th century has made it impossible for the House of Commons to make any effective examination of it or exercise any appreciable influence on its composition. Increasing attention has therefore been given in recent years to the activities of Select Committees of the House in this role. The numbers and terms of reference of these committees, normally consisting of 11-15 members, reflecting the party composition of the House of Commons, has varied, but the present system includes:

(a) the Public Accounts Committee, originally established in 1861, with a continuous but developing interest in the examination of departmental and other accounts laid before Parliament, and the related conduct of financial management (see Chapter 7);

(b) a number of departmentally related committees, charged with 'shadowing' the policies and operations of the main government departments and scrutinizing their Estimates, e.g. defence, trade and industry, transport, energy, health and social services;

(c) as a special example of group (b), the central Treasury and Civil Service Committee which oversees the operations of the Treasury in expenditure control and its conduct of economic and monetary policy as well as the central control and management of the Civil Service, now the responsibility of the Cabinet Office (Management and Personnel Office);

(d) the Liaison Committee, consisting of the chairmen of all select committees, which coordinates their activities.

All these committees select the subjects they will examine within their terms of reference, take written and oral evidence, usually from senior officials but occasionally from Ministers, and make public reports. Their recommendations are backed by no formal powers, but are considered on their merits by the government. Some such system is the only way of involving Members of Parliament in a detailed and informed way with the departmental conduct of expenditure and other policies.

Under the new Supply procedure introduced in November 1982, the Liaison Committee recommends specific estimates for debate by the House of Commons on an Estimates Day, usually on the basis of reports from the departmentally related committees. However their value as a means of more effective Parliamentary scrutiny of expenditure proposals remains to be established.

The chapter so far has been confined to the main constitutional and statutory controls exercised by Parliament over spending by the central government. Parliament's relationship with the local authorities and the nationalized industries (the two other main parts of the public sector) needs separate examination. This will lead to consideration of the planning and control of public expenditure as a whole by the government. The funding, financial control and accountability of the local authorities and nationalized industries themselves is dealt with fully in the chapters which follow.

2.3 LOCAL AUTHORITIES

Local authorities are elected bodies accountable to their own electorates, not Parliament, for their policies and administration. But Parliament has a major, and ultimately decisive, role in their powers and responsibilities as the sovereign legislature. That role is currently exercised mainly in the following ways.

(a) Services provided by local authorities are authorized by statute, e.g. education and housing Acts, which lay down, in considerable detail, what is to be or may be provided and how services are to be administered.

(b) Legislation also provides for the way in which local authority expenditure is to be financed, including arrangements for central government contributions by way of block grants or specific grants, and the financial relations between central and local government generally.

(c) Parliament holds accountable to itself the government departments responsible for national policy on locally provided services – education, housing, personal social services, roads and transport – and, in the case of the Department of the Environment, policy on relations generally between the central and local authorities. This accountability is usually pursued through the Select Committees who may examine Ministers and officials on the exercise of their responsibilities under the governing statutes.

Parliament also determines the whole structure of local government in the country, both geographically and in respect of other features of its organization.

2.4 NATIONALIZED INDUSTRIES

The nationalized industries and other public corporations, for example the Scottish and Welsh Development Agencies, have the following distinguishing characteristics:

(a) They are established by Act of Parliament, which lays down their constitution, powers, responsibilities and relations with the government.

(b) Subject to (d) below, their boards are not directly answerable to Parliament, but are subject to the control of their sponsoring Ministers as provided for in legislation, those Ministers in turn being accountable to Parliament for the discharge of their statutory duties in respect of the industries.

(c) As a corollary of this constitutional position the industries are fully backed by the Exchequer and have no independent credit standing of their own.

(d) Their annual reports and accounts are required to be laid before Parliament, which brings them formally within the purview of the Public Accounts Committee. In practice Parliamentary examination of the industries' operations is undertaken by the Select Committee shadowing the government department sponsoring the industry (see Chapter 5). Note that this right to question Boards and to report on their operations depends on convention and not on the statutes establishing the industries.

(e) Though by agreement with other Select Committees the Public Accounts Committee has in general not examined the industries (except in recent years the British National Oil Corporation as a special case) the Committee has been showing an increasing interest in the sponsor departments' actions in relation to their industries.

2.5 THE PUBLIC EXPENDITURE SURVEY SYSTEM

Until the early 1960s the control of expenditure was focused mainly on the annual Estimates of departments. The Treasury discussed new policy developments and proposals with the departments as they arose; if approved, any necessary legislation would be prepared and submitted to Parliament and the resulting expenditure would be provided for in the next annual Estimates or, if they were agreed to be sufficiently urgent, in Supplementary Estimates. The Treasury required individual projects or services to be submitted to them, even within approved policies, if they were not covered by departments' delegated authority; and they paid close attention to matters of regularity and propriety, that is conformity to Parliamentary rules and requirements, and to departmental instructions governing such matters as the administration of social security benefits or schemes of assistance to farmers. There was already some formulation of longer-term expenditure plans, for example by the defence departments, which necessarily had to look forward several years in relating their manpower and equipment needs to military requirements and the resources likely to be available. But for most programmes the time profile was short.

The Treasury was aware that current planning and control arrangements for public expenditure – not just those for central government – were inadequate; the Select Committee on Estimates had reported in the same sense in 1957-58. The government accordingly set up a committee under Sir Edwin Plowden to examine the system and recommend necessary action. The committee's report, *The Planning and Control of Public Expenditure*, issued in 1961, was a major landmark. The system it recommended has formed the basis of successive governments' approach to this area of policy ever since, though the techniques have been progressively developed and modified. The central recommendations of the Plowden Committee were that 'regular surveys should be made of public expenditure as a whole, over a period of years ahead, and in relation to prospective resources; decisions involving substantial future expenditure should be taken in the light of these surveys'.

These recommendations were accepted by the government, and the Treasury, in consultation with the spending departments, set up machinery to implement them. Central to this machinery was the Public Expenditure Survey Committee, a group of senior officials from all major departments, responsible for making an annual survey of public expenditure plans as the basis for ministerial decisions on its total and composition. Its initials –

PESC – became by somewhat inaccurate but general usage the term describing the whole system. The essential task of the committee was to summarize and cost as accurately as possible all public expenditure programmes on the basis of 'existing policies'. The costings were to cover the current year and a number of years ahead, which has varied from two to four. Departments were allowed, later in the development of the system, to include 'additional bids' for further expenditures they wished to make but for which approval had not yet been given; and in some years the committee included 'costed options' in their report, i.e. costs which would be saved by cutting out or reducing the least essential services in expenditure programmes. During the 1970s, the system changed from a costing of 'existing policies' to a projection forward of existing levels of approved expenditure on them. Thus the question ceased to be 'how much will this cost' and became 'how much can you buy for this level of expenditure?'. Additional bids and costed options were then related to this 'survey baseline'.

Important features of the Survey Report were the following:

(a) It was factual; explanation and costing of the expenditure programmes it covered were agreed between the departments and the Treasury, except where specific disagreements could not be resolved, e.g. whether a service was or was not covered by the definition of 'existing policy'.

(b) The figures were at constant prices, normally those of the autumn preceding the Committee's report, which was compiled by the early summer of 'Year 1' – the current year. The use of constant prices, and the control of a large proportion of public expenditure in the corresponding volume terms, were the subject of considerable difficulty and controversy, and are discussed below.

(c) 'Public expenditure' covered not only the expenditure of central government and its closely related agencies, but also the expenditure, both capital and current, of local authorities, and, for some years, the capital investment of the nationalized industries. The total external financing needs of the industries are now included in the survey figures in place of the cost of their investment programmes. The exact definition of public expenditure, and its rationale for various purposes, have also been the subject of much discussion.

(d) Whereas the figures for central government and for nationalized industries, while subject to varying degrees of estimating uncertainty, could be used for subsequent control purposes as well as for planning public expenditure as a whole, the figures for local government spending were derived from a complex estimating procedure involving representatives of the local authorities and government departments concerned, and could not be regarded as control figures. Central government exercised control only over local capital expenditure and not over current expenditure, by far the larger component.

(e) The PES committee took no decisions about the scale or content of public expenditure. Its report was intended simply to provide an agreed, comprehensive and factual basis for Ministers' consideration and decisions. This was nevertheless a major task each year, given the range of the public sector, its widely varying components, and problems of pricing and estimating.

When the completed survey was circulated to Ministers, the Chancellor of the Exchequer put forward his own proposals for levels of public expenditure in relation to his judgement of the prospects for the economy. This was in accord with one of the Plowden Committee recommendations. The intention was that the demands of the public sector should not be excessive, at any part of the survey period, in comparison with the expected growth of national output and other competing demands on it. The way in which this judgement was made, and the methodology used, have varied over the years. The following alternative methods have been used:

(a) The expected growth rate of the national output (gross domestic product) was compared with the estimated growth of public expenditure, generally with the object of avoiding the latter exceeding the former.

(b) An assessment was made of the demands of 'prior claims' on the national output – the resources required for productive investment and the balance of payments – and a view was taken of the desirable division of the remainder, itself the bulk of the total, between public expenditure and private consumption. This work centred on the 'medium-term economic assessment' and was essentially related to the use of resources in the economy rather than to financial objectives.

(c) Linked to (b), attention was concentrated on the implications for personal and company taxation of public expenditure plans, to see if prospective tax levels appeared acceptable or not.

(d) The proportion of the national output likely to be taken by public expenditure was estimated, to enable Ministers to judge whether its growth rate was acceptable or excessive.

(e) The present Government (1985) has, since 1979, planned public expenditure within the context of a medium term financial strategy. This places the main emphasis on control of certain monetary aggregates, which imply in turn a certain level of Government borrowing and thus, given the objective of reducing taxation, a certain level of public expenditure.

(f) More recently, in addition to continuing concern for levels of taxation, the government's policy has been dominated by the importance they have attached to controlling public expenditure in cash rather than in volume or resource terms; and cutting down the size of the public sector.

The technical problems involved in making these various assessments are formidable. For example, different types of public expenditure have very different economic effects; social security payments transfer purchasing power from taxpayers to the beneficiaries; investment in the nationalized steel industry increases productive capacity; purchases of land transfer existing assets from private to public ownership; and so on. But the final decisions by Ministers are to some extent subjective, and certainly political; there are no demonstrably 'right' answers to questions about public spending.

When Ministers had taken the main decisions about the totals of public spending in the next years ahead, and its distribution among the main functional programmes, the annual Public Expenditure White Paper was prepared. Recently it has been the practice to publish the expenditure programme and public expenditure planning totals in November, in the Autumn Statements, with an expanded public expenditure White Paper published much nearer to the start of the next financial year. But the broad tax and borrowing implications of public spending plans are much in Minister's minds when they take public expenditure decisions, and the Autumn Statement now brings the public expenditure plans together with forecasts for the economy so that these implications are apparent. At the time of the Budget the government brings together all the salient figures on both sides of the government's central accounts in the 'Financial Statement and Budget Report'. Parliament is now considering proposals from one of its Select Committees for a 'green book' to be published in the autumn, setting out the government's detailed expenditure and taxation proposals in draft. These would then be modified in the light of Parliamentary and public comment, before the Budget was introduced in the spring.

The Public Expenditure White Paper now provides a great deal of information about the government's forward spending plans and their relationship to other objectives of economic and financial policy. Figures for all the spending programmes are broken down to show the individual services; they are analysed by spending authority – central or local government, public corporations, and by economic category – capital investment, current spending on goods and services, transfer payments and so on. The policies and purposes which all the principal services are intended to promote are described and some output measures provided. The changes in expenditure plans and out-turns compared with the previous White Paper are explained. Information about the nationalised industries' capital investment and financing is included.

The White Paper, looking ahead for up to four years, has been presented to Parliament every year since the late 1960s, but it does not itself carry any Parliamentary authorization. The plans it contains are the government's plans, or in some cases the government's estimates of what is likely to be spent. As already indicated, however, Parliament does exercise formal control in various ways over public sector spending:

(a) by legislating to provide for defined services, e.g. assistance to industry and agriculture, provision of housing, health, education and transport, subsidies for some nationalized industries;

(b) by providing funds each year through the Supply procedure for most of central government spending, including the block grant and other financial support to local government;

(c) by authorizing certain permanent charges directly on the Consolidated Fund, e.g. payments to the European Communities, which it would be inappropriate to subject to annual Vote procedures.

2.6 FINANCING OF PUBLIC EXPENDITURE

This book is not concerned with the theory or practice of taxation, but mention must be made of the ways in which the government and other public authorities raise revenue or borrow to meet their expenditure. They are:

(a) Central government taxes, imposed or changed under the

authority of the annual Finance Act, following the Budget.
(b) Local authority rates, charged on domestic, commercial or industrial property, and imposed at levels decided under statutory powers by all rating authorities.
(c) Charges for goods or services sold by the nationalized industries, the water authorities, other public corporations or bodies, and central and local government. While the nationalized industries are primarily very large commercial undertakings, which are expected wherever possible to operate profitably, there are also sizeable trading activities carried out by central government – for example in the Stationery Office, and the Royal Mint – and by local government – for example bus services. Moreover both central and local government and the National Health Service raise a wide variety of charges for goods or services provided to the public, ranging from council house rents to prescription charges and passport fees.
(d) Sales of surplus assets, for example land or buildings, equipment or stores.
(e) Borrowing on the private capital or money markets; or, in the case of most governmental agencies, from the central government itself.

In addition, the large sums received on privatization of publicly owned undertakings, e.g. Cable and Wireless, British Telecom, reduce the Government's borrowing requirement.

Central government capital expenditure is financed through Votes whatever its economic category, but that part of capital investment by the nationalized industries which cannot be financed from their own internal resources is mostly financed by borrowing. Moreover, capital investment apart, the government has for several years incurred heavy deficits on its own spending/revenue balance, and the local authorities also borrow to finance much of their capital spending. The public sector borrowing requirement is the total of these components. It is increased by higher revenue deficits and larger externally financed capital investment programmes. It can be reduced by lower spending, higher taxation, higher nationalized industry prices, and sales of public sector assets. It size and management have been a major concern of government policy in recent years.

The central government's statutory power to borrow, in the National Loans Act 1968, sets no upper limit to the total which may be borrowed, nor specifies the manner or terms of borrowing. These are matters which 'the authorities' – i.e. the Treasury and the Bank of England – will decide in consultation, with final decisions in the hands of Ministers as always.

Parliament does not at present set any overall limits on government borrowing. It does, however, impose periodic limits on borrowing by each of the nationalized industries and certain public corporations, usually estimated to meet their external capital financing needs for three to four years ahead. All lending to the industries, apart from some short-term bank finance, to other public corporations and the local authorities is centralized through the National Loans Fund in the interests of monetary management.

2.7 PROBLEMS OF THE PUBLIC EXPENDITURE SURVEY SYSTEM

The public expenditure survey system summarized above greatly improved the technique for managing and presenting this crucial area of policy, and the understanding of its complexity. In these respects the United Kingdom probably led the world. But the technique was no substitute for Ministerial decisions, often difficult, on the scale of public expenditure, priorities between programmes and services, and the relations of government with other public sector authorities. Moreover, as the system was progressively implemented and developed, substantial problems emerged. The most significant were the following:

(a) While the White Paper figures for central government spending were control figures, those for local authorities were not, except in so far as they related to capital expenditures controlled by government loan sanctions, or direct allocations. The government had no direct control over the total spending plans of the individual local authorities, though they account in total for large parts of some of the main expenditure programmes, e.g. education, housing.

(b) As the difficulty of reconciling strong pressures for additional public expenditure with low rates of economic growth and industrial performance worsened, the total forward cost estimates which the survey produced, even on the basis of 'existing policies', were often found to be unacceptably high for one or more of the future years it covered. Moreover by the time the survey report was completed, around June, there was little time for the necessary Ministerial decisions, often controversial, to be taken and the consequent reworking of figures completed before preparation of the White Paper could start.

(c) These decisions, and their reflection in the White Paper, could not preclude further decisions to increase expenditure being taken in advance of the next annual survey. The figures for a particular year therefore came to show large increases in successive White Papers. This was not necessarily indefensible, depending on the course of the economy, but when repeated it strongly suggested that the government had been unable to maintain their earlier judgement and that public expenditure was 'out of control'. The setting aside of a substantial unallocated 'contingency reserve' in an attempt to meet unforeseen spending demands without breaching the totals proved inadequate until it was itself used as an instrument of positive expenditure control and combined with other measures in the middle and late 70s.

(d) The price basis of the survey figures caused difficulties. Each survey was conducted at constant prices, but the constant prices were updated between one survey and the next, and even between programmes there was some variation in the base dates used. It was therefore difficult to compare expenditure plans and outturns for any particular year in successive White Papers.

(e) The whole concept of planning and presenting public expenditure plans in constant prices, or volume terms, rather than in the actual prices ruling from year to year – i.e. current prices – caused serious problems of control once inflation rose above comparatively modest levels of say 4-5%. When it reached 25% and more in 1973-75, with price increases varying considerably from one component of expenditure to another, and thus from one programme to another, control was seriously affected. This was not only because control figures set in volume or resource terms made no effective use of cash budgeting, but because with such big pay and price movements it was very difficult for the Treasury to judge whether expenditure had not in the event exceeded even the original volume figures for individual programmes.

Two criticisms of a rather different type were also made:

(a) Some Ministers considered that the PES system gave them little help in comparing the benefits from various spending proposals, or therefore in deciding on their priorities.

(b) Select Committees complained that while the system gave

figures of spending plans and outturns it provided little or no information about the outputs planned and achieved; i.e. measures of what are now called the goals or objectives of public spending.

Both these points are of major importance in public expenditure planning and control, but as criticisms of the public expenditure survey itself they largely misconceive its purposes, or at least the extent to which its already complex methodology could be extended to meet yet further aims. Decisions on priorities between public spending programmes require careful cost/benefit studies and an effective system, yet to be devised, for collective Ministerial consideration of their results. The development of output measures is one objective of the Financial Management Initiative, referred to below (2.9).

2.8 THE CASH LIMIT SYSTEM

The major problem of technique in public expenditure control to emerge in the mid-1970s was the absence of an effective cash budgeting system. Some programmes were necessarily planned and controlled in cash terms, for example the large social security schemes and other types of transfer payments. Local authorities' spending was determined by their own cash budgets for the year ahead. The allocations to individual health authorities, from within the total health programme, were also made in cash terms. In addition, cash controls were superimposed on some other types of government expenditure when exceptionally high cost inflation made this necessary, for example building and construction in 1973. But the greater part of central government spending was not subject to cash, as distinct from volume or 'real term', limits: pay and price rises were provided for as they occurred. The Parliamentary procedures did ostensibly provide for full cash control: departments were not allowed to overspend their original estimates without submitting a Supplementary Estimate. But in practice Parliament had no option but to grant the extra funds, so that the formal control was illusory.

Control in resource or real terms had advantages. It enabled departments to staff, build, equip and supply the projects and services that had been authorized without risking shortfalls and disruption due to their cash provision falling short of actual inflation. But if all wage and price increases were 'for free' so far as departmental managers were concerned, there was less incentive to keep cash costs within bounds and the discipline of firm cash allocations was absent. More seriously, the government had no means of knowing, within wide margins, how much would actually be spent at a time when financial policy was moving strongly towards monetary controls.

The working out of the cash limit system in 1974 to 1975 and its application from 1976 to 1977 was designed to remedy these problems. It had the following essential features:

(a) Cash limits would be set for as many central government programmes as possible, for the next financial year.

(b) they would be worked out from the volume figures agreed by Ministers for the Public Expenditure White Paper, applying the government's assumptions about inflation for the period in question.

(c) This inflation rate would be broken down into separate estimated inflation rates for different parts of public spending – for example civil service pay, industrial pay, construction/equipment programmes.

(d) The cash limits would be regarded as firm, not to be increased save in highly exceptional circumstances, and then only with Treasury permission.

(e) Consideration would be given to extending cash limit control to as many further programmes and services as possible. The main exclusions were services which were 'demand-determined', such as social security benefits and grants for industrial and agricultural assistance, where the sums paid out followed automatically from the numbers of qualified recipients and the levels at which benefits were set from time to time by policy decisions.

It should be noted that, although Parliament was informed of the cash limits and subsequently of any changes or excesses, the system was a purely administrative one, decided and applied by the government, and that it provided for no formal Parliamentary endorsement. It was another illustration of the extent to which the Parliamentary machinery for expenditure control, in its essentially 19th century form, failed to match up to modern circumstances; hence the greater reliance on the role of the Select Committees.

Cash limits could not be applied to the current expenditure of individual local authorities without extensive machinery for approving the plans of over 450 authorities. It was therefore decided to apply a cash limit to rate support grant (block grant) which had previously been redetermined in the course of the year to take account of actual pay and price changes. Block grant is now fixed in cash and is cash limited. In order to influence local authorities' spending the government has set targets for local authorities' 'total expenditure' (broadly expenditure from the rate fund after deduction of specific and supplementary grants). Spending over target has meant grant penalties. From 1985 to 1986 the government has powers to limit the rates – and hence broadly the expenditure – of individual local authorities selected for rate limitation. The government will also have reserve powers to limit the rates of local authorities generally. Cash limits were not applied originally in any form to the nationalized industries and other public corporations, but later the system was extended and the limits for the nationalized industries are now known as external financing limits (EFLs).

At the same time as the cash limit system was being developed, attention was given to the information about actual government spending, during each financial year, which was available to the departments and particularly the Treasury. The Treasury knew very soon how much money had been issued from the Exchequer accounts to those of the departments but not till much later how their expenditure was broken down by Vote detail. Keeping track of the outturn against the provisions for public expenditure as a whole raised even wider problems, owing to the diversity of spending authorities and the varying systems of accounting. Departments had their own financial information systems to meet their own control needs, but these were not integrated with information available to the Treasury. In 1974–1975 a new central Financial Information System was worked out by the Treasury, in consultation with the main spending departments, to provide early and accurate information about current central government spending in relation to both the Vote provision and the Public Expenditure White Paper figures. The course of actual expenditure was analysed on a monthly basis so far as its most important features were concerned. This analysis was compared with expected 'profiles' of expenditure for the year as a whole, since the rate of spending may not be uniform either throughout the year or by different types of service. Any necessary corrective action could thus be considered in good time. It was clearly essential that, for the cash limits to be monitored and enforced, an effective financial reporting system of this kind should be in operation.

Cash limits are essentially the same system as the cash budgetary arrangements in force in many other countries. But they are closely related to the broader public expenditure survey system, some of whose limitations they were designed to remedy; and they were not imposed where they could not have been enforced. Both systems have continued to evolve. The main developments in the cash limit system have included:

(a) extension of cash limits to some other services not originally covered – for example, certain forms of assistance to industry where as a policy decision an overall limit was imposed to override the 'demand-determined' criterion;

(b) over the financial years 1979-80 and 1980-81 cash limits covering Supply expenditure were aligned with Votes in the Parliamentary Estimates – before then some cash limits covered more than one Vote;

(c) as a practical consequence, some squeeze on real spending when inflation rates proved to be higher than those allowed for fixing the cash limits.

From 1982 to 1983, a major change was made by the government in the basis of the public expenditure survey itself, and its relation to cash limits. Up till then cash limits had been grafted on to the volume system of planning public expenditure as a whole; no change had been made in the constant price or real terms basis of the survey. From 1982 to 1983 the survey itself has been conducted in cash terms for all the years it covers. This required complicated calculations to bring the 'survey prices' used in the last White Paper up to date and then to feed in the government's assumptions about inflation in deciding expenditure figures for the future years of the Survey. Plans in volume of physical units of service or provision now take second place to the cash which is made available for the programmes. They are no longer sacrosanct whatever happens to prices; on the other hand, improved efficiency in departmental operations enables more goods or services to be provided. (For a clear explanation of these changes, see *Economic Progress Report No. 139* for November 1981, published by the Treasury.)

2.9 THE FINANCIAL MANAGEMENT INITIATIVE

The public expenditure survey, Ministers' decisions thereon, periodic policy reviews, and the discipline of cash limits should suffice to determine and control the total of public spending and its allocation between competing services and programmes. The vote accounting system and associated Parliamentary procedures should guard against spending without constitutional authority and misappropriation of public funds. But essential as they are for these purposes these arrangements do little of themselves to secure the maximum efficiency and cost effectiveness in day to day budgetary management in departments. The government's financial management initiative (FMI) was designed to meet this need. It was first publicly described in 1982 in the government's reply to a report from the Parliamentary Treasury and Civil Service Committee on efficiency and effectiveness in the Civil Service (Cmnd 8616).

The FMI is not a new technique, though in many areas of government business it is a new approach. It reflects the belief, stimulated by the need to work within firm cash limits, that agreed policies can be carried out in alternative ways and with greater or lesser expenditure for essentially the same results. It owes something to the results of the efficiency studies instituted by Sir (now Lord) Derek Rayner which examine in depth specific activities with a view to cutting costs and staff and streamlining methods of work without detriment to results.

It is both a financial and a management initiative. Its object is to promote in each government department an organization and a system in which civil servants in a managerial capacity at all levels have a clear view of their objectives, well defined responsibilities, and the necessary information, including financial information, to help discharge them. Clearly the nature of these responsibilities will vary greatly according to the particular job. Senior officials in the Treasury, responsible for advising on matters of monetary policy, may have virtually no expenditure under their direct control, and few staff. An under secretary in the Department of Trade and Industry may supervise the distribution of many millions of pounds in measures of industrial assistance and have scores of people working on their detailed administration. A project manager in the Ministry of Defence may be in charge of the development and procurement of a complicated weapons system for whose success a variety of military, scientific, financial and administrative skills have to be satisfactorily combined. The management approach, and allocation of budgetary and other managerial tasks, must be adapted to the reality of each such situation.

Adequate, timely and relevant financial information is clearly one important requirement for successful management. The annual appropriation accounts obviously cannot meet it. Nor for that matter can the commercial accounts produced by departments which operate as Trading Funds. Even if their structure was fully consistent with the allocation of responsibilities within departments, these accounts could not display the necessary degree of detail, and in any case they are produced only annually, some time after the end of the year to which they relate.

The Treasury's internal financial information system, referred to above in connection with the working out of the cash limit system, does provide prompt expenditure figures throughout the year, but it was designed to meet broader objectives of monitoring and control than those which directly concern many middle managers responsible for specific parts of departmental programmes. Their need has to be met by the development and use of additional management information and accounting systems. They can vary in form from a full costing of a specific activity, say the acquisition, nurture and training of police dogs, to set against the outputs of these particular public servants, to the enumeration and costing of the multiple activities of a large department, such as the MINIS system (Management Information for Ministers) developed in the Department of the Environment. The aims of this type of analysis are to know what is being done in the pursuit of policy objectives, what it costs, and whether an alternative procedure could produce efficacious results more cheaply: better value for money, not a lower standard of service. But value cannot be judged without some measure or assessment of what is produced. Sustained effort is therefore necessary, and is being applied, to the development and improvement of measures of output and performance. The greatly improved annual reports of some departments, for example the report 'The Health Service in England' published by the Department of Health and Social Security in 1984, contain numerous examples.

The FMI is not however simply a collection of financial and management techniques, however sophisticated. It also sets out to promote people's self-reliance and enthusiasm and to increase their job satisfaction, by giving them as much independence and personal responsibility for the achievement of their objectives and management of their staff and budgets as is consistent with accepted policy and with their individual freedom of action. Granted that there are inevitable constraints on such freedom in large public service organizations, which have to operate within set policies and procedures and often with wide internal and external consultation, the FMI in practice is nevertheless demonstrating that there is more scope for it than had previously been thought. Progress on the FMI and its application in all the main government departments has been made public in successive White Papers.

2.10 ACCOUNTING FOR PUBLIC EXPENDITURE

It remains to indicate how public expenditure is accounted for, as distinct from controlled. There is no general accounting system for the public sector as a whole: its component parts are too diverse, both constitutionally and operationally, for that. Local government has its own accounting system, which varies from authority to authority with the range of services for which each is responsible, and is fully described in Chapter 4. The nationalized industries and those public corporations that are predominantly commercial in character, such as the Scottish and Welsh Development Agencies and the Civil Aviation Authority, produce their accounts in full commercial form. They also provide a great deal more information in their annual reports than commercial enterprises do in the private sector, to meet the requirements of public and Parliamentary accountability. A summary of central government arrangements follows.

The annual Appropriation Accounts of government departments and closely related bodies follow the form of the Estimates – Votes and subheads – and show how much cash has been spent against the amounts provided by Parliament; the composition of shortfalls, and occasionally excesses; receipts appropriated in aid of the Votes, or surrendered to the Exchequer; and supporting information, including statements of losses, special payments and so on. They are audited by the Comptroller and Auditor General (C&AG – Chapter 7) and presented to Parliament, where they may form the basis of examination by the Public Accounts Committee.

For 60 years or more those departments that carried on commercial or industrial activities were required to produce, in addition to the relevant vote accounts, Trading Accounts to exhibit the results of those activities in commercial form. Examples were the Royal Ordnance Factories, the Stationery Office and the Royal Mint. A separate volume of such trading accounts is produced each year, and they are also audited by the C&AG. The financing of some of these bodies was changed, by the Government Trading Funds Act 1973, from the cash vote system to a trading fund, under which they are suitably capitalized, and are exempt from the requirement to surrender any surplus cash at the end of the year, though they may have to pay dividends to the Exchequer from their profits.

The government also maintains the central Exchequer accounts: the accounts of the Consolidated Fund and the National Loans Fund. Further, there are a number of Government services financed by statutory funds which are known collectively as

White Paper accounts. Two important examples are the National Insurance Fund showing the position with regard to the contributing social insurance schemes, and the Redundancy Fund which provides for rebates to employers who have made redundancy payments to staff. But there are no accounts as such relating to the Public Expenditure White Paper. So far as the central government services in it are concerned, the following information is produced about the out-turn:

(a) the running check, and end year figures, produced by the financial information system described above;

(b) the figures for actual expenditure in the past year or years, analysed by programme and in other ways, which appear in each successive White Paper. As already noted, the price basis on which this information is provided has recently undergone substantial revision.

This set of accounts and financial information has been criticized, in Parliament and elsewhere, for not giving sufficient basis for an assessment of outputs, as distinct from inputs into the various services and activities of departments. It shows cash spent, for example on schools, hospitals, agricultural research and all the other functional activities of government, but not what has been achieved in any area in relation to plans or budgets. But there is a limit to the purposes which a Parliamentary set of accounts can be expected to serve. Accounts showing how money has been spent in relation to money voted cannot also show full costs, including depreciation of assets and provisions for losses. Moreover the final objectives or outputs of much government activity are not quantifiable and cannot even be readily assessed. It is therefore frequently necessary to concentrate on 'intermediate objectives', for example miles of motorway constructed, number of school or university places provided, rather than on the ultimate goals these public operations are meant to serve. These are matters to which the Financial Management Initiative is in part directed.

EXAMINATION QUESTIONS

2.1 What are the major differences between controlling public expenditure and controlling spending in private sector organizations?

2.2 Explain the relationship between Parliamentary control of expenditure and control by cash limits.

2.3 Can Parliament really control public expenditure?

2.4 The Appropriation Accounts of government departments show cash spent on various heads and subheads compared with cash voted by Parliament. What additional types of accounts would you expect a department to maintain for its own use?

2.5 What do you understand by a management accounting system in central government?

2.6 The government uses the Public Expenditure Survey Committee process in planning and controlling public expenditure. Discuss the usefulness and importance of this process to the government. (CIPFA. Policy Making in the Public Sector. November 1980)

2.7 Outline the Public Expenditure Survey System. In what ways does it influence or control the policies of public sector organizations? (CIPFA. Policy Making in the Public Sector. November 1979)

2.8 Discuss the reasons for and against greater flexibility in the control of public expenditure.

2.9 Why has value for money become so important for monitoring central government activities? Why is it difficult to measure in some cases?

2.10 'Financial information provides the basis for decision-making.' Discuss this statement in relation to central government financial reporting.

APPENDIX 2.1 ACCOUNTANTS AND FINANCE OFFICERS IN CENTRAL GOVERNMENT

Professional accountants in central government are part of the Government Accounting Service (GAS) which provides accounting advice to government departments. Members of the GAS work within a department, but may move to other departments in the course of their career and may also be promoted into the senior administrative grades of the civil service.

Many other posts with the words 'accountant' or 'finance officer' in the title are not held by professional accountants, but by civil servants without formal accounting training. Some of these posts are:

(a) *The Accounting Officer.* Normally a post held by the permanent secretary at the head of a government department or equivalent official head of other government agencies – e.g. research councils. The Accounting Officer is responsible to his Minister and by tradition to the Public Accounts Committee for the proper use and sound management of the funds voted to the department by Parliament.

(b) *Departmental Principal Finance Officer.* Responsible for financial policy, expenditure control and accounting work within a department. He liaises with the Treasury and the National Audit Office. Most of his staff are not professionally qualified accountants.

(c) *Treasury Officer of Accounts.* Among other duties, supervises accounting methods and constitutional propriety throughout government departments, and liaises with the National Audit Office. Is the main Treasury witness before the Public Accounts Committee.

(d) *Treasury Accountant.* Manages the government's bank account with the Bank of England and the outflow of money to departments.

APPENDIX 2.2   ACCOUNTING AND CONTROL ISSUES IN CENTRAL GOVERNMENT

There is very little published material about issues in UK government accounting. This is partly no doubt because it is a subject which is largely of concern to those who are practitioners and because these practitioners' deliberations are conducted almost entirely within the government. This is in contrast to some other countries, especially the United States, where there has been a great deal of public debate over many years on central government accounting and finance issues.

Information on some issues is available in reports of House of Commons Select Committees, notably the Public Accounts Committee and the Treasury and Civil Service Select Committee. Otherwise articles on central government accounting and finance matters sometimes appear in journals such as *Public Finance and Accounting* and *Public Money*, both published by CIPFA, as well as in the press and in more general economic and accounting publications. The arguments put forward on each side in the issues mentioned below come from these sources.

The two major sources of information about accounting techniques are:

(a) *Government Accounting*, HMSO, 1974, reprinted 1981 (with supplements 1-3),

(b) *Management Accounting in the Civil Service*, HMSO, 1976.

Form of accounts

The way in which central government accounts are prepared has evolved over many years, influenced to some extent by successive demands for more or clearer information from Parliament. These demands have increased in recent years, partly as a result of calls for greater clarity of information in all types of accounts, and partly because of the changing nature of scrutiny by Parliament through select committees.

As a result of the work done by the Treasury itself, the House of Commons Treasury and Civil Service Committee since 1979, and the Expenditure Committee before that, considerable changes have been effected in the way in which financial information has been presented to Parliament. Pressure for change and suggestions for further changes in presentation are likely to continue from those inside and outside Parliament who wish to have a better understanding of the figures. One problem has been that because it is not as easy for central government as it is for the private sector to define the needs of users, and because the results of government operations can be presented in different ways, it has been difficult to establish exactly what the form of the accounts should be, and how the form of accounts can best be improved.

Role of accountants

The formation of the Government Accounting Service in 1974 remedied a longstanding need for a proper professional structure for accountants within the Civil Service. It has been said that accountants, nevertheless, still do not have the professional prominence in central government finance work which the relevance of their qualifications justifies. It has also been said that there are major difficulties in recruiting enough suitable accountants for central government service because the rates of pay are significantly lower than those available in the private sector. On the other hand, it has been argued that the lowering of barriers between the government accountancy service and the administrative Civil Service which took place in 1982 helped to improve the career prospects for accountants within the Civil Service. It has also been said that, while pay is certainly a problem, there are other considerations such as job satisfaction and career prospects which are as important in deterring accountants from coming into the Civil Service.

It is worth putting this debate in context. Much government

accounting is of a different type from commercial accounting, reflects different kinds of activity, and serves different ends. Commercial accountants therefore cannot simply apply private sector techniques to government work, and would not necessarily be cost-effectively employed in some areas of government accounting. In other areas, notably trading and production operations (where commercial accounting methods have long been applied) and the development of management information systems, it is increasingly recognized that professional accountants – once they have appreciated the environment in which government works – should have much to offer.

Flexibility and control

As described in this chapter, one of the main principles of central government accounting is that cash is allocated for a particular year. Normally, if not spent in that year, funds may not be carried forward. It has been argued that this control system is too rigid and that it results in distortion. One danger, for example, is that some expenditure of low priority is artificially boosted at the end of a financial year to ensure that a budget is not underspent. Another objection is that some programmes are consistently underspent because there is fear of overspending. It has also been said that with a system based on cash there is a danger of distorting expenditure patterns if inflation is different from the forecast, since more or less goods and services from those planned can then be bought for the total amount of money available.

Many of these concerns are common to any control system, whether in the public or the private sector. The argument against greater flexibility is that this weakens central control and makes the planning of public expenditure and, for the government, monetary policy more difficult. It is also said that while the disadvantages of having a rigid system are clear, the difficulties of introducing flexibility are even greater because of the impact on planning and control. Nevertheless some limited flexibility has been built into parts of central government expenditure.

One particular aspect of the control system which has aroused considerable criticism is the tendency for government to underestimate the wage increases paid to their employees during the course of the year. It has been said that estimates are kept deliberately low in order to set the 'tone' for wage negotiations in the coming year since the government cannot be seen to be encouraging high wage settlements. If this is true, expenditure as a whole is affected because if the estimated wage settlement is exceeded, expenditure for a particular programme will be squeezed.

On the other hand, it has been pointed out that it is very difficult for a government to acknowledge in advance the real rate of increase in wages it believes may occur, since this tends to be treated as the starting point in wage negotiations. But the evidence from recent years is that the rate of increase which has been included in plans has generally been lower than the level of actual settlements.

Value for money

Because of pressures over a number of years on resources in the public sector, and the absence of the straightforward yardstick of profit or loss, there have been persistent calls for investigations into value for money in central government. The term 'value for money' is not always clearly defined, but is now generally taken to cover the pursuit of economy, efficiency and effectiveness. The MPO, which is attached to the Cabinet Office, and the Treasury are centrally responsible for improving value for money in the Civil Service.

It has been said that central government does not give value for money, that it is over-staffed and inefficient, and that the numbers employed by central government and expenditure on manpower ought to be drastically cut. On the other hand there are those who say that there is little evidence of such inefficiency, that the officials in central government provide an excellent service, and that such criticisms are based on a dislike of any kind of public expenditure. These generalized arguments are difficult to resolve because it is in practice almost impossible to compare value for money for services which are not exactly paralleled anywhere else. Much work has been done in the departments and externally (see also Chapter 7) in promoting more efficient forms of financial management and control in wide ranging areas of government.

The MPO, and its predecessor, the Civil Service Department, have been criticized on the ground that they are not effective enough in pressing for improved value for money in central government. Once again, however, this is difficult to prove either way, but there is general consensus that effective machinery is essential to make sure that ways are constantly sought to improve value for money.

BIBLIOGRAPHY

The basic accounting material is covered in outline in a self-instruction package *Government Accounting* first published by HMSO in 1985. The set comprises five parts – Public Expenditure Survey: Supply Estimates: In-Year Monitoring: Appropriation Accounts and Outturn: Using Resources Well. This is a package for internal government use and while it is very clear it is purely descriptive. To get a balanced view, original documents and comments need to be studied. To get an idea of what the documents look like, it is important to skim the latest Public Expenditure White Paper, a volume of the Estimates and the Financial Statement and Budget Report, all published by HMSO and normally available in larger reference libraries.

Details of the constitutional position of Parliament and the government in the raising and spending of money can be obtained from any one of a number of books covering the field of public administration, government and public finance.

Some basic books covering aspects of public expenditure are:

Clarke, R.W.B. (1978) *Public Expenditure Management and Control* (Ed. Sir A. Cairncross), Macmillan.

Diamond, Lord (1975) *Public Expenditure in Practice*, George Allen & Unwin.

Goldman, Sir S. (1973) *Public Expenditure Management and Control*, HMSO.

Heclo, H. and Wildavsky, A. (1981) *The Private Government of Public Money*, 2nd edn., Macmillan.

Likierman, J.A. (1981) *Cash Limits and External Financing Limits*, Civil Service College Handbook No. 22, HMSO.

Prest, A. (1979) *Public Finance in Theory and Practice*, 6th edn., Weidenfeld and Nicholson.

and two books covering developments are:

Barnett, J. (1982) *Inside the Treasury*, Andre Deutsch.

Pliatzky, L. (1982) *Getting and Spending*, Basil Blackwell.

Most of the continuing discussion of financial reporting appears in the reports of and evidence to House of Commons Select Committees. Some of the most important reports in recent years are:

Expenditure Committee
14th report Session 1977-8 HC 661, Financial Accountability to Parliament.

Procedure (Supply) Committee
1st report Session 1980/1 HC 118.

Procedure (Finance) Committee
1st report Session 1982/3, HC 24.
Public Accounts Committee
3rd report Session 1976/7 HC 274: Cash Limits.
4th report Session 1977/8 HC 288: Supply Estimates and Cash Limits.
3rd report Session 1978/9 HC 232: Parliamentary Control of Public Expenditure.
13th report Session 1979/80 HC 570: Parliamentary Control of Public Expenditure.
27th report Session 1979/80 HC 766: Carry-Over of Cash Limits at the End of the Financial Year.
14th report Session 1980/1 HC 376: Treasury. Carry-Over of Cash Limits at the End of the Financial Year.
18th report Session 1981/2 HC 1981/2 HC 383: Publication and content of Appropriation Accounts.
Treasury and Civil Service Committee
6th report Session 1980/1 HC 325: The Form of the Estimates.
3rd report Session 1981/2 HC 236: Efficiency and Effectiveness in the Civil Service.
6th report Session 1981/2 HC 137: Budgetary Reform.
2nd report Session 1984/5 HC 110: The structure and form of financial documents presented to Parliament.

These Committees have a regular programme of work, and their reports should be monitored regularly. In particular the annual investigation of the Treasury and Civil Service Select Committee into the major expenditure reports (Autumn Statement, Public Expenditure White Paper and Budget) yield important information about reporting practices.

The Annual Reports of some Central Government bodies are also worth studying. The Department of Health and Social Security has improved its reports in recent years and the Department of the Environment tried a private sector style report in 1983. But generally the reports of central government bodies have tended to be either public relations documents or to be designed to comply strictly with the requirements in force.

Other literature in the area of government accounting, reporting and control includes:

Allen, D. (1981) 'Raynerism: strengthening Civil Service management', *RIPA Report*, Winter, Vol. 2. No. 4 .
Anthony, R.N. and Herzlinger, R.E. (1980) *Management control in*

non-profit organizations, Richard D. Irwin.

Bevan, R.G., Sisson, K. and Way, P. (1981) 'Cash limits and public sector pay', *Public Administration*, Vol. 59.

Carty, J. (1981) 'Accounting standards and central government', From *Public Finance and Accountancy*, October.

Drebin, A.R., Chan, J.L. and Ferguson, L.C. (1981) 'Objectives of accounting and financial report for governmental units: A research study', National Council on Government Accounting (USA).

Else, P.K., and Marshall, G.P. (1979) The Management of Public Expenditure, Policy Studies Institute.

Financial Accounting Standards Board (1980) *Objectives of financial reporting by non-business organizations*, FASB (USA).

General Accounting Office (1980) *Exposure Draft, Objectives of accounting and financial reporting in the Federal Government, GAO (USA)*.

Hardman, D.J. (1982) 'Models of government accounting', *Accounting and Finance* published by the Accounting Association of Australia and New Zealand, May.

Hills, J. (1984) Public assets and liabilities and the presentation of budgetary policy, *Public Finances in Perspective* (Ed. H. Ashworth), Institute of Fiscal Studies.

Institute of Fiscal Studies (1980) Report of a Committee on Budgetary Reform in the UK chaired by Lord Armstrong,, Oxford University Press.

Jones, R. and Pendlebury, M. (1984) *Public Sector Accounting*, Pitman.

Likierman, J.A. (1983) 'Maintaining the credibility of cash limits', *Fiscal Studies*, Spring, Vol. 4, No. 1.

Likierman, J.A. and Vass, P. (1984) *Structure and form of government expenditure reports*, Association of Certified Accountants.

Metcalf, L. and Richards, S. (1984) 'Raynerism and efficiency in government', *Issues in Public Sector Accounting* (eds A. Hopwood and C. Tompkins), Philip Allan.

Rutherford, B.A. (1983) *Financial reporting in the public sector*, Butterworths.

Sharp, K. (1981) 'Accounting standards and central government – Against,' *Public Finance and Accountancy*, October.

Steiss, A.W. (1982) *Management control in government*, Heath.

GLOSSARY*

Accounting Officer   An officer appointed by the Treasury historic-

* Taken from Supply Estimates 1982/3. Reproduced by permission of the Controller, Her Majesty's Stationery Office. Crown copyright.

ally in compliance with Section 22 of the Exchequer and Audit Departments Act 1866, to sign the Appropriation Accounts and any other accounts within his responsibility; and by virtue of that duty, the duty of being the principal witness on behalf of the department before the Committee of Public Accounts to deal with questions arising from those accounts, now covering financial management in its widest sense as well as matters of accuracy and regularity.

Ambit (of a Vote)   The description in Part I of a Supply Estimate, or of a Supplementary Supply Estimate, of the purposes for which provision is made. The ambit appears in the Schedule to the Appropriation Act and Parliament authorises specific sums of money to each ambit.

Appropriation Account   An end of year account of government departments' spending of monies voted by Parliament which compares the Supply Estimate (and any Supplementary Estimates) with actual payments made and receipts brought to account, and explains any substantial differences. An Appropriation Account is prepared for each Vote.

Appropriation in aid   Receipts which, with the authority of Parliament, are used to finance some of the gross expenditure on the Vote, thus limiting the amount to be issued from the Consolidated Fund to the net Vote.

Capital expenditure   Expenditure on new construction, land and extensions of and alterations to existing buildings and the purchase of any other fixed assets (e.g. machinery and plant) – including vehicles – having an expected working life of more than one year, and stocks. Also includes grants for capital purposes and lending.

Cash limit   The limit on the amount of cash that can be spent on certain specified services during one financial year.

Class   A group of Votes which broadly correspond to the voted expenditure element of one of the main programmes in the public expenditure survey.

Consolidated Fund   The Exchequer account into which are paid gross tax revenue, less repayments, and all other Exchequer receipts not specifically directed elsewhere. Issues from the Fund include issues to meet Supply services shown in Supply Estimates.

Contingencies Fund   A fund which can be used for urgent expenditure in anticipation of provision by Parliament becoming available. The Fund is limited to 2% of the previous year's total authorized Supply. Drawings on this fund must be repaid when Parliament has voted the additional sums required.

Economic classification   An analysis of public sector accounting transactions according to their economic character. It is based on the classification used by the Central Statistical Office for compiling the accounts of national income and expenditure.

Extra receipts by the Consolidated Fund   Receipts related to expenditure in the Supply Estimate which Parliament has not authorized to be used as appropriations in aid of the Vote.

Financial year   The year from 1 April one year to 31 March the next.

General administrative expenses   Current expenditure, other than pay, directly related to administration such as post and telephones, stationery, etc.

Grant   Money voted (i.e. granted) by Parliament to meet the services shown in Supply Estimates. Also used in individual subheads of Supply Estimates to describe an unrequited payment to an individual or body, in the private or public sector. (See also Subsidy.)

Grant in aid   A grant from voted monies to a particular organization or body where any unexpended balances of the sums issued during the financial year will not be liable for surrender to the Consolidated Fund. In such cases the chief official of the grant-aided body normally accounts in detail for expenditure, and the Accounting Officer of the department issuing the grant has the broader responsibility of ensuring that the conditions of grant are met.

Main programme   One of 17 main functional programmes within the public expenditure survey, for example defence, housing, social security. Most main programmes are further divided into sub-programmes.

National Audit Office (formerly Exchequer and Audit Department) The department of the Comptroller and Auditor General. Officers of this department carry out the audit of Appropriation and Trading Accounts (other than that of their own department), many related accounts, and by agreement a number of international accounts such as those of some of the specialized agencies of the United Nations.

Net subhead   A net subhead is created when receipts are offset against expenditure in a specific subhead, rather than appropriated in aid of the vote as a whole. In most cases the receipts equal or exceed the expenditure and only a token £10 is shown to be voted.

Outturn   Actual expenditure, normally in a financial year.

Programme   See Main programme.

Section   A group of subheads in the same programme and Vote. Sections provide a means of summarizing a Vote if, for example, it covers more than one programme.

Subhead   Expenditure within a Vote which is separately identified in the Appropriation Account. (See also Net subhead.)

Subsidy A grant (i.e. an unrequited payment) to a producer or trader which is deemed to benefit the consumer by reducing the selling price of the products. (See also Grant.)

Supply Estimate A statement presented to the House of Commons of the estimated expenditure of a department during a financial year (i.e. 1 April to 31 March) asking for the necessary funds to be voted.

Token subhead See Net subhead.

Token vote In some cases receipts of a kind that could be appropriated in aid of the vote are expected on a scale equal to or greater than the expected gross expenditure. In these circumstances, sufficient of the expected receipts are shown as appropriations in aid to leave only a nominal balance, usually £1000, to be voted as Supply. Part IV of the Estimate shows the balance of the receipts expected which are payable to the Consolidated Fund as extra receipts (see above). In addition, a Supplementary Estimate for a token sum may be presented, for example to transfer some existing provision to a new service in the same vote.

Vote An individual Supply Estimate.

Votes on Account Monies granted by Parliament to carry on public services from 1 April of the next financial year until the passing of the Appropriation Act, which authorizes the issue of the amount required for the full year.

3

Local government and its financing

3.1 SCOPE

Finance and accounting in local government is probably more complex than in any other part of the public sector, not least because it has developed in a quite distinctive way. It is therefore not possible to make a fully comprehensive presentation on all the many aspects which are covered. The aim is rather to provide an introduction, highlighting points of current debate and relating them to the other parts of the public sector, where appropriate.

Because local government finance and accounting have developed in a distinctive fashion, they have also developed a terminology that may be unfamiliar even to those with experience of finance in either the public or the private sector. A glossary of terms and a guide to sources are provided at the end of Chapter 4. There is also a list of abbreviations on pages 285-6.

This chapter outlines the structure of local government and goes on to examine the main aspects of the financial relationship between central and local government. Chapter 4 reviews the internal control and external reporting of local government.

It has to be borne in mind that British local government is not homogeneous. There are different systems of local government in England, Wales, Scotland and Northern Ireland. It is not possible to take full account of this variety and the material below specifically refers to England, although for most purposes this also covers Wales. Scotland has a broadly similar system of local government but a different legislative framework (and legal system). Northern Ireland has, at present, a much more limited form of local government. Parish councils (community councils in Wales) are local authorities and an important part of the fabric of local democracy – there are over 9000 in the UK. But as they are not major spenders, they are not covered in depth and more details of their operations are described in Ousby and Wright (1976).

3.2 THE ENVIRONMENT OF LOCAL GOVERNMENT – STRUCTURE AND FUNCTIONS

Local authorities in Great Britain provide a very wide range of services which, as with the nationalized industries, have a daily impact on almost everyone. They are labour-intensive, employing over two million people, and account for about one eighth of gross domestic product. Just under a third of all houses in Great Britain are rented from local authorities.

The functions of local government are diverse and the allocation of functions between authorities as of 1985 is summarized in Table 3.1. This is not a definitive guide, but is intended to indicate just how disparate is local government. Unlike the health service and major nationalized industries, local government does not have one broad unifying service or function. Any local authority is responsible for a range of functions, often with no apparent link except that they are in fact provided by a single body.

Even within English local government, which forms the main frame of reference for this chapter, taking a particular group of authorities, e.g. metropolitan districts with the same basic functions, it is important not to underestimate the variety of practice and style of operation. Each has a different set of problems, of aspects, of elected members and of staff. Local government is not uniform. This is the idea behind *local* government, although it is not always appreciated and certainly not always supported by those involved in commenting on, consuming or even providing local government services.

It is not possible here to devote much space to the history of local government and how it developed into present day structure and functions. It may perhaps suffice to say that local government has evolved gradually from a pre-19th century system of counties, boroughs and parishes.

Local government's recent history has been dominated by a major reorganization in 1974 in England and Wales outside London (1975 in Scotland), which altered structures – amalgamating authorities – and the allocation of functions both between types of authority and between local government and other public bodies. Since that reorganization, the economic climate faced by local authorities has deteriorated, despite few reductions in public

Table 3.1
Main Functions of Local Authorities as at 1985

Function	Metropolitan		England and Wales non-metropolitan		London		Scotland	
	County	District	County	District	GLC	Borough	Region	District
Consumer protection	X		X				X	
Education		X	X		(Inner London)	X	X	X
Environmental health		X		X		X		X
Fire service	X		X		X		X	X
Housing		X		X	X	X	X	X
Industrial development	X	X	X	X	X	X	X	X
Libraries		X	X	X	X	X	X	X
Passenger transport	X		X		X		X	X
Planning								
Structure plans	X		X		X		X	
Development control		X		X	X	X	X	X
Police	X		X		X (Central Government)	X	X	X
Rate collection								
Recreation		X		X		X	X	X
Refuse disposal	X	X	X	X	X	X	X	X
Social services		X	X		X	X	X	
Transport and highways								
Policy and principal roads	X		X		X		X	
Non-principal roads		X		X		X	X	X

The aim of this list is to give a brief summary of the distribution of the main functions. There are many footnotes possible in a list of this type and a detailed summary can be found in Byrne (1981).

expectations about service provision. The tensions caused by these conflicting pressures have contributed to further calls for a review of structures and functions, particularly in London, which was reorganized in 1965, and in metropolitan areas, and in respect of 'regional' government. But there is little consensus about the outcome of any change or indeed whether the costs of undertaking changes outweigh the benefits. Certainly the experience of the 1974 reorganizations led many inside local government to question whether effort devoted to restructuring – even for admirable ends – could be fully justified when there were pressures to devote the maximum effort actually to managing services.

Notwithstanding such reservations, it appeared likely at the time of writing that a Bill would pass through Parliament in 1985 with the aim of abolishing the Greater London Council and the metropolitan counties. This would involve transferring services to districts and boroughs, to ad hoc bodies such as fire boards, and in some cases outside local government altogether. The details of Chapters 3 and 4 are based on the pre-abolition situation.

There are a number of useful texts on structure and history noted in the further reading, with Byrne (1981) being a particularly accessible and wide-ranging summary.

3.3 LOCAL AUTHORITY INCOME AND EXPENDITURE – A SUMMARY

Local authority income and expenditure can be categorised in a variety of ways, and each of the most important categories is highlighted below. In most cases, these categories have significance either for resource allocation at the national level or locally or for control mechanisms. To make the summaries readily comprehensible, concepts and definitions have been presented in a simplified form, and fuller details will be found in the original sources.

The first major subdivision is between capital and revenue expenditure. The trends in the two types of expenditure are shown in Fig. 3.1. It can be seen that over the period concerned capital expenditure bore the brunt of the cuts in local government services, particularly those falling on housing capital expenditure.

Because local authorities are subject to a variety of legislative requirements, their expenditure has to some extent to be subdivided into separate funds. There are essentially four broad types of fund. Their relative importance is shown in Table 3.2. It

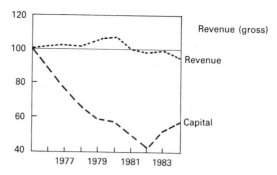

Fig. 3.1 Local authority expenditure in Great Britain at 1984 prices (Derived from *Public Expenditure White Paper 1985-86 to 1987-88*, Cmnd 9428. Reproduced by permission of the Controller, Her Majesty's Stationery Office. Crown copyright.

Table 3.2
Distribution of Gross Revenue and Capital Expenditure between Funds

Fund	% of gross revenue expenditure	% of gross capital expenditure
Rate fund services	81	56
Housing revenue account	14	33
Trading services	2	4
Special funds (superannuation, capital, etc.)	3	7
Total	100	100

Reproduced from *Local Government Financial Statistics England and Wales 1982/83* (1984), Department of the Environment, by permission of the Controller of Her Majesty's Stationery Office. Crown copyright.

can be seen that for revenue expenditure the rate fund overshadows all others, whereas, for capital, Housing Revenue Account expenditure is very important.

The rate fund dominates local authority finance and is accordingly analysed in more detail. The distribution of its gross revenue expenditure is shown in Fig. 3.2 and the sources of its gross income in Fig. 3.3. It can be seen that rate fund expenditure is dominated by the education service.

Turning to the sources of rate fund finance, it can be seen that the rates are very much a minority source of finance. Central government grants of one type or another represent about half total income. It is perhaps hardly surprising that central government takes so much interest in the details of local authority

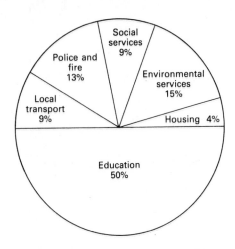

Fig. 3.2 Where the money goes: rate funded services. (Derived from *Local Government Financial Statistics, England and Wales 1982/83* (1984), Department of the Environment, by permission of the Controller of Her Majesty's Stationery Office. Crown copyright).

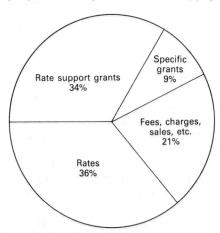

Fig. 3.3 Where the money comes from: rate fund services. (Derived from *Local Government Financial Statistics, England and Wales 1982/83* (1984), Department of the Environment, by permission of the Controller of Her Majesty's Stationery Office. Crown copyright).

expenditure. The importance of sales, fees, charges and similar types of income is sometimes overlooked and this is an area that has received increasing attention (Glasby, 1981; Coopers & Lybrand, 1981). The relationship between grants and rates means

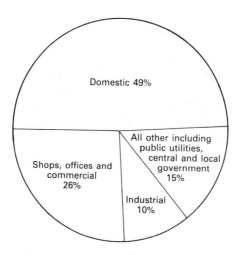

Fig. 3.4 Analysis of rateable values in England and Wales at 1 April 1983. (Derived from *Local Government Financial Statistics, England and Wales 1982/83* (1984), Department of the Environment, by permission of the Controller of Her Majesty's Stationery Office. Crown copyright).

that relatively small changes in government grant received can have a quite dramatic effect on rates levied. The distribution of rateable values (Fig. 3.4) shows the importance of commercial and industrial ratepayers, and it should also be noted that public sector bodies are also major ratepayers. A very brief guide to the rating system is set out in Appendix 3.1.

The Housing Revenue Account has a quite different type of financial profile from the rate fund. Its revenue expenditure is dominated by loan charges, representing the cost of borrowing to create the housing stock. About a quarter of its income is from government subsidies, although these are reducing in importance and rents have generally been increased substantially in real terms in consequence.

Local authorities' past borrowing is reflected in the very large volume of debt outstanding – well over £30,000 million. This does not represent authorities being in deficit on revenue account – there are only very limited powers to borrow for this purpose – but instead reflects the creation of social infrastructure. The loans financing this debt derive from a variety of sources (Table 3.3) with the Public Works Loans Board – part of central government – being the major source. In any one year, local authorities will use funding other than loan, and the major sources of capital finance are shown in Table 3.4.

Table 3.3
Summary of Debt Outstanding by Source of Finance
(England and Wales)

Source of loans	% as at 31 March 1983
Public Works Loans Board	41.4
Bonds and mortgages	14.0
Internal sources	24.1
Temporary loans	8.5
Stock issues	1.6
Local bonds	6.7
Other	3.7
Total	100.0

Reproduced from *Return of Outstanding Debt as at 31 March 1983*, CIPFA SIS (1984), by permission.

Table 3.4
Sources of Capital Finance

	% of gross capital financing resources
Loans	49
Capital receipts from the sale of fixed assets	35
Capital grants from central government	6
Revenue contributions to capital outlay (RCCO) – capital funded directly from revenue	3
Other, including transfers between funds, authorities and lotteries	7
	100

Leasing is not included here but is a not insignificant source of finance. (Reproduced from *Local Government Financial Statistics, England and Wales 1982/83* (1984) Department of the Environment. Reproduced by permission of the Controller of Her Majesty's Stationery Office. Crown copyright.)

3.4 THE LEGISLATIVE BASIS OF LOCAL GOVERNMENT

Almost all local government's powers are derived from legislation and, in contrast to the arrangements in some other countries, local authorities do not have the power to spend on any purpose they see fit, except for a 2p rate 'in the interests of their area' under Section 137 of the 1972 Local Government Act. The legislative framework is of great importance to the finance, accounting and audit of local government, and local finance has become increasingly subject to the legislative decisions of Parliament.

In some of the major current issues surrounding local government, there is a close link between constitutional, legislative and financial matters and it is therefore necessary to examine the background to these and indeed to touch on the rationale for local government, as it is difficult to make judgements about the efficiency and effectiveness of local government and its finance merely by examining structure and functions.

The legislative framework covers three broad areas:

(a) duties or powers to provide *services*,
(b) specification of the *structure* of local government,
(c) specification of the arrangements for *financing* local authorities.

Some Acts of Parliament have touched on all three areas; for example, the 1972 Local Government Act restructured local government boundaries and functions in England and Wales, consolidated legislation relating to powers and duties, and contained some financial clauses. But the 1972 Act did not in fact reflect a simultaneous and systematic review of services, structure and finance. It was really about structural review. One of its great faults was that it did not also reform finance.

Financial changes were made in 1948, 1958, 1966, 1976, 1980, 1982 and 1984, but were concerned only with parts of local government finance, such as rating or grants, and were in no sense comprehensive measures of financial reform. And when it comes to powers and duties, these have accumulated through literally dozens of Acts of Parliament passed over many years. Powers and duties are also affected by secondary legislation – regulations and statutory instruments – which are also extensive in scope.

Even though Acts of Parliament may contain reference to financial implications, there is no close or necessary relation between the powers and duties which have accumulated over many years and the equally ad hoc financial framework which has developed.

Two aspects of the legislative basis of local government need to be highlighted because of their far-reaching implications. The first is the degree to which legislation categorizes local authority powers between 'mandatory' powers, which impose a duty on local authorities to do something, and 'discretionary' powers, which allow them to provide a service at their own discretion. If it were possible to separate powers, and hence expenditure, into such categories it would assist in the clarification of many important aspects of local government finance. The Layfield Committee (1976) reviewed this question in some depth, and the review is contained in Annex 12 of their Report. It repays reading in full.

The conclusions reached were of great signifiance and the key aspects, summarized below, demonstrate the complexity of the influences on local government spending:

> The respective responsibilities of central and local government for local services could not at present be expressed in terms which could form a reliable base for the allocation of financial responsibility.
>
> The difficulty we encountered throughout was that the categories of local government expenditure which are manifestly either totally discretionary or totally mandatory are very limited; the bulk of local government expenditure falls somewhere between the two extremes, being determined not by formal requirements alone nor by free local choice alone but by a complex mixture of pressures and influences. Informal advice and exhortation from government departments, inspection, nationally accepted standards, accumulated past practice, professional attitudes, political influences and actions by various pressure groups, national and local, all play a part in determining local government expenditure, along with the statutory provisions. (Layfield Committee (1976) pp. 403-404)

The second aspect of local government legislation which has become a matter of note is the marked extent to which topics relating to local authority expenditure have become the subject of dispute in the courts. Up to the late 1970s this was a rare occurrence, but by the early 1980s there had been a variety of court cases on local authority expenditure, the best known being the case brought by Bromley LBC against the Greater London Council over the legality of a supplementary rate levied primarily to enable a fares reduction to be made on London Transport. But there were also cases brought by industrial firms and ratepayers' groups over rates and expenditure being too high, as well as by consumer or pressure groups over failures to provide services. Local authorities also began to use the courts to try to reverse decisions of the Secretary of State for the Environment which were, in their opinion, unreasonable. The variety of this litigation demonstrated the extent to which local government finance had become a matter of confrontation rather than consensus. (See Appendix 4.1.)

3.5 THE NEED FOR LOCAL GOVERNMENT

Though virtually all developed countries have a system of local government, some systems involve considerable local autonomy, while others involve less. On a spectrum, the English and Welsh systems probably involve less, rather than more, autonomy.

But why have local government at all? This question and the answers are important because they reflect the type of financial framework required. One summary of the case for local government is L.J. Sharpe's (1970):

> To sum up: the participatory value, if not the liberty value, still remains as a valid one for modern local government. Not perhaps in the full glory of its early promoters, but as an important element in a modern democracy nonetheless. But as a coordinator of services in the field; as a reconciler of community opinion; as a consumer pressure group; as an agent for responding to rising demand; and finally as a counter-weight to incipient syndicalism, local government seems to have come into its own.

The Layfield Committee (1976, p. 53) lists the following points in local government's favour.

(a) It provides democracy.
(b) It acts a a counter-weight to the uniformity inherent in government decisions. It spreads political power.
(c) It embraces accountability because it brings those resonsible for decisions close to their electors.
(d) It is efficient because services can be adjusted to local needs and preferences, and because responsibility can be more decentralised.
(e) Central government would be overloaded by more functions.
(f) It provides a vehicle for formulating new policies and pioneering ideas. Scope for these are limited in centralized organizations concerned to apply policies uniformly.

It is noticeable that at a time when many inside local government felt that constitutional and financial developments were challenging the traditions of local government, there was a growth in publications justifying the bases of local government (Stewart, 1983 and Local Government Training Board, 1984).

3.6 INTERNAL ORGANIZATION AND STRUCTURE

Of the over 500 principal local authorities in the UK, probably no two have exactly the same internal organization and structure. *Local* authorities will be organized to best reflect *local* situations.

But, in practice, there is considerable similarity in terms of the general principles of organization and structure, which tend to group around a few broad types.

One of the distinct features of local government, which has widespread implications for both financial policy and operations, is the predominant and often detailed role played by elected councillors (or elected members as they often are also called) in management. This has few parallels in central government where most Ministers cannot, by reason of time, become overinvolved in detailed operations.

But in local government the committee, composed of elected councillors, advised by officers, not only performs a monitoring role but also has executive powers. Although the roles of committees may have gradually changed, it would be unwise to underestimate their continuing importance. And although the relative 'strength' of officers and members is as lively a topic of debate now as it was in the 19th century, there is little indication that local authorities are becoming more dominated by their full-time paid officers.

3.7 CORPORATE MANAGEMENT

The idea of corporate management gathered momentum in local government in the 1960s. It was stimulated by the Maud Management Committee Report (Committee on the Management of Local Government, 1967), which was critical of the lack of professionalism by elected members and the lack of a corporate approach by both members and officers. The tradition of separate committees and departments was strong, and indeed continues to be so. Maud's well thought out but radical ideas found favour only in a few authorities initially and it has to be said that much of his critique still holds true today. But by the time the Bains Report (1972) was published, there was at least acceptance of the need to set up a structure which could promote corporate management even if the structure alone was not enough. Such structures included a Chief Executive with a clear brief to coordinate and lead, a management team of Directors to provide a vehicle for coordination, and a greater number of interdepartmental working groups to promote closer working between staff at a variety of levels.

Authorities today do tend to have corporate management structures. The Policy and Resources Committee, recommended by Bains as a central unifying influence, is found almost universally. So, too, is the Chief Executive. He or she is no longer the old Town Clerk *primus inter pares* with fellow chief officers, but clearly head of the paid service. Almost all authorities now have chief officer management teams chaired by the Chief Executive (perhaps also now with elected members present) to coordinate the Council's day-to-day affairs. Whether or not these structures do lead to effective corporate management is quite another matter and they certainly do not guarantee it.

At the time of reorganization there was much concern among chief financial officers that corporate management would put them in a subordinate position, subject to consensus decision making, and even to the lowest common demominator. This has happened in some places and it has been felt to happen in others; but overall a tremendous amount depends on the calibre and personality of the Chief Financial Officer and his staff. And corporate management has brought advantages to the finance department because they are at the centre of the system. Problems of overlap do occur, e.g. 'What is the role of the Chief Executive or Director of Personnel in budgeting?', but in practice the advent of corporate management has not usually weakened the influence of a good Chief Financial Officer.

3.8 LOCAL AUTHORITY ASSOCIATIONS

One aspect of local authority structure that is particularly important is the role of the local authority associations. In Scotland there is a single association representing all authorities – Regions, Islands and Districts – particularly in relations with central government. An equivalent to this single Confederation of Scottish Local Authorities (COSLA) does not exist in England, where the different types of local authority have their own associations, namely:

ACC: Association of County Councils (non-metropolitan counties);

ADC: Association of District Councils (non-metropolitan districts);

AMA: Association of Metropolitan Authorities (metropolitan counties and districts and London Boroughs);

In London political differences led to the splitting of councils into two groups, though confusingly some authorities belong to both:

LBA: London Boroughs Association

ALA: Association of London Authorities

The associations play a key role in representing and advocating their members' interests, particularly with central government. They are convenient to central government who would find difficulty negotiating with a large number of individual authorities. The associations are political bodies with a majority party, whose view will generally predominate in major policy issues. Since at any one time the English associations may be under differing political control, this has often made it difficult for local government to present a common stand on major financial issues. United opposition to the passage of the 1980 Local Government Planning and Land Act through Parliament was diffused when the Association of County Councils in essence agreed with the Government to reduce the scale of their opposition to the legislation.

3.9 LOCAL AND CENTRAL GOVERNMENT – FINANCIAL RELATIONS

The sections above outline the way local authorities are structured and managed, and briefly indicated sources of finance and types of expenditure. Attention is now directed to probably the single most important topic in local government finance and accounting – the relations between central and local government. This topic has, directly and indirectly, been the subject of a large and increasing literature, including the report of a major Commission of Enquiry (the Layfield Committee). It has also been one of the key issues upon which the Economic and Social Research Council has directed its research resources.

The very magnitude and complexity of the subject makes it difficult to summarize in an introductory text. It has also latterly been an area subject to frequent, if not over-frequent, policy changes and legislation. This means that not only points of detail, but also points of principle can rapidly become out-dated. In general, therefore, the discussion below tries to emphasize general principles. These are accompanied by relatively brief descriptions of the grant and resource allocation systems in force at the time of writing (mid-1985). For those requiring a more detailed and up-to-date explanation of a particular area, further sources are indicated in the bibliography.

Three areas are examined to illustrate the nature of the central-local relationship, and how it is changing. They are the main areas in which central government sets financial targets, either for local government as a whole, or for individual authorites:

(a)   the Public Expenditure White Paper;
(b)   rate support grant;
(c)   capital programmes.

Other areas of importance with their own particular legal or policy context, but which are not examined here, are housing and transport finance, education pooling, borrowing controls, charging policies and direct labour organizations.

The question of the central-local financial relationship has been a source of concern on both sides for the hundred years that modern local government has existed. Formal and informal reviews and reports have been produced, typically with few changes actually arising from them. In 1974 the then Government set up a Committee of Enquiry into Local Government Finance (the Layfield Committee) which was to undertake the most thorough review of local government finance yet seen. Its report published in 1976 will remain essential reading for many years whenever the broad principles of finance are discussed. The report discusses many areas of local government finance and a few key points relating to the central-local relationship are outlined below, discussing the three types of financial target.

An early discovery of the Layfield Committee was that:

We were asked to consider the whole system of local government finance and we have come to the conclusion that there is at present no coherent system. (p. 49)

Layfield categorized the requirements of a coherent financial system as:

Accountability
Fairness between individuals
Fairness between areas
Balance between consumption and investment
Efficiency
Stability
Flexibility
Comprehensibility

and also pointed out that finance could not really be reviewed in isolation from the structure and functions of local government.

The Government's reaction to Layfield was set out in a May 1977 Green Paper (DOE, 1977) and proposed moving forward in areas such as Unitary Grant and an Advisory Committee on Audit. The main proposal on a new grant system was subject to great hostility from the local authority associations and was dropped. The incoming Government of 1979 reintroduced both the block grant and new controls on capital and direct labour organizations in the Local Government, Planning and Land Act of 1980. Further alterations to block grant and a new audit system were brought in with the Local Government Finance Act of 1982. These measures were intended to secure greater control by central government on the one hand and greater accountability to local communities on the other. It was agreed by individual members of the Layfield Committee (Raine, 1981) that this outcome intensified the confusion inherent in the old system. And with another Green Paper, on Alternatives to Domestic Rates (DOE, 1981d), again concentrating on just one aspect of local government finance in isolation, there was powerful evidence that the lessons of Layfield had not been learnt.

In order to clarify the central-local relationships the Layfield Committee had set out two alternative systems of local government finance:

(a) *Based on greater central responsibility* – under this, both the total of local expenditure and the priorities between local services would be decided by the government, which would be seen to carry the main responsibilities for expenditure control.

(b) *Based on greater local responsibility* – the responsibility for control of expenditure would rest primarily with local authorities. They would be responsible to their electorates for expenditure incurred and revenues raised. Grants would not play a dominant role and the local tax base would need to be widened. The government's powers would only operate to meet the needs of national economic management, of which local authorities should have full understanding.

The Committee did put a strongly-held view among their members that the only way to sustain a vital local democracy was to enlarge the share of local taxation to make councillors more accountable to local electorates. A local income tax for this purpose would be justified.

Since Layfield reported, the local income tax has been rejected by government, though it has been argued that it could have been viable (Bennett, 1981). Most of those involved in local government in England would argue that the incoherent system of finance discovered by Layfield was becoming even more incoherent in the 1980s.

A further review was set in motion in 1984 with a view to reporting during 1985. This was set up as an internal departmental review by junior ministers at the Department of the

Environment. The government's belief was that this would lead to more chance of useful progress than would occur through the full panoply of a formal enquiry. There were no formal terms of reference as such. Ministers indicated the studies would be concerned with the main features of local authorities financial arrangements, including rate support grant distribution, the balance between exchequer and local financing of local authorities, measures for improving local accountability, and how local revenues might best be raised. Initial indications suggested that quite major constitutional issues might be raised in this perhaps surprisingly informal set of studies.

3.10 THE ROLE OF CENTRAL GOVERNMENT

Central government's perception of its role in relation to local government was set out clearly in its response to Layfield:

> Because of their responsibilities for the management of the economy, central government must concern themselves with total local government expenditure and taxation. They also have responsibility for the development of policy for particular services. Central government's role is therefore:
> — to ensure that the local services (education, personal social services, housing, etc.) reflect national priorities and national policies and are provided at broadly comparable standards;
> — to ensure that, in aggregate, local government's spending plans are compatible with the government's economic objectives;
> — to ensure that activities of one authority do not have adverse effects on the area of another;
> — to promote cooperation between local authority and other complementary services;
> — to ensure that the financial arrangements promote efficiency;
> — to safeguard the interests of vulnerable minority groups whose interests may get a proper hearing only at national level;
> — to encourage and maintain local democracy.

(Reproduced from Department of the Environment Green Paper *Local Government Finance* (1977) by permission of the Controller of Her Majesty's Stationery Office. Crown copyright.)

The government's response to Layfield's 'central' and local options was to define a middle way – which Layfield had rejected as a possibility. It proposed to develop a block grant and to 'strengthen' financial machinery for four reasons:

(a) expenditure control — central government needs to be able to exert more effective influence over total local authority expenditure;

(b) equity — ratepayers should pay a similar rate poundage for a comparable level of service wherever they live;

(c) accountability — local electors need to have some improved way of assessing local spending decisions and of requiring local authorities to account for them;

(d) policy control — in some services the government needs to have additional financial powers to promote particular policies.

In Layfield's terms, these conclusions probably represented an implicit move towards a more centrally based approach, and with the coming into effect of the 1984 Rates Act, which introduced rate capping, this centrally based approach became even more explicit.

3.11 THE MACRO-ECONOMIC CASE FOR CONTROLLING LOCAL GOVERNMENT SPENDING

The Layfield Committee supported the Government's objective of controlling the total of local authority expenditure – neither local authorities nor local tax payers being in a position to assess the competing claims on national resources or the pressures which local authority expenditure may generate.

There are, however, other views, as Barlow (1981) describes in his useful review of the various Keynesian, monetarist and structuralist arguments for macro-economic control. He concludes:

> If local democracy is to be valued highly, then this freedom (to make choices about the provision of services) is essential to local government, and if local government is to be preserved, local authorities should no longer accept unequivocally the argument that control over their levels of expenditure by central government is essential to economic management. (p. 12)

There is not space here to consider these macro-economic questions in more depth, but it is certainly the case that within local government there is no longer the near-unanimous agreement to the government's right to control total local spending that there once was. Most local authorities do take note of the government's broad wishes, but the essence of local democracy is to be able to act according to local needs and preferences, if necessary. This is why there is widespread hostility to specific controls even by authorities who would generally have no need to worry about the adverse impacts of such controls themselves.

3.12 THE PUBLIC EXPENDITURE WHITE PAPER

The production of the Public Expenditure White Paper is discussed in Chapter 2. It took some time for the government to relate together explicitly public expenditure plans and the rate support grant settlement. Not until the 1975 White Paper was there a direct reconciliation between the two sets of figures. 1975 was also the year that the Consultative Council on Local Government Finance (CCLGF) was set up. Its purpose is to promote regular consultation and cooperation between central and local government on major issues of common concern, with special emphasis on the deployment of resources both in the long and short term. The CCLGF is the forum for all ministerial-level meetings on the RSG and is supported by various groups of officials representing both central government and the local authority associations. The subgroups examine the *service* implications within planning targets set by the Consultative Council. The interim reports of the subgroups go to expenditure steering groups which consider the implications for *policy*. Reports setting out steering groups' preferred distribution of expenditure and the achievability of the planning targets then go to the official steering group and the Consultative Council.

Some of the topics regularly discussed at the Consultative Council are set out below. Approximate timings are shown but latterly experience has shown that there are no 'normal' years:

March — Setting the terms of reference for the officer working groups on grant and expenditure for the ensuing year.

May — Consideration of the DOE/CIPFA return of expenditure and rates.

July — Local authorities' input into PESC.

October — Negotiations on expenditure considered relevant for RSG.

December — The statutory meeting on RSG.

The local authority associations have pressed for some time for more involvement in the public expenditure survey process because:

(a) Local authorities only provide an input in describing the policy implications of different funding levels. They play no part in the actual decisions on plans.

(b) Local authorities are actually responsible for a very significant section of public expenditure.

(c) If the central government were to win local government's confidence and support in pursuing national policies, local government would have to feel it had participated in the deliberations whereby those policies are fixed.

(d) Local authorities are directly in touch with the real needs of the public and are best able to assess the impacts of government policies on their own environments.

The Layfield Committee recommended the establishment of a new joint forum to improve communication between central and local government, and provide detailed analysis of the impact of central policies on local government finance. The government, in its 1977 Green Paper rejected this proposal, instead preferring to see the CCLGF and its subsidiary committees developed.

The CCLGF does enable local authorities to put their views to a variety of Ministers but whether it, and the subsidiary committees, really provide effective two-way consultation is another matter. During the economic constraints which have characterized most of the period since the 1974 local government reorganization, central governments of different political persuasion have often been seen by local authorities as directing rather than consulting.

One commentator (Taylor, 1979) has noted:

> The public expenditure survey in the UK treats local authority expenditure in a much more detailed way than the equivalent process in other countries. Participation by the local authority associations in that process, albeit in a very circumscribed way, can only give spurious legitimacy to the centre's desire at a time of economic stringency to specify the precise use of PESC finance.

In the absence of what they regard as genuine consultation, it is perhaps hardly surprising that the local authority associations refuse to frank the government's detailed decisions. For example, in one RSG Report (Local Authority Associations, 1981) they pointed out:

> Annexe A to the RSG Report, 1980, sets out a breakdown of expenditure between services, which is stated to be tentative, and one which will be affected by individual local authorities' decisions taken in the light of their judgement of local needs and conditions. The associations do not endorse this or any breakdown of local authority expenditure. (p. 33)

Having noted the local authority associations' misgivings about their own role in the public expenditure survey, there is no doubt that the White Paper has been an important document for local authorities for several reasons:

(a) Given the importance of central government decisions on rate support grant, and over capital expenditure allocations, any indications of the government's intentions will assist planning.

(b) The relative priority given to local government spending, as opposed to other areas of public expenditure, can be seen.

(c) Though there is a general feeling in local government that they retain the right to make their own decisions, local authorities are responsible bodies who will often wish to take the government's wishes into account in finalizing their expenditure plans.

(d) The breakdown of expenditure for services is useful in this context for deriving *overall* changes for different types of authority.

There are, however, problems of both principle and latterly of practice, which have tended to reduce the relevance of the Public Expenditure White Paper to local government. For example, the Director of CIPFA (Hepworth, 1980, pp. 5-6) has set out the main problems which local government sees in the public expenditure survey system.

(a) Local government is not involved in the preparation of the basic plans. Although it comments on the consequences of the plans, any modifications are not agreed with local government.

(b) The public expenditure survey is not only a national economic planning document, but also an expression of the political views of the central government. Local government may therefore have no 'emotional' commitment to supporting the plan.

(c) The public expenditure survey presents the national position, but national figures are impossible to interpret at local level.

(d) Although expenditure plans have been reconciled to rate support grant totals, the reconciliation is for one year only.

(e) Definitional problems, e.g. over price base, cause a lack of understanding of what the public expenditure survey is trying to do, or even ought to do.

(f) The short-term basis of planning presents local government with major problems of logistics in deciding how it should cope with decline or growth.

(g) Because central government has more direct control over capital than revenue expenditure, it has tended to use the former as a regulator, which has led to 'a greater arbitrariness in capital investment decision making'.

The 1981/82 and 1982/83 White Papers contained alterations to style and format which began to erode seriously their utility to local government. It seems to have become the custom for the White Paper to be published in the New Year rather than in November, as was the original intentenion. Since local authorities have already been notified of their RSG and capital allocations before Christmas, the first year of the plans are of limited relevance. What are more useful are the second and subsequent years. But the 1981/82 White Paper reduced the number of future years from three to two and did not subdivide local authority expenditure by service for these years, only into blocks of expenditure within the overall programmes. The 1982/83 White Paper did not even analyse future spending by spending authorities, only by programme area. These reductions in future year information were justified by the government because of the uncertainties faced, even though the lead times for major changes in direction, and for capital programming, are considerably more than 12 months ahead.

The move to cash planning in the 1982/83 White Paper and the complete absence of constant price forecasts reduced the usefulnesss of the White Paper for most kinds of planning in the local government sector. In central government services, the rate of pay and price inflation is to some extent controlled by government itself. But local government is autonomous and cannot always be expected to conform to government pay and price norms (even where it wishes to). If the government puts 'unrealistic' inflation factors into the forecasts, local authorities will not feel committed to the plans. It could appear that the government itself no longer places much importance on providing medium-term planning information to local government.

Despite their own reservations, the local authority asociations have pressed for more involvement in the PESC process, but it is increasingly being argued in local government circles (see Raine, 1981) that, in fact, local authorities' own expenditure should be removed from the Public Expenditure White Paper, which should be concerned only with the expenditure directly under the control of central government (e.g. grants and loans to local government). This is because local authorities are autonomous bodies with a right to set their own local tax and responsible for carrying out legislation in the ways felt to be necessary by them in relation to local interpretation of needs. It will only be a coincidence if the totality of local government expenditure, arrived at by hundreds of local decisions, equates to a national planning figure over which local government has no real influence.

It can be seen that the Public Expenditure White Paper process, which during the 1970s had some measure of acceptance, albeit grudging, from local government, by the 1980s had been seen to take on an increasingly unhelpful, and indeed threatening, role.

3.13 RATE SUPPORT GRANT — BACKGROUND

The rate support grant (RSG) is one of the most significant financial mechanisms in the public sector. It involves some £9 billion cash being transferred from central to local government in England alone. The overall size and distribution of the RSG has always involved controversy and often disagreement between the government and local authority associations. The intensity of this controversy heightened after 1979 as the RSG became the focus of disagreements betwen central government on the one hand, and both individual authorities and some or all associations on the other. The RSG has developed over a long period and has been subject to changes of principle and detail, sometimes even within a single year. Its main objective had always been relatively clear, namely to subsidize local services by redistributing central taxation to compensate local authorities for:

(a) differences in spending needs,
(b) differences in their ability to raise local revenue from their taxable resources.

These objectives reflect a relatively homogenous society. In the USA, for example, much less emphasis is placed on the second objective. There has been considerable debate over alternative methods of financing local government and these are well summarized in sources indicated in the bibliography. The aim in this section is to examine how the main aspect of central-local financial relations has operated in recent years.

In order to understand the present grant system, it is important to see what went before, and why it was replaced. The rate support grant system that applied from 1974 to 1981 was broadly as follows. Firstly, the government decided on a national total of expenditure for local government. A percentage of this – around 60% – was funded by the government as rate support grant. From this total cash available as RSG were deducted specific and supplementary grants. The net cash remaining was distributed to authorities in three elements:

(a) *Domestic element* — A reduction of rate poundage for domestic rate payers. This has been 18.5p for a number of years.
(b) *Resources element* — This enabled all local authorities who received it to spend a similar amount per head for the same local rate poundage. Authorities with rateable values below a 'national standard' received sufficient grant to bring them up to the national standard.

(c) *Needs element* — The largest element in the grant. Its aim was to compensate for differences in authorities' needs to spend. Measuring 'needs' is inevitably subjective and this was done by a formula based on an analysis of the relationship between local expenditure and indicators of local needs. It utilized the statistical technique of multiple regression analysis.

The needs element was a fixed amount not affected in the year in question by the Council's own level of expenditure. The resources element depended on the Council's spending. The more was spent, the more resources element was received.

In the Department of the Environment's submission to the Layfield Committee, they suggested 'Unitary Grant'. This was to replace the resources and needs elements and would have the following advantages:

(a) It would be payable to all authorities, promoting clearer accountability.

(b) Under the resources element there was no limit to an individual Council's grant entitlement. But there was a national cash limit. So if authorities put in grant claims collectively totalling more than the cash limit, the government would pro-rata reduce *all* authorities' grant. This process, known as 'clawback', affected low-spending Councils as much as high-spending ones. With Unitary Grant, high-spending Councils should be penalized without affecting low-spending ones.

(c) It would be possible fully to equalize needs and resources with a smaller total of grant than with needs and resources elements.

(d) It would arguably be more comprehensible.

These were not inherently unreasonable objectives and the Layfield Committee did not rule out a Unitary Grant, although it pointed out that a more explicit assessment of individual authorities' spending needs would be required. Equalization of resources should relate to total personal income rather than total rateable value. Layfield also strongly emphasized:

> Although the amount of grant will influence local authorities' plans in the medium term, it should not be used as a means of short-term regulation of local expenditure or tax level. Stability from year to year in the distribution of grant would help to ensure that changes in local tax closely reflected local spending policies. (p. 233)

It was, for example, quite possible for an authority to reduce expenditure but have a large rate increase because of a loss of grant due to changes in the operation of, in particular, the formula for calculating the needs element.

In the 1977 Green Paper responding to Layfield, the government enthusiastically embraced the Unitary Grant proposal, but rejected Layfield's idea of equalizing on personal incomes, not rateable values, and ignored the proposal for more stability. The Green Paper realistically recognized that the history of Exchequer support for local authorities showed 'how difficult it is to provide solutions to major problems which do not themselves create further problems' and proposed in-depth discussions with the local authority associations to remedy any deficiencies identified.

The local authority associations were, in fact, extremely hostile to the Unitary Grant, largely because they feared that the publication of assessed expenditure needs for individual authorities would threaten the independence of local government. Layfield had shown how the Unitary Grant could be used to promote a more centralist approach. In the face of this opposition, the government withdrew the Unitary Grant proposals. The government elected in May 1979 had a strong commitment to reducing public expenditure. It also declared that it wanted to reduce the detailed scrutiny of central government over local authorities, and to encourage greater local discretion. In terms of grant, the solution proposed was the Unitary Grant, now called the Block Grant. This was brought in as part of the large Local Government Planning and Land Act 1980. The four main stated aims of the Block Grant were:

(a) to introduce a simple, readily understood grant distribution system;

(b) to place a limit on the extent to which an authority increasing its expenditure could thereby increase its entitlement to grant – the 'problem of the overspenders';

(c) to end the system whereby needs element was distributed solely on the basis of an analysis of past expenditure;

(d) to stimulate greater public interest in local government and reinforce local accountability.

The needs and resources elements were combined. A new system of needs assessment – Grant Related Expenditure Assessment (GREA) – would be introduced, no longer wholly based on levels of past expenditure. The penalty for 'overspending' would not be implemented immediately an authority's expenditure exceeded GREA. Because expenditure assessments are of necessity imprecise, the government envisaged a 'threshold' of 10% above the GREA before the penalty was incurred. To moderate both grant losses and grant gains, a 'multiplier' would be applied in the calculations but it could not be used to reduce grant except to moderate grant losses.

The Grant Related Expenditure Assessments have assumed considerable significance under the Block Grant system. The process for producing GREAs is summarized in Table 3.5. They are built up from individual service analyses. The indicators fall into five main categories concerned with:

(a) people in the area,
(b) physical features of the area,
(c) social and environmental problems,
(d) differences in the costs of providing services, and
(e) special requirements of particular services.

Table 3.5
Deriving the Grant Related Expenditure Assessment

National service totals for GRE derived from RSG settlement

↓

Identify measurable factors which influence the costs to authorities of providing services (e.g. number of premises from which refuse must be collected)

↓

Assess the relative importance of the different factors for each service

↓

Allocate the national total of GRE to each authority in accordance with the relative size of the factors in its area

---

In theory, the size of any individual service component of GRE for any authority gives no indication of what the authority should spend on that service. It is simply a contribution to the authority's overall GREA. And even the overall GRE is not supposed to *direct* what authorities should spend, but rather to serve as the mechanism for allocating grant. In practice, the fact that penalties are incurred for spending over a certain amount above GREA means that it inevitably begins to have a prescriptive effect, although some councils can and do make their budget decisions without much, if any, reference to GREA.

The local authority associations were united in their opposition to Block Grant. They supported the Government's four objectives, however, but considered Block Grant would only partially fulfil them. And it would be at the expense of a fundamental constitutional change in the relationship between central and local government.

The association's main objections (Local Authority Associations, 1981, p. 58) were:

(a) There was no way in which *any* centrally operated formula-based needs assessment could ever be good enough to enable the government to use it to specify what individual authorities ought to be spending.

(b) Low-spending authorities would be put under enormous pressures to improve service to the level of assessed needs.

(c) Most authorities would still get more grant, the more they spent.

(d) Block Grant would therefore encourage overspending and there would still need to be 'clawback'. But this would apply to all grant (not just resources element as in the past) and hence increase uncertainty.

(e) The wide powers for the use of mutlipliers would make it possible for the grant distribution to be manipulated in quite unaceptable ways.

(f) Block Grant was so complicated as to 'make a mockery of the Secretary of State's aim of simplicity and comprehensibility'.

3.14   RATE SUPPORT GRANT IN PRACTICE

The first years of operation of the Block Grant demonstrated that the fears of the local authority associations had, in many ways, materialized. The government had failed to heed the warnings of the Layfield Committee and *had* begun to use the Block Grant system to exert short-term control over individual authorities.

In 1981, not long after Block Grant had started, two wholly new concepts were introduced. The first was the idea of an expenditure target. This was calculated by reference to quite different criteria than GREA, typically a percentage reduction off a Council's previous years budget. In subsequent years the target was renamed expenditure guidance, but it served the same function. This was that Councils who spent above their target would be subject to a much more severe set of penalties than applied for spending above GRE threshold. These penalties were known as 'holdback'.

The rate of grant loss for spending above target became proportionately greater as the holdback system developed, and proved a major disincentive to spending for many authorities. Councils which spent above target faced large rate increases. Councils with high rateable resources could lose as much as £4m grant for every £1m spent above target, and the introduction of holdback led to a number of such authorities losing rate support grant altogether.

The essence of the Block Grant after the introduction of target and holdback is explained in Fig. 3.5. The actual shape of this schedule varies from authority to authority, and some authorities have radically differently shaped schedules. The one shown is for authorities with targets in excess of GREA and relatively high rateable values. It can be seen that grant is paid at a constant percentage up to expenditure at the threshold. Above that the first stage of grant loss comes into effect. As soon as spending goes above target, steep penalties come into effect until the point of zero grant is reached.

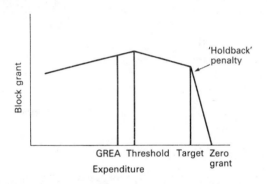

Fig. 3.5 An example of the relation between expenditure and block grant.

A Local Government Finance Bill was drawn up to consolidate holdback. It also included a proposal to require referenda before supplementary rates could be approved. The latter proposal was dropped after Parliamentary pressure, and the outcome was the 1982 Local Government Finance Act which involved:

(a) abolition of supplementary rates;
(b) allowing the Secretary of State to adjust Block Grant generally to achieve any reduction in the level of local authority expenditure 'which he thinks necessary'; and
(c) allowing the Secretary of State to increase or decrease the amount of block grant payable to an authority according to whether or not they have complied with his overall guidance.

A green Paper was also published on 'Alternatives to Domestic Rates', carrying a fairly clear threat that local authorities' source of independent tax could be at threat or at least curtailed. Proposals for a separate Block Grant for the Education Service were raised in the Green Paper and found considerable favour from the Treasury and the Department of Education and Science, who saw distinct advantages in gaining more direct control over local education authorities, particularly higher-spending ones. It was also supported by some education officers including those from lower-spending authorities.

The 1984 Rates Act enables the Secretary of State for the Environment to limit rate increases in individual authorities (the selective scheme) or across the board (the general scheme). The selective scheme starts by the Secretary of State deciding which authorities are to be capped. The principles used have to be consistent within a class of authorities.

There are two criteria which allow many authorities to avoid the selective scheme altogether if they do *not* have expenditure which:

— exceeds Grant Related Expenditure or £10 million, whichever is the greater

— is 'excessive having regard to general economic conditions'.

The £10 million figure may vary based on charges in national relevant expenditure.

Specific criteria used to identify rate capped authorities in its first year of operation were for councils

— spending more than 20% over GREA and also

— spending more than 4% over target.

The process of rate capping is both formalized and complex, and is summarized in Fig. 3.6. There are really two broad routes open to a council. The first is either to concede the Secretary of State's decisions *or* to ignore them. The second is to appeal against these decisions at each stage.

In practice in the early operation of rate capping, no authority used the appeal (re-determination) route, largely because under clause 3(6) of the Act, the Secretary of State then has the power to 'impose on the authority in question such requirements relating to its expenditure or financial management as he thinks appropriate'.

A number of authorities chose to ignore rate capping, and not co-operate with the process. This places increased emphasis on the stage after the issue of a notice of a maximum rate level in December or January. A council can still at this stage seek to have

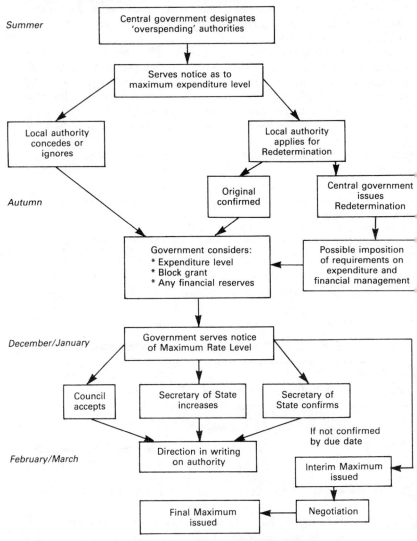

Fig. 3.6 The rate capping process.

a higher rate limit. In one classic case a council was able to obtain a substantial increase in rate limit because it overspent the previous year and needed, on the auditors' advice, to replenish balances.

Rate capping further increased the conflict element in central-local relations and further blurred local accountability. Only time will tell if its macro-economic objectives are met by capping a relatively small number of councils, or whether a much wider application will emerge.

The first comprehensive review of the block grant was undertaken by the Audit Commission (1984), using its Section 27 powers to examine the effects of legislation on local government efficiency. Though the review saw the basic logic of the rate support grant as 'fundamentally sound', it did highlight a variety of shortcomings of the system in practice. These are summarized in Table 3.6 and the Commission's very positive recommendations for reform of the block grant are shown in Table 3.7.

Table 3.6
Audit Commission's summary of block grant shortcomings

---

1. *The effect of new uncertainties*
   Extent of system induced uncertainties.
   Higher rates caused by councils' response to uncertainties.
2. *The impact of a potentially sound approach to grant distribution*
   Distorting effects of grants and penalties.
   Unresolved questions with Grant Related Expenditure (GRE).
   Unreliable information on needs and resources.
   Complexity.
3. *Lack of necessary pressures and incentives*
   Blurred local accountability.
   Lack of positive incentives to reduce costs.
   Frustrations of detailed central intervention in local affairs.

Table 3.7
Audit Commission's proposals for reform of block grant

---

1. Central government to fix its cash support for three years ahead; particularly the percentage of relevant expenditure.
2. Improve information on needs and local property values.
3. Introduce more robust and simpler GREs and up-to-date property values.
4. If the government wants to cut total council spending it should do so primarily by reducing the percentage of expenditure met by RSG.
5. Expenditure targets separate from GRE should be abolished to reduce perverse incentives.
6. Local market forces (the electorate) should determine local spending, after strengthening local accountability.
7. Close ending should be abandoned as should mid-year adjustments to councils spending within budgets.
8. Councils should be left to change their allocation of resources without detailed intervention from central government; specific priorities to be achieved via specific grants or legislation.

It is likely that the severity of the critique from the Audit Commission was one of the factors leading to the inception of the ministerial reviews of local government finance in 1984-85.

The conclusion of the developments in Block Grant must be that problems that have occurred have not so much arisen from the theory of the grant, but from the fact that too much was expected of it in practice. In particular, the Government saw it both as a vehicle for allocating grant and as a vehicle for penalizing overspending Councils. Major legislative changes were rushed through with inadequate consideration and the Block Grant system was subjected to precisely the kind of manipulations feared by all the local authority associations. The basic problems addressed by the Layfield Committee, and demanding a coherent approach, were not resolved; in particular the account-ability of local authorities was not, in fact, strengthened.

There were, however, alternative approaches put forward which it was argued would have led to a more effective system of grant and finance, such as those summarized in Jones *et al.* (1982), pp. 31-32:

(a) There should be a clear separation between expenditure for which the central government is responsible and accountable and that for which local government is responsible and accountable.

(b) The centre should control its grant and borrowing by local government. It should not seek to influence, other than by general exhortation, current and capital expenditure of local government as long as it is financed out of taxes levied by local authorities on their local voters, without resort to deficit financing and borrowing.

(c) Grant should be reduced to well below 40% of local government rate-fund income, compared to the 56% at present.

(d) The non-domestic rate should be transferred to the centre, since it is not appropriate as a local government tax. It does not encourage local accountability, and complicates the process of equalising the resources of local authorities.

(e) Domestic rating should be retained as an ideal local government tax, but assessments should be based on capital not rental valuation and subject to a regular, at least every three years, revaluation.

(f) To make up for the reduction of grant to well below 40%, and for the loss of non-domestic rating, local government should receive as a supplement to domestic rating the proceeds of local income tax, collected through the Inland Revenue on the basis of place of residence. The rate of tax is to be set by the local authority, which will inform Inland Revenue of the rate.

(g) If a two-tier structure of local government is retained, then LIT will be used to finance the big spending authorities and domestic rates the low spending, so that each authority is allocated its own visible local tax.

From 1986/87 the expenditure target was abolished, but greater levels of penalty were incurred for spending above GREA, leaving the block grant curve still broadly as in Fig. 3.5.

3.15   CAPITAL EXPENDITURE – ITS PLANNING AND CONTROL

Major changes to the system of capital expenditure planning and control were introduced under Part VIII of the Local Government Planning and Land Act 1980. The previous system, which had been initiated in 1970, placed controls on local authority borrowing but in general allowed freedom to undertake capital expenditure not financed by borrowing. Local authorities used this freedom to supplement borrowing, particularly using leasing, capital receipts and revenue resources.

The logic behind these changes was that the government wanted greater control for macro-economic reasons over what it regarded as high levels of local authority capital expenditure. It also wanted to reduce some of the detailed controls over individual capital projects.

The new system was detailed in Circular 14/81 (DOE, 1981e). It defined 'prescribed expenditure', which was to become the basis for control, rather than just the element financed from loan. In other words, the Government sought to impose a national cash limit on total local authority capital expenditure. In fact, the government was subject to heavy pressure from a variety of interests inside and outside local government, and made a number of exclusions from 'prescribed expenditure' for control at an individual local authority level. The most significant were police services expenditure, lottery proceeds, finance leasing, leaseholds of under 20 years and expenditure on equipment under £5000. However, although the government did not regard these items as standing to be controlled for individual authorities, it took some of them into account when calculating the national cash limit.

The process of allocating capital resources to authorities had as its central feature the designation of five service 'blocks' – housing, education, transport, social services and 'other services'. The government's aim was that authorities could aggregate the allocations given in each of these five blocks and spend the total as they see fit – the allocations were not limited to the service blocks on which they were given. Though this flexibility works at the margin, there are powerful pressures against authorities making fullest use of it. Each block falls under the purview of a different central government department and they can feel that it is necessary to 'protect their block'. It is certainly not unknown for representatives of one particular central government department to warn authorities that if they transfer allocations out of 'their' block the authorities will lose allocations in the following year.

An authority may supplement its allocation by four main methods:

(a) the application of a prescribed proportion of capital receipts from the sale of assets;
(b) carrying forward underspendings from the previous year, or anticipating next year's allocation, up to a limit of 10% of the current year's allocation;
(c) transfers from another local authority's allocation;
(d) adding an amount equal to the profit of trading undertakings, as measured on a current cost accounting basis.

This last method caused significant controversy because it applied CCA principles to an area where the accounts are not kept on a CCA basis.

The procedure for making allocations for housing, education, social services and transport involves each local authority making a bid for funds to the four appropriate government departments. The bids are then analysed and allocations made to individual authorities at cash limit prices about the time of the rate support grant settlement. The 'other services' block is allocated on the basis of recommendations made by the local authority associations. The criteria for making allocations are a mixture of the political and technical – regard is paid to existing commitments, past achievement of programmes, statistical factors and pure political preference. Some blocks involve lengthy bids, in particular housing, where housing investment programmes (HIPs) have to be prepared; and transport, with transportation plans and programmes (TPPs).

There are various provisos and qualifications to the operation of capital expenditure controls, explained in annually updated circulars from the Department of the Environment. Several areas are treated as special cases, namely the Inner Urban Programme, Airports, Joint Financing with Area Health Authorities, Coast Protection and Derelict Land Schemes. These have their own allocation and approval processes albeit within the same broad framework. Authorities may also receive an additional allocation for projects of 'national or regional importance'. There has been some reduction in controls on detail of individual projects, albeit that the housing project control system still requires a sizeable document to explain it.

The monitoring of capital expenditure programmes has had to become both more extensive and more sophisticated as a result of the system. Councils have to make more frequent returns to the government, and the Department of the Environment monitor for likely overspending. Overspending is not in itself *ultra vires* but if the Secretary of State issues a directive, because of actual or likely overspend, the authorities must have his specific permission to make capital payments. It is perhaps paradoxical that before the end of the first year of these new powers, introduced to restrain local authority capital expenditure, the Secretary of State for the Environment was making speeches complaining that local authorities had fallen well short of his forecast level of spending on capital account.

There were in fact three main reasons for this. The first was that a more extensive cash limit system with fairly draconian powers of direction is bound to cause authorities to err on the side of underspending rather than overspending. Secondly, local authorities' actual capital *allocations* fell short of the Secretary of State's *forecasts*. The latter included assumptions about how councils were to apply additional resources, and in particular capital receipts. As it turned out, authorities chose a cautious approach – not least in case there were future reductions in allocations – and preferred to retain capital receipts rather than apply them to new capital expenditure. Thirdly, capital expenditure is rarely without additional revenue implications either for debt charges or for running cash for employees and maintenance. Given that local authority revenue expenditure was being particularly put under pressure by the new block grant system and its penalties, there was a natural reluctance to incur increased revenue commitments through increased capital expenditure.

The first two years of this capital controls system saw local authorities underspend the national cash limit. However by 1983-84, local authorities had begun in aggregate to spend in excess of that cash limit. There were, as with the underspend, a mixture of reasons. Firstly, the previous exhortations from ministers had at last, due to the long lead times for capital schemes, found their way into actual expenditure on projects. Secondly, there had been a major reduction in the national cash limit in 1983-84, making it that much harder to achieve.

But the major reason for the overspend was that the whole system used quite different criteria to decide whether individual councils were on target, as opposed to the national criteria. Indeed under the rules it was not possible for an individual council to overspend as such.

The key to this paradox lay in the treatment of capital receipts. Councils may augment their block allocations by the 'prescribed proportion' of capital receipts from the sale of land and other assets. It did not matter in which year the receipts arose, as long as they had not been already used to 'justify' expenditure. On the other hand, the national cash limit only took into account the current year's receipts, and not the unused justifications from previous year's receipts which had been of considerable significance locally.

As soon as the new system had settled down and councils were better aware of how it worked, they began to consume these previous years justifications. And they therefore almost inevitably caused a national 'overspend' of the cash limit in 1983-84. A similar occurrence was likely in 1984-85 for the same reasons. In the summer of 1984 a system of voluntary restraint was introduced, with warnings of a full moratorium and/or deductions from future years block allocations for those not observing the restraint.

The 1985-86 capital control system considerably reduced the percentage of capital receipts that councils could use in justification in any given year, and carried out the threat, though not in a very major way, to reduce allocations of authorities not conforming to the previous restraint.

The system of control that was supposed to put an end to the stop-go cycle in capital spending that was common before 1980, had in practice ended up having the same effects, if not worse. It was hardly surprising that the Audit Commission (1985) were as highly critical of this system's impact on local authority efficiency, as they had earlier been of block grant.

EXAMINATION QUESTIONS

3.1 'After many decades of uncertainty in the realm of local government finance, the time has come for a choice on the issue of responsibililty.' Explain what the Layfield Committee meant by this final sentence in their report. (CIPFA. Policy Making. December 1976)

3.2 Local authorities should provide the standards of service they regard as appropriate despite central government policy towards public expenditure. Discuss. (CIPFA. Law and Finance. November 1976)

3.3 Prepare a draft report to the appropriate committee on the implications of externally imposed cash limits in a public sector organization of your choice. (CIPFA. Policy Making. November 1980)

3.4 Critically describe the methods by which the government allocates resources to either local authorities through RSG, or health authorities through RAWP. (CIPFA. Policy Making. November 1978)

3.5 Explain and critically discuss the various elements of the rate support grant. (Association of Certified Accountants)

3.6   What controls has the central government over local authority capital expenditure?

3.7   Should the central government make greater use of central grants to local authorities?

3.8   What are suitable characteristics for additional sources of local government income?

3.9   'Central government should control local authorities' borrowing rather than their capital expenditure'. Discuss in relation to the changes brought in under the 1980 Local Government, Planning and Land Act.

3.10   'Which of the present problems and strains on local government finance are temporary in nature and which are symptoms of longer-term weaknesses or deficiencies?' (Layfield Report)

3.11   Who ultimately pays local authority rates? (CIPFA. Public Finance. November 1981)

3.12   What principles should guide the allocation of government grant for local authorities given that the total sum has been fixed?. (CIPFA. Public Finance. December 1982)

3.13   You are required to draft a report to the Local Policy Committee of Abel District Council on the current methods available to authorize and finance its capital programmes for Housing Services and Other Services Block. (CIPFA. Public Sector Accounting. December 1983)

3.14   It has been asserted that local rates are tolerable because the alternatives are worse. Discuss. (CIPFA. Public Finance. December 1983)

APPENDIX 3.1   THE RATING SYSTEM

The rate is a local property tax whose roots go back to medieval times. It is levied and collected by district councils and London Boroughs in England and Wales and by regional councils and islands in Scotland. However, all local authorities are entitled to rate income and the authorities not responsible for collection levy a 'precept' on the rating authority. The total amount of rates could therefore be derived as in the following hypothetical example:

District Council rate	20p
Add County Council precept	80p
Add Parish Council precept	1p
Council rate poundage	101p

The occupiers of all non-agricultural land and buildings are liable for rates. These are calculated by reference to the rateable value (RV) of the property. This rateable value is set by the Inland Revenue (in England) and is based on the notional annual rent which the property might have.

The Government gives a grant – the domestic rate relief grant – to reduce domestic rates by 18.5p. There is no relief for industrial and commercial premises except for 'mixed' properties which are partially domestic in nature, such as a shop with a flat over it. For those on lower incomes a rebate system (unified housing benefit from 1983) reduces the cost of rates.

Rates are calculated as follow. On industrial and commercial property:

Rates payable = Rateable value × General ratepoundage

On domestic property:

Rates = Rateable value ×
(General rate poundage − Domestic rate relief)

e.g. for a house with a rateable value of £500 and general rate poundage of 101p,

$$\text{Rates} = 500 \times (101 - 18.5)\text{p}$$
$$= \text{£}412.50$$

Occupiers also pay water and sewerage rates, which may be collected with the local authority rate demand, but in England and Wales these are no longer part of local government finance.

A good layman's guide to rating is published by the Consumers' Association (1980).

BIBLIOGRAPHY

Audit Commission (1984) *The Impact on Local Authorities' Economy, Efficiency and Effectiveness of the Block Grant Distribution System.*

Audit Commission (1985) *Review of Capital Expenditure Controls System.*

Anthony, R.N. and Herzlinger, R.E. (1975) *Managerial Control in Non-profit Organisations*, Richard D. Irwin.

Barnfield *et al.* (1981) *Rating Law and Practice*, Rating and Valuation Association.

Bains Report (1972) *The New Local Authorities: Management and Structure*, HMSO.

Barlow, J. (1981) 'The Rationale for the Control of Local

Government Expenditure for the Purposes of Macro-economic Management', *Local Government Studies*, May/June 1981, 3-13.

Bennett, R.J. (1981) 'The Local Income Tax in Britain: A Critique of Recent Arguments against its Use', *Public Administration*, Autumn 1981, 295-312.

Bonner G.A. (1977) 'The Case against Local Income Tax', *Public Administration*, Spring 1977, 27-33.

Burgess, T. and Travers, T. (1980) *Ten Billion Pounds*, Grant McIntyre.

Byrne, T. (1981) *Local Government in Britain*, Penguin Books.

CBI (1980) *A Businessmans Guide to Local Authority Finance and Expenditure*.

CIPFA SIS Vol. 4: *Budgetary Processes*.

CIPFA SIS (1984) *Return of Outstanding Debt as at 31 March 1983*.

Committee on the Management of Local Government (1967) *Report* (Maud Management Report), HMSO.

Consumers' Association (1980) 'Rating', *Which Reports*, June 1980, 334-341.

Coopers and Lybrand (1981) *Service Provision and Pricing in Local Government: Studies in Local Environmental Services*, HMSO.

Davies, R.U. (1977) *Parish Council and Town Council Accounts*, Charles Knight.

Dearlove, J. (1979) *The Reorganisation of British local Government: Old Orthodoxies and a Political Perspective*, Cambridge University Press.

DOE (1977) Green Paper, *Local Government Finance*.

DOE (1981a) *Local Government Financial Statistics, England and Wales 1978/79*.

DOE (1981b) *Alternatives to Domestic Rates*.

DOE (1981c) *Capital Programmes*, Circular 14/81.

Foster, C.D., Jackman, R. and Perlman, M. (1980) *Local Government Finance in a Unitary State*, George Allen & Unwin.

Glasby, J. (1981) 'Principles of Charging in Local Government' *Public Finance and Accountancy*, February 1981, 13-15.

Grant, M. (1984) *Ratecapping and the Law*, Association of Metropolitan Authorities.

Grey, A., Hepworth, N.P. and Odling-Smee, J. (1981) *Housing Rents, Costs and Subsidies*, CIPFA.

Hepworth, N.P. (1978) *The Finance of Local Government*, George Allen & Unwin.

Hepworth, N.P. (1980) 'Local Authority Expenditure', *Three Banks Review*, September 1980, 3-24.

Holtham, C. (1977) 'Ratepayers Reports Reviewed', *Public Finance and Accountancy*, October 1977, 346-9.

Jones, G., Stewart, J. and Travers, T. (1982) *The Way Ahead for*

Local Government Finance, INLOGOV.

Jones, R., (1981) *Local Government Audit Law*, HMSO.

Layfield Committee (1976) *Local Government Finance: Report of the Committee of Enquiry*, Cmnd. 6453, HMSO.

Lee, D. and Johnson, R.W. (1977) *Public Budgeting Systems*, University Park Press.

Local Authority Associations (1981) *The Rate Support Grant (England) 1981-82*, ACC, AMA, ADC, LBA and GLC.

Local Government Training Board (1984) *Why Local Government?*

Mackie, P.J. (1980) 'The New Grant System for Local Transport – the First Five Years', *Public Administration*, Summer 1980.

Marshall, A.H. (1974) *Financial Management in Local Government*, George Allen & Unwin.

Minogue, M. (Ed.) (1977) *The Consumer's Guide to Local Government*, Macmillan for the National Consumer Council.

Ousby, W.H. and Wright, B.G. (1976) *A Practical Guide to Local Council Administration*.

Phillips and Drew (1981) *Local Authorities in Britain: A Survey for Lenders and Investors*, Phillips and Drew.

Raine, J.W. (Ed.) (1981) *In Defence of Local Government*, Institute of Local Government Studies, Birmingham.

Sage, N. (1979) *Local Authority Capital Finance*, Charles Knight.

Sharpe, L.J. (1970) 'Theories and Values of Local Government', *Political Studies* 18 (2) 153-74, Butterworths.

Snyder, J.C. (1977) *Fiscal Management and Planning in Local Government*, Lexington Books.

Stewart, J. (1983) *Local Government. The Conditions of Local Choice*, George Allen & Unwin.

Taylor, J.A. (1979) 'The Consultative Council on Local Government Finance – A Critical Analysis of its Origins and Development' *Local Government Studies*, May/June 1979, 7-36.

Tomkins, C. (1981) 'Financial Control in Local Authorities: Research Issues', in *Essays in British Accounting Research* (A. Hopwood and M. Bromwick, Eds.).

Vargo, R.J. (1977) *Readings in Government and Non-profit Accountancy*, Wadsworth.

Woodham, J.B. (1980) 'Local Government – Central Control and Local Stewardship', *Local Government Studies*, September/October 1980, 3-16.

4

Local government: internal control and external reporting

Chapter 3 examined the environment of local government finance, and some of the issues arising from its financial relationships with central government. In this chapter, attention is directed to the planning, budgeting and control mechanisms of local authorities – the vehicles of internal control. Internal audit is not covered in any depth and readers are referred to CIPFA's relevant publications, mostly stimulated by the Institute's very active Audit Panel. This section is followed by a review of external reporting, in which local government practice has developed in a quite distinctive way.

4.1 THE DEVELOPMENT OF NEW FORMS OF BUDGETING

Whereas the National Health Service has a planning system whose form is devised centrally and to some extent imposed on Health Authorities, in local government planning and budgeting systems are normally devised locally, albeit with regard to external needs. Before analysing present practice, it is necessary to explain the context which has influenced the practice.

Through most of the 1960s and 1970s there was continuous concern with the nature of local authorities' planning and budgeting systems, heavily influenced by American writings commending more rational planning systems, and from the implementation of planning, programming, budgeting systems (PPBS) in American federal government and some state and local governments. Advocates of systems such as PPBS (e.g. Stewart, 1971) pointed out that there was confusion between planning and budgeting. The essentially short-term financial process of annual budgeting was also being used for policy planning. There was insufficient strategic thinking and long-term planning. Local authorities were not clear on their objectives or local needs and had not orientated their financial information to an objective-based (programme) format. Too little attention was given to measuring outputs and to monitoring the outcomes of policies.

In place of this relatively unsystematic approach, Norton and Wedgewood-Oppenheim (1981) described how PPBS:

> was a comprehensive model of integrated procedures for analyses of government objectives and activities within an output-orientated programme structure, leading to a multi-year programme and financial plan and a reformed budget which would incorporate both input and output data. There was a strong emphasis on spelling out objectives of programmes, developing alternatives and evaluating these by systematic costs and benefits. It assumed that the analysis would be carried out for the organisation as a whole and was therefore essentially a corporate approach. (p. 58)

PPBS was rarely tried in a pure form, but from the Institute of Local Government Studies (INLOGOV) at Birmingham University, as well as from private sector business consultants, emerged the concept of corporate planning. The Institute of Municipal Treasurers and Accountants (IMTA) actively promoted discussion of programme budgeting (IMTA, 1967, 1971). Many members of treasurers' departments became involved in developing new types of management and budgeting sytems.

Just as PPBS and corporate planning had their advocates, so too had they critics (e.g. Wildavsky, 1975). Most pointedly, they referred to failures to implement PPBS successfully in America, particularly President Johnson's ill-fated attempt to introduce it in the federal administration. To local government officers and councillors, whose perspective of local government expressedly related to a single profession or service, the idea of a corporate approach carried worrying overtones. And even authorities who had had some success in introducing new management systems, found that more rational systems involved a lot more work.

During the 1970s, variations to PPBS were advocated, particularly zero base budgeting (ZBB) which is an approach more geared to a climate of restraint and cutback than PPBS. Sarant (1978) defined it as follows:

> ZBB is a flexible approach to budget formulation by which budget analysis and justification shifts away from *increments above* the baseline represented by existing programmes to systematic review of *decrements below* that baseline, i.e. financial requirements for both *new* and *existing*

programmes or activities are justified and analysed by the decision-makers. (p. 4)

As Sarant admits, ZBB is a misnomer because in most large organizations a complete zero-base review of all elements in a budget is not feasible in a single budget period; it would result in excessive paperwork and be an almost impossible task. A base level has to be chosen usually representing the minimum level of service consistent with providing services legally.

Though very few authorities would admit to having formal PPBS or ZBB systems, there is little doubt that there has been a gradual but significant change in local authorities' planning and budgeting systems. Compared to a very extensive review carried out before reorganization (Danziger, 1978), many local authorities have now restructured their budgets so that they are more policy-orientated. There has been a greater use of multi-year planning, and a clearer presentation of options to committees.

There is little doubt that planning and budgeting systems in British local government have evolved out of the relatively formalistic procedures and systems contained in PPBS to more flexible systems attuned to adverse economic circumstances and indeed to the local characteristics of individual authorities. (Stewart, 1983 and Holtham, 1984).

4.2 THE FINANCIAL CYCLE

Fig. 4.1 summarizes the main documents involved in financial reporting. Documents are only a means to an end, but they are a visible aspect of the financial cycle. There are many similarities among all authorities, with a basic annual cycle containing most of the elements shown.

The main point at which all authorities inevitably have the same document is the one-year budget. This may be a policy budget and/or a very detailed line-by-line budget. A policy budget will tend to summarize the detailed budgets. All authorities produce periodical reports on spending to date, which go out to the relevant departments. If adverse trends are spotted a report may in due course go before members.

The final accounts show what was actually spent during the year. They are of course compulsory and an important element in stewardship, with some policy implications at the aggregate level in connection with the level of surplus or deficit achieved.

Returning to policy-making, the multi-year policy plan may cover main political priorities only, or be comprehensive. Where

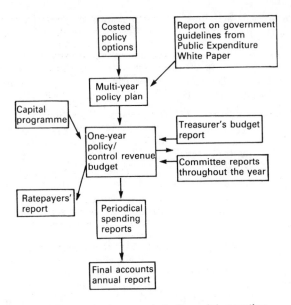

Fig. 4.1 The main documents in financial reporting.

there are multi-year plans, the annual budget will generally be based on the updating of the 'first year' of the plan. Virtually all treasurers now report on the Public Expenditure White Paper; this may be an important element in a policy or financial planning process which begins in, say, April. Of great importance also is the treasurer's report on the Annual Budget itself.

The capital programme is typically a separate document from the revenue budget. In some cases in the past there was an almost complete policy and even financial split between capital programmes and revenue growth or savings. But now the capital planning process is increasingly integrated as fully as possible with revenue planning. The capital programme follows from general policy decisions on financial priorities within the framework set by central government, rather than being considered entirely separately.

4.3 THE BUDGET TIMETABLE

No two councils have identical financial processes, though there are inevitably major areas of similarity. Fig.4.2 sets out a budget

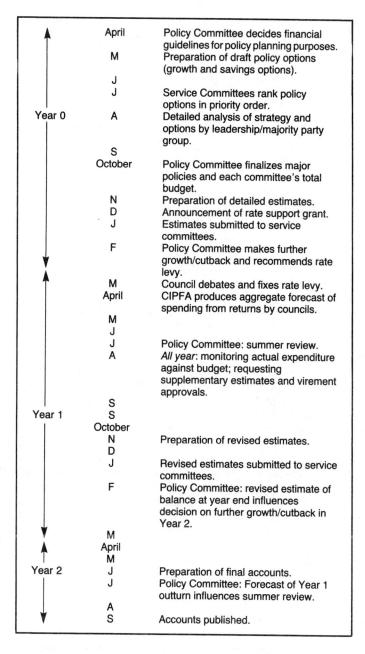

Fig. 4.2 A typical financial planning and control timetable.

timetable which is increasingly common. It relates to a district council but the only difference for a county is that it has to fix its precept early in the new year. The main point of this example is that planning, spending and accounting for Year 1's budget is spread over no less than 30 months.

Year 0 is taken up with the policy planning and finalization of the budget. Year 1 is devoted to spending the money, but at the policy level there is a summer review and the revision of estimates in the autumn; either could in theory lead to revised policies, and hence revised financial allocations. During Year 1, there is continuous monitoring of actual expenditure against budget. The preparation of final accounts begins in earnest at the end of financial year 1 and should be completed within six months of that year end.

The main variants on this cycle are really only related to Year 0. Traditionally, there have been no budget guidelines, and committees' estimates have been bids, which the Finance Committee has usually had to prune. This process neither suits a climate of restraint, nor promotes policy planning. A half-way house between the 'traditional' cycle and that illustrated is to issue budget guidelines in the autumn, but not to have gone through a policy planning process earlier in the year. This still leaves relatively little time to implement policies at the start of the coming year.

4.4 BALANCING THE BOOKS

Having undertaken all the work of detailed budgeting, the time comes when the books need to be balanced; i.e. the final decisions on expenditure made, with the consequent rate levy (or precept) being fixed. The key factors in budget preparation can be easily summarized in a very simple diagram (see Fig. 4.3); each factor will then be considered in turn.

The allocation of government grant is a factor which is largely outside an authority's control. Once the block grant settlement has been announced in November, the degree of uncertainty involved is reduced, but not eliminated. The November settlement sets out the framework for the grant, giving authorities' schedules of rate poundages, threshold and penalization rules, etc., permitting an initial grant forecast. However, since the final block grant may not be known until two Novembers later, a degree of skill and judgment is still required by the treasurer in forecasting likely final levels of block grant.

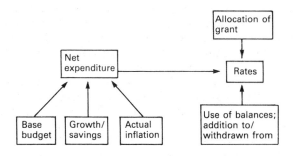

Fig. 4.3 The key factors in budget preparation.

The term 'balances' is capable of a number of meanings, but is here shorthand for the surplus on the rate fund account. As far as the rate fund is concerned, the decisions on the use of balances are wholly within the control of the authority, though account has to be taken of legal, quasi-legal or good financial management considerations surrounding surpluses and deficits.

Net expenditure is all rate fund expenditure to be financed by rates, block grants and balances. There are, in summary, only two types of variation to the base budget – growth/savings and inflation. The forecast level of inflation, already discussed above, is almost wholly outside the control of any individual authority. This is not to say that there is no action which councils can take in consequence; they can alter their mix of goods and services or they can take explicit or implicit policy decisions not to provide for the full effect of inflation (i.e. cut the real level of service provision). Simplifying all the many elements that make it up, therefore, the area over which the local authority does have control is the 'growth/savings' policy decision component. Hence the importance of the policy planning process to budgeting and also the need for the budget to enable fine tuning (or in extreme cases, coarse tuning) of the policy plan.

Of the four key factors in budget preparation – government grant, use of balances, net expenditure and rates – it is if anything rates which is the balancing factor of the four. The two single largest influences on the rates are usually the level of government grant allocation and the actual level of inflation suffered. Broadly speaking, neither is directly within the authority's control. The two factors that are – use of balances and real/growth savings – are all the more likely to reflect political decisions.

It was sometimes the case in the past that elected members would decide on a rate poundage and then set expenditure allocations for committees based on these predetermined pound-ages. This was known as 'rate rationing'. But the now inevitable uncertainties over block grant and inflation do not encourage rate rationing in its purest form. Expenditure alone does not determine the rate. Indeed, it is perfectly possible for councils to follow government's expenditure guidelines, yet have rate increases greatly in excess of the government's target. This is generally because:

(a) arbitrary changes are possible in grant allocation;
(b) balances have been run down and are to be rated for;
(c) the council has provided for a 'realistic' level of inflation which may be higher than the government's target implicit in the block grant settlement.

For authorities who face grant penalties, legal advice and possibly counsel's opinion may be sought to determine whether a rate could successfully be challenged in the courts. Some of the important issues involved in judicial decisions in this area are set out in Appendix 4.1.

4.5 BUDGETARY CONTROL

The basic principles of budgetary control do not vary significantly across the public and private sectors. The need is to define a structure of accountable management, produce budgets which are as realistic as possible, and set up a monitoring system to provide the managers with relevant and timely information to help them make decisions. However, the problems encountered and the major issues in budgetary control can vary from organization to organization, even within local government. There is ample discussion in Chapter 6 on the general problems of accountable management and budgetary control in health authorities, much of which is equally relevant to local government. More detailed information on local government's particular problems can be found in CIPFA Financial Data Processing Panel (1980) and CIPFA's FIS Volume 4.

To summarize briefly the position in local government: once the budget has been fixed by the council, officers responsible for spending it receive detailed figures of their budgets, against which the actual trends in spending can be monitored on a periodic basis, usually monthly. Local authorities invariably use computerized systems to handle the large amount of data involved. A particularly good example is outlined in Hollis (1981).

Councillors may become involved in this process when some adverse trend is discerned at a detailed level, e.g. if income from a particular council service is considerably below forecast, a policy change may need to be considered. Alternatively they may become involved at a global level, e.g. if pay awards have exceeded the provision in the contingency fund, the policy committee must consider the options open to the council.

The responsibility for budgetary control usually lies with service chief officers, with the treasurer's role relating to the collation of data and global monitoring and forecasting. Since it is physically impossible for individual chief officers to control all details of spending, except in the smallest departments, there should ideally be a formal structure of accountable management, defining the roles of resource and service committees, the treasurer, chief officers and the named line managers directly responsible for controlling spending. Accountable management is often introduced with the aim of delegating responsibility to those nearest the actual provision of services, e.g. headmasters, officers-in-charge of residential homes, area superintendents. Whatever the extent of delegation – and some authorities permit remarkably little – the principle of accountable management should still be promoted. Improved financial information systems are now increasingly paying attention to ensuring that data can be presented flexibly to meet the wide needs of different types of manager.

One of the most significant issues in budgetary control is the way inflation is treated. Some authorities budget at outturn prices i.e. allocate out inflation at the beginning of the financial year. Others may allocate the sums in respect of inflation on request from committees. If actual spending is to be compared with something comparable, then generally some element of inflation must be allocated, unless there is an overriding reason, e.g. if no cash is available to allocate!

Another area receiving increasing attention is the attitude of the authority to virement – permission to spend more on one budget head matched by a corresponding reduction on some other head. A few authorities permit no virement at all. Others allow almost unlimited virement. Two points need to be stressed. The first is that fortuitous savings are not appropriate for use in virement. Second, increased commitments should not be generated by virement. Having said that, with an increasing climate of restraint, a flexible approach to virement – which in many authorities still needs to be sanctioned by elected members – can act as a powerful motivation to seek value for money and should be encouraged.

Budgetary control has tended to relate solely to financial information. But a number of authorities are introducing systems which integrate financial and non-financial data. This may involve the production of unit-cost information, e.g. cost per resident-week in homes, cost per swimmer in baths, cost per square yard of road patched, and so on. Such data are more concerned with the measurement of efficiency and effectiveness than a purely financial system which relates to stewardship and to ensuring that cash limits are not exceeded. This leads on to the broader question of performance measurement.

4.6 PERFORMANCE MEASUREMENT

As part of the development of improved planning and budgeting systems during the 1970s, quite a lot of effort was devoted to improving the measurement of performance in meeting authorities' objectives. These objectives are largely non-financial in nature. Unlike the nationalized industries, few key performance measures can be reduced to a financial basis, perhaps an exception being the rate of return for direct labour organizations. Most objectives laid down by statute are of a general nature such as 'to secure efficient education to meet the needs of the population', and explicit performance measures cannot be readily derived from them.

Considerations of performance measurement tend to focus on two issues; efficiency and effectiveness. Effectiveness relates to how far authorities are actually meeting their ultimate objectives. Efficiency concerns whether, for a given level of achievement, the use of resources is being minimized. Considerable effort has been put into examining the measurement of effectiveness and into how, if at all, the 'outputs' of services can be measured. In particular, IMTA's Output Measurement Working Party published an important series of reports and articles. The main conclusion of these reports (*IMTA Output Measurement Working Party*, 1974) was that it was not possible or desirable to incorporate output measures into planning and budgeting systems in the precise and regular way possible with financial measures. Successful use of output measures requires the establishment of a recognized management process, and does not present a total picture of the organization's output at one time. The Working Party developed a simple categorization of different types of output data (see Table 4.1).

Given the problems of measuring effectiveness, latterly more

Table 4.1
Categories of Output Data

Type of decision	Type of output data	Frequency of decision
Introduction of new policy or major change in existing policy	Quantified final output measures where possible and other sorts of quantitative assessment (usually produced by detailed studies)	Ad hoc
In-depth review of existing policies	As above, plus opinion of staff and clients	Periodic
Budget	A few key statistics on need for, and use of, services	Annual
	Simple performance measures	
	Unit Costs	
Routine implementation of policies	Workload and throughput data targets and simple achievement measures	Regular, but frequency depending on the subject
Review of management performance	As above, plus evidence of effectiveness available from other types of decision-making	Periodic

Reproduced from IMTA Output Measurement Working Party (1974), *Public Finance and Accountancy* Vol. 10 (October), pp. 339-42, by permission.

attention has been directed to measuring efficiency, particularly by central government. In local government, as elsewhere, *comparison* is at the heart of measurement of efficiency. Inter-authority comparisons have been the subject of much interest, and in the Code of Practice on Publication of Information (DOE, 1981) an annex is devoted to 'performance statistics'. Authorities are asked to provide comparisons with the average for their class of authority, and with other authorities chosen by the authority as having similar characteristics.

The Code of Practice recognizes that the performance statistics listed need to be interpreted with care, and often provide only a starting point for analysis of relative performance. Also the statistics measure different aspects of performance, including the cost, scale and quality of service, the demand for service, a degree of client satisfaction, relative efficiency, and so on. Most of the list relates to the cost and scale of service, which is a somewhat limited aspect of performance.

A broader perspective has been taken in the study by Hatry et al. (1979) which, in addition to undertaking a number of in-depth studies, also proposes a general approach to comparison for performance measurement, suggesting:

(a) comparisons over *time*;
(b) measures compared *between* geographical areas or institutions *within* an authority;
(c) comparison of actual performance with '*standards*', particularly in relation to standardised procedures;
(d) comparison of actual performance with performance *targeted* at the beginning of the year;
(e) comparison with similar *private sector* activities;
(f) *inter-authority* comparisons.

This range of comparisons highlights the importance of performance measures as internal tools of control rather than just as measures for an external audience. A number of local authorities have been developing improved internal performance measurement systems. One example of this is Bexley LBC, where chief officers present to committees a 'Quarterly Operations Report'. Typically this might include:

(a) service demand and deliveries – general,
(b) key performance indicators for the last quarter,
(c) finance: latest position for the current year,
(d) manpower,
(e) capital programme monitoring.

Another approach to the use of performance data is outlined by Hill (1981).

4.7 VALUE FOR MONEY

Considerable attention has been devoted to the question of value for money in local government in recent years, not least because of a perception that local government is not giving value for money (CBI, 1980). A large number of recommendations has been made to promote its achievement. These include strengthened external audit, a greater use of management consultants, more publication of more information, more participation of the public and of industry and commerce, 'privatization' of services, and the development of zero base budgeting. The problem with most such recommendations is that they tend to treat value for money as an extra – achieved by a particular approach – rather than as a basic aspect of management. Many approaches such as those outlined have a contribution to make, but as integral parts of the management structure, process and performance of an authority.

In developing an overall framework for action (Holtham and Stewart, 1981), the following themes have been identified as critical:

(a) Value for money involves comparisons, not as ends in themselves, but as a means of developing beyond the apparent necessity of the present.

(b) Value for money involves changes in individual activities, but changes will not be achieved without adequate management processes which are dependent on the working environment.

(c) Management processes must clarify accountability and promote the managerial initiative that achieves real value for money.

(d) Over-detailed control systems can prevent the search for value for money.

(e) Selectivity is the key to tackling value-for-money work. The resources are there for such work but they have to be realised, and an action plan can structure the overall process.

CIPFA has played an important role in stimulating thinking about value for money, particularly in two studies (CIPFA, 1979, 1980b). It has in particular collaborated with LAMSAC and SOLACE on a joint local authority value for money project. This involves a looseleaf handbook containing actual reports from individual authorities, details of district audit efficiency and management exercises, editors' comments and a bibliography (CIPFA, 1982a).

Since its creation in 1983 the Audit Commission has been extremely active in promoting the search for value for money in a variety of ways. There have been in-depth national reviews of topics such as rent arrears, fleet management and care of the elderly. These are followed up within each authority by auditors.

The 1982 Local Government Finance Act places a duty on auditors to review whether a council has made 'proper arrangements for securing economy, efficiency and effectiveness in the use of resources'.

The Commission publishes material of a more general nature on value for money, particularly its annual 'yellow book' on economy, efficiency and effectiveness (Audit Commission, 1984a).

It also produced comparative statistics for each authority in a 'profile'.

An innovative approach has been value for money reviews of councils as a whole, the first two being at the request of Basildon and Wansdyke councils. This uses comparative statistics to highlight areas for more detailed review, and comparisons are then applied in more detail.

A wholly new provision in the 1982 legislation enabled the Commission to undertake reviews of how statutory provisions, or Ministerial directions and guidance, were affecting value for money in local government. This has been used to great effect in studies of the block grant system (Audit Commission, 1984b) and capital expenditure controls.

4.8 LOCAL AUTHORITY EXTERNAL REPORTING

Local government external reporting has developed in a distinctive fashion, with few similarities to central government's methods, and in parallel to, rather than derivative of, private sector methods; and it has developed its own principles, practices and terminology. Since the mid-1970s there has been some movement in relating local government external reporting more closely to generally accepted private sector accounting principles and practice. But there still remain many areas of importance and debate in local government external reporting which cannot be readily discussed within the framework of private sector principles. The attention devoted here to the external reporting of local authorities should enable readers to be able more readily to follow any particular set of local authority external reports.

Whereas in private firms external reporting is almost synonymous with the published accounts, in a democratically elected local authority a vast range of external reports is produced, and a rich variety of reporting mechanisms exists. Fig. 4.1 illustrates this fact, which is often overlooked and misunderstood. Certainly in introducing new legislation to increase further the volume and nature of local authority external reporting in 1980, the Department of the Environment appeared not to understand the worries of many people inside local authorities that they suffered from too much accountability and reporting, not too little.

On the other hand, though local authority accounting has reached a high degree of sophistication, it has been argued that in its reporting to the public this sophistication may have been a barrier to comprehension. It is interesting to see what the

Departmental Committee on Accounts (1907) had to say on this topic:

> It is generally agreed that as wide publicity as practicable should be given to the accounts of local authorities and that they should be published in such a form as to be intelligible to ratepayers possessed of average ability but without special knowledge of accountancy. (p. 19)

It is perhaps an indication of at least partial failure that 69 years later the Layfield Committee (1976) still found it necessary to point out in almost identical language:

> We believe that there is an obligation on local authorities to devise a means of providing the electorate with financial information about services in reasonably simple and straightforward terms. (p. 102)

It should be noted that the distinction between trading and nontrading accounts of local authorities is taking on increasing significance, with a very clear trend towards the former conforming as closely as possible to Companies Act accounts. At this stage it is important to set the formal external financial reports of local authorities in context. They are not the only source of information to users and indeed in the present day context of British local government they are not necessarily their most important source of information. Even though local authorities publish comparisons of expenditure with that of other local authorities in their formal reports, this tends to be at a fairly broad level on a few indicators and with a relatively small group of comparator authorities. Unions, pressure groups or researchers examining comparative expenditure on particular services will tend to use the CIPFA statistical information service which contains details of *all* authorities expenditure on, say, education. The absence of such publicly and readily available comparative information for companies is one reason why their individual company reports are more significant.

Local authority accounts – not just the published external reports – are in addition uniquely openly available. The 1982 Local Government Finance Act continues the longstanding rights of public inspection:

> At each audit . . . any person interested may inspect the accounts to be audited and all books, deeds, contracts, bills, vouchers and receipts relating to them.

Local government electors also have the right to question the auditor about the accounts. In practice those who wish to make detailed enquiries into one or more aspects of a particular authority's finances are able to use the rights of inspection to such a degree of detail that the level of disclosure in the published accounts is of no great significance to them. Recent years have seen what is felt to be a significant increase in the volume of public inspection and questioning, particularly about controversial projects or policies.

The 1984 Rates Act introduced the requirement for local authorities formally to consult with commercial and industrial ratepayers. The Access to Information (Local Government) Bill aims to provide freedom of information over a whole variety of previously unpublished documents. If passed it would further confirm local government as the most open and accountable part of the public sector, not least in respect of financial and accounting data.

4.9 STATUTORY BASIS OF EXTERNAL REPORTING

Before the second world war, most local authorities were subject to very detailed specification by central government of the form and content of their accounts. But as local authorities became more visibly competent in financial administration – not least through the efforts of the IMTA – and as specific grants reduced considerably in scope, so too did this detailed control reduce. Only with the passing of the Local Government Planning and Land Act 1980 did a greater degree of prescription again enter into external reporting, and this was for different motives than those of 50 years earlier.

The major legislation relating to local authority accounts is the 1982 Local Government Finance Act. This essentially carried the previous legislation forward without innovation. It does not itself touch on more than some very general areas of accounting. More detailed accounts regulations are made by the Secretary of State. The current accounts and audit regulations are in fact considerably shorter than their main predecessor, The Accounts (Borough and Metropolitan Boroughs) Regulations 1930. It is perhaps a direct reflection of the successful self-regulatory activities and the absence of any major structural shortcomings in local authority accounts that the regulations contain so little detail compared to, say, the Companies Acts.

A further source of guidance comes in the Local Government Audit Code of Practice (Audit Commission, 1983). This sets out the framework for external auditors and includes reference to the more important matters to which an auditor should draw attention; these include a number of aspects relating to accounting.

Most local government expenditure and income relates to general rate fund or county fund services. Other accounts must, however, be kept separate under statutes relating to various services including housing revenue, housing advances, police, reserve funds, superannuation, lotteries and loans funds.

One of the most significant developments in local government accounting was contained in Part III of The Local Government Planning and Land Act 1980. This introduced wholly new concepts into the operation and accounting of direct labour organizations (DLOs). From an accounting viewpoint the most radical approach of Part III of this Act was that it explicitly introduced 'true and fair view' concepts into local government, and required DLOs to apply current cost accounting principles to calculate their rates of return. DLOs were also required to prepare their accounts by 30 September – no such timescales for preparation had previously been included in local government legislation.

In the more general area of external reporting, as opposed to accounting, further radical changes were also introduced in the Local Government Planning and Land Act 1980 relating to the need to prepare annual reports and other documents in a format laid down by the Secretary of State. The draft legislation would have involved the Secretary of State *prescribing* the detailed form and content of annual reports but this met very hostile criticism from the local authority associations and CIPFA, not least because of the speed with which new mandatory requirements were proposed for implementation. The Government then conceded the principle of a code or codes of practice though still warned that if local authorities were dilatory in conforming to the code it might have to take more positive action.

Four codes of practice have been published:

(a) information to be issued with rate demands,
(b) annual reports and financial statements,
(c) manpower information,
(d) information for publication at quarterly intervals e.g. planning applications.

The single most significant is the second on annual reports (DOE, 1981). It was based largely on suggestions put forward by CIPFA and the Society of Local Authority Chief Executives (SOLACE). Its objectives, which are important enough to warrant further consideration, are:

(a) to give ratepayers clear information about local government's activities,

(b) to make it easier for electors, ratepayers and other interested parties to make comparisons of and judgements on the performance of their authorities,

(c) to help councillors form judgements about the performance of their own authority.

The objective of the annual report is, through the use of narrative and financial statistical data, to integrate the total management and financial reporting of the authority. It should also account for the resource costs implicit in the policies of the authority and as far as practicable the performance and efficiency of the local authority. The documents should be designed as a statement of stewardship for the benefit both of members of the council and of the public. (pp. 2-3) (Reproduced by permission of the Controller of Her Majesty's Stationery Office. Crown copyright.)

It is stressed that the publications covered by the code are only one part of the whole range of information made available by local authorities in, 'for example, budgets, structure plans, corporate plans, policy reports and minutes'. In many authorities the annual report is an enhanced version of the abstract of accounts. In others, the two documents have been separated, with the annual report tending to concentrate on corporate policy achievements, rather than the details of financial performance, and often with a strong 'public relations' approach as opposed to the traditionally more technical approach of abstracts.

The government wanted to promote comparisons both between authorities and over a period of years, as a starting point for the analysis of relative performance. 34 performance statistics were specified, all of a relatively unsophisticated nature, e.g. pupil/ teacher ratios, social work staff per 1000 population. The government also advised authorities that 'it will be at the discretion of the authority to decide if any further statement is necessary when the document is published'. A number of authorities have taken up this offer by including sections in their reports which are less than complimentary about the impact of government policies on their locality.

The annual reports have not yet been in existence long enough for an authoritative analysis of their impact to be identified, although there is the beginning of an 'industry' in such analysis (INLOGOV, 1981). In a review of the implications of the code, Long (1981) confirms that the objectives set out above are relevant as much for internal management purposes as for external accountability. But:

On the negative side, account must be taken of the various financial costs involved in publication. There is also the danger that the statistics may be misinterpreted. Finally, there is the danger that both managers and the public may ignore the publications with the result that the costs have been incurred without any of the benefits being gained. (p. 26)

Her overall conclusion is that, given the considerable discretion allowed under the code, authorities are likely to vary in the extent to which the information in the new publications is used. But it provides a basis for much more questioning of existing policies and practices in many authorities, and could lead to a strengthening of the corporate approach as a result.

4.10 THE DEVELOPMENT OF LOCAL AUTHORITY ACCOUNTING

The annual reports are an important innovation but do not eliminate the need for continued development of the fundamental vehicle of financial reporting, the financial accounts, commonly published as an 'abstract of accounts' (i.e. a condensed version). A number of authorities still formally publish detailed accounts that are effectively a line-by-line analysis of outturn. Though these will now usually be accompanied by a short abstract, it was not so very long ago that such lengthy accounts were the norm in local government.

Legislation, regulations and the various audit and information codes of practice provide a broad framework for accounting but they do not wholly constrain discretion and indeed they cannot if definitions of good practice are to be allowed to change and develop. 'Proper accounting practices' as referred to in Section 15 of the 1982 Local Government Finance Act are therefore something that have gradually evolved during the era of modern local government and which are particularly evolving as CIPFA responds to its full membership of the Accounting Standards Committee, touched on later.

A landmark was the publication of *The Standardisation of Accounts: General Principles* (IMTA, 1963). To develop the 'general principles' in depth relative to individual services, detailed standard analyses of income and expenditure were prepared for 17 services. The success of CIPFA in achieving uniformity in the form of accounts is indicated by the widespread use of the CIPFA standard form in completion of returns to central government and, of course, in the completion of returns of CIPFA's own statistical information service. The content of the standard form in relation to the analysis of income and expenditure, and to the

101

structure of the abstract of accounts, should be examined in IMTA (1963).

Although *General Principles* was reprinted as late as 1979, and is still regarded as authoritative in respect of matters of principle, it could not be expected to survive unscathed major reorganizations, the introduction of computerization and the increased demands for management information. A major review of the general principles and of the standard form was, therefore initiated with a view to completion by 1985 (see Sypula & Gray, 1981). This aims to codify fully CIPFA's recommendations on accounting, and to provide a comprehensive manual of principles and practice for local authority accounting. Three major discussion papers were published to promote debate on the content of this manual (CIPFA, 1983a, 1983b and 1984a, and see Rogers, 1985).

To recapitulate, local authority accounting had developed to a high degree of specialization, involving a terminology that was unfamiliar even to experienced private sector accountants, and accounting concepts that derived from the particular statutory and functional requirements of local government services. In particular the treatment of capital expenditure, its financing and depreciation, applied an approach that was based on the methods of capital financing typically found in local government, rather than on any generally accepted commercial principles.

But local authority accountants were not isolated from private sector accounting and did not necessarily believe that the well tried and tested accounting principles codified in 1955 would last for ever. Because of the magnitude of the issues involved, experiments were mounted on the application of CCA to trading undertakings (Brooke, 1981). In addition, a major study was commissioned by CIPFA and the ASC into CCA in the non-trading sector, and the role of depreciation (if any). The outcome of this research by Woodham (1982) involved a controversial proposal to adapt the principles of CCA to local authority non-trading services based on the need to maintain the 'equity' of the authority.

4.11 CRITIQUES OF LOCAL AUTHORITY ACCOUNTS

On one occasion the then Secretary of State for the Environment, Mr. Michael Heseltine, described local authority accounts as 'abysmal', but no detailed evidence was produced in justification. In a more structured review which compared company and local authority accounts (Walls, 1980) an external auditor identified the following shortcomings.

(a) Local authorities tend to publish too much information and in a form which creates confusion rather than clarity.

(b) A greater use should be made of unit cost data.

(c) There is insufficient detail and explanation of capital programmes, including revenue implications.

(d) Local authority accounts do not show the historic cost of acquiring capital assets and the matching principle is not met where capital assets funded by, say, capital receipts do not show any costs in the revenue accounts.

(e) For trading undertakings, current replacement costs should be recognized in the revenue accounts.

(f) There is no standard definition of a trading surplus or deficit for trading undertakings, and no obligation to be consistent with company accounting, e.g. over depreciation accounting.

The first three areas refer more to presentation than to fundamental accounting principles and all are areas where the requirements of the 1980 code of practice have had an effect since Walls made his criticisms. It must also be said that CIPFA's Public Sector Accounts Award, initiated in 1980, has spurred local authorities towards improving their standards both in the spirit of competition and also as a result of the greater publicity given to the high quality winning entries. The judges for the 1981 Award noticed a 'great improvement in the quality of local authority reports over the last year'.

The last three areas concerning accounting principles are all ones where CIPFA has been devoting effort to reviewing existing practice as decribed above. It should also be noted that Walls' criticisms are similar to those made by some accountants in local government. They do, however, fall short of the views expressed by the Institute of Chartered Accountants in England and Wales (ICAEW) that local authority accounts should conform to the 'true and fair view' standards of company accounts. These views will now be examined in more depth.

There had been considerable discussion within the IMTA and CIPFA on the form and content of local authority accounts but one emerging factor after the mid 1970s was the attention devoted by members of other accountancy bodies to the perceived shortcomings of these accounts. In particular, the ICAEW has taken a close interest in developments in local authority accounting and makes no secret that this has some relation to extending the use of their members' talents in relation to both external audit and consultancy exercises in local government. Their recommendations cannot be regarded as wholly unbiased, but they do reflect a different perspective and their views have not been uninfluential. Their views on a variety of topics, including financial accounting, are in particular set out in three memoranda to the Department of the Environment (ICAEW, 1976, 1977, 1979). The significance of these memoranda lies in the apparent overriding presumption of the ICAEW that achievement of commercial accounting standards is effectively an end in itself and that failure to comply with commercial standards is a sign of failure. The main recommendations on the form and content of financial accounts themselves were as follows (ICAEW, 1977, paras 7-13):

Form of Accounts

We believe that the present information available to the public is inadequate for it to judge the financial performance of its local authority.

The methods of accounting used by local authorities have evolved on an individual basis and there is need for greater comparability of accounts between authorities.

This requirement has already been recognised by Water Authorities who have responded by themselves agreeing with the Department of the Environment a standard form of accounts.

We, therefore, recommend that a standard form of published accounts supported by statements of standard accounting practices should be developed by local government and adopted by the Department of the Environment. The accountancy bodies are in a position to advise on how far such standards would be compatible with national and international practices.

Publication of Accounts

Under the Local Government (Scotland) Act 1973, accounts must be available for audit by 31 August in each year. This regulation should be extended to England and Wales. The objective should be that audited accounts are published by 31 October in each year so that the public is informed of financial results promptly and so that the budget for the following year can be prepared on a sound basis. If accounts are for any reason not available by the set date, a mandatory audit report should be issued, setting out the reasons.

To conform with accepted conventions for other organisations, the 'accounts' of the local authority should be defined as those which are to be published. Unaudited accounts should not be published except for the purpose of public inspection.

Published accounts should not include only the actual results of the year under review but should disclose the original budget, fundamental assumptions thereon and reasons for major variances.

In its 1979 paper (paras 19, 21 and 25) the ICAEW developed some of the individual points in more depth and the recommendations on the publication of information foreshadowed what later emerged in the code of practice.

In relation to working balances and reserves it was proposed that the commentary in the abstract of accounts 'should deal with variances in the budgeted movement of working balances and reserves during the year and the general policies of the authority in relation thereto. In addition, the accounting presentation of working balances and reserves should be reviewed with the intention of simplifying them on lines similar to the 1967 Companies Act'. For the purpose of unit costing, 'the allocation of overheads to identifiable units is a problem and guidance will be required in order to achieve sufficient standardisation to make costs reasonably comparable between authorities'.

The abstract should be divided into two parts – a clear and concise summary of the 'consolidated' accounts of the authority, together with detailed accounts and other information for each service. The ICAEW then put forward a key recommendation:

> The presentation of the 'consolidated' accounts should be standardised. More importantly, their method of presentation should be based on the general concept of 'true and fair'. Aspects of the accounts which require alteration to present a true and fair view include the disclosure of past capital expenditure and the treatment of reserves. At present, most authorities provide no analysis of past capital expenditure. It is therefore impossible to identify the amounts spent on council houses, roads, schools or any other assets. Moreover, authorities may charge various items of expenditure directly against reserves with the result that their revenue accounts do not readily disclose the total expenditure during the year.

In fact, although the comments of the ICAEW were by no means openly welcomed by local government accountants, CIPFA itself was in essence working along the broad lines sought by the chartered accountants, albeit that there might be disagreement over both the pace and objectives of change. This has been exemplified by the joint working between CIPFA and the ICAEW in the Accounting Standards Committee.

In early 1984, the Department of the Environment produced a lengthy consultation paper on standardized statements of accounts by local authorities (DOE 1984). This covered a number of areas of proposed change. The paper met a barrage of criticism from CIPFA, the Audit Commission and local authority associations. It contained a number of erroneous statements, and wholly ignored many of CIPFA's recent proposals in favour of a highly prescriptive approach. Detailed pro formas of accounts were subject to particular criticism given the background of successful self-regulation in local authority accounts.

By the end of 1984, the DOE effectively withdrew the consultation paper and set up a technical working group to advise on the drafting of new regulations. The target date for such regulations was for the accounts for 1986-87 and subsequent years.

The government decided that the regulations should provide for statements of accounts which should:

(a)   contain both consolidated and fund based accounts,
(b)   contain a service based analysis of income and expenditure,
(c)   have a balance sheet prepared on the 'deferred charges' basis,
(d)   contain notes to the accounts providing additional information, e.g. disclosure of salaries in high income bands, and members' allowances,
(e)   be in a form suitable for integration with annual reports (P.J. Fletcher, 1984).

These were much less radical than the original proposals, and in particular the controversial pro formas had been eliminated. Even so, the proposals contained two items which raised some degree of debate. The first was the proposal for 'service analyses'. Councils normally prepare their budgets and accounts on a *committee* basis. The use of a nationally prescribed *service* basis does not assist in local accountability except through easier inter-authority comparisons. However, such service-based comparisons can already be made from CIPFA's statistical publications. There is thus also some risk of local confusion, particularly if accounts are shown on both a committee and a service basis.

In relation to preparing balance sheets on a deferred charges basis, this will promote greater comparability between councils but only in relation to expenditure financed by borrowing. Given the increasing significance of capital receipts and other non-loan sources of finance, capital accounting emphasising only loan finance is unlikely to give a balanced view, particularly in relation to inter-authority comparisons.

4.12   APPLICABILITY OF ACCOUNTING STANDARDS TO LOCAL AUTHORITIES

A major CIPFA statement on accounting standards (CIPFA, 1980a) started off with three paragraphs that showed how far by then CIPFA had moved towards accepting the relevance of the accounting standards which had primarily been initiated for private sector trading organizations.

> The Accounting Panel, through its Local Authority Accounting Sub-Group, has given consideration to the applicability of Statements of Standard Accounting Practice (SSAPs) issued by the Accounting Standards Committee (ASC) to local authority accounts in England and Wales. Local authorities, for this purpose, are as defined in the Local Government Act 1972, but excluding town, parish or community councils and meetings.
>
> The Accounting Panel is of the opinion that there are advantages in applying these standards in the interests of good accounting practice and the general movement towards increasing standardization of financial information. CIPFA is a member of the ASC and, as such, should encourage the application of agreed standards. In practice, it is not thought likely that there will be much need for change in accounts preparation.
>
> As SSAPs apply to accounts intended to give a 'true and fair view', it was originally thought that it was not appropriate to apply them generally to the accounts of local authorities, which are based on 'proper accounting practices'. Following consultation with interested parties, including the Chief Inspector of Audit, there would not appear to be major difficulties in applying most SSAPs to local authority accounts. (p. 19)

The proposals to apply SSAPs reflected the changes that had been taking place anyway in CIPFA's approach during the 1970s and which had perhaps been accelerated by the exigencies of the direct labour organisations legislation. It was decided that CIPFA would state clearly for each SSAP its degree of applicability, normally:

(a) apply in total,
(b) apply partially with reasons, or
(c) not apply – with reasons.

CIPFA subsequently arranged that its own observations would be fully integrated into the standard setting process, so that as SSAPs were developed a panel of local authority specialists would advise the ASC on the extent to which the standard was applicable to local government. Material departures from the standards as applied to local government need to be disclosed in a note to the accounts. A consolidated summary of ASC guidance was then produced (Accounting Standards Committee, 1983).

4.13 SOME KEY ISSUES IN LOCAL AUTHORITY ACCOUNTING

Having reviewed the general development and current position of local authority accounting, some of the key issues will be briefly touched upon. The four areas of capital accounting, revenue charges for capital expenditure, depreciation and inflation accounting are all closely related, and this was recognized by CIPFA in initiating via the ASC a major research project in this area.

Capital accounting

The area of capital expenditure is perhaps the most contentious of all aspects of local authority accounting. From both within CIPFA and outside local government there have been criticisms of current practice as already noted. Local authority capital accounting has been closely related to the method of capital finance used and the relevant part of Chapter 3 should be reviewed again if necessary before considering some of the detailed points raised below.

The distinction between 'capital outlay' and 'other long-term outlay' is of particular significance in examining CIPFA's recommended approach to capital expenditure which was set out in the 1963 *General Principles* as follows:

> *Capital Outlay*. This refers to capital expenditure which creates tangible, saleable assets such as land, buildings and equipment. CIPFA recommended this should be retained at cost in the accounts until the asset was disposed of.
> *Other Long-Term Outlay*. This is capital expenditure that does not produce saleable assets; the most obvious examples are highways and sea defences. The recommendation has been to segregate this type of expenditure in the accounts and write it off at the end of the loan period. There is no suggestion that the 'life' of the asset necessarily coincides with that of the loan — it is a rough and ready method for establishing a date of write off.

CIPFA's recommendation here is unambiguous. All assets, however financed, should be shown in the accounts at historic cost until disposed of or until the end of their 'notional' life. In practice, this recommendation is not followed in many authorities (see Sypula & Grey, 1981) and it is clear from *General Principles* (IMTA, 1963, p. 12) that the recommendation would be unacceptable to some authorities even at the time of its drafting. Many authorities still show only the cost of assets net of loan repayments and assets not financed by loan are not shown at all. Some do so as a matter of principle. But for others if not most it is expediency. To operate the CIPFA recommendation requires full scheduling of all capital assets. Where such scheduling has long existed, it is possible to follow CIPFA's recommendation. But there was a local government reorganization in 1974. Where several authorities with differing accounting practices merged and one did not adopt the 'historic cost' recommendation, it was not an easy matter to reconstitute an assets schedule. So successive councils may have had to move over to a 'net written down' (deferred charges) system by default. And once such a system becomes established it is that much more difficult to return to a full historic cost system.

This was found to be of particular significance during the 1974 reorganization when water authorities, whose finances had in general to follow commercial accounting principles, had to try to create assets schedules in a situation where there were very few data in some cases on historic cost or even on the existence of assets that had been fully written down.

The continued failure to resolve the basis of local authority capital accounting led to a further review being initiated and published for comment (CIPFA 1983a). Particular emphasis was based on meeting the needs of 'reasonably informed' readers and those interested in inter-authority comparisons. Needs were related to accountability, including efficiency and economy in operation.

The shortcomings of the status quo were highlighted:

— It is inconsistent and arbitrary in the charges which appear in the revenue account.
— It may meet basic stewardship criteria but it cannot promote accountability for efficiency.
— The comparison of performance between authorities and over time is compromised.
— It fails to demonstrate the authority's financing policies.

The working party concluded, the 'weaknesses are sufficiently serious to warrant urgent changes'.

As an alternative the review concluded:

There is a *prima facie* case, based on accountability for efficiency, for charges to revenue based on asset *use*. There is also a case for comprehensive asset valuation, but more evidence of the potential benefits is needed before a firm recommendation can be made to include such values in the balance sheet. An appreciation of the potential value of assets for their alternative use is important in encouraging efficiency, but we have some reservations about constructing an accounting system on alternative use values. Existing use values may be more appropriate. Existing capital maintenance concepts are not yet acceptable as a basis for forcing a charge, for asset consumption, in the revenue account on which the rate levy is based. The question of spreading the burden of capital expenditure between different years' ratepayers is political and not technical, and the accounting system should highlight the political choices made. Debt charges accounting, in its present form, is not suitable as a basis for charging for the use of assets in service revenue accounts. It is inconsistent and does not satisfy the accountability for efficiency criterion. Depreciation accounting, whilst having some strengths, is not suitable as a basis for charging for the use of assets in service revenue accounts. It is based on capital maintenance concepts which are not, in themselves, acceptable and it does not fully satisfy the accountability for efficiency criterion.

The review argued that a system of asset rents could be devised which would be particularly attractive for charging to service revenue accounts, and that such a system should be adopted as a longer-term objective following practical tests in a range of authorities.

CIPFA received many submissions about the proposals and there was no unanimity over the way forward. There was considerable concern about the practical implications of making any change. As a result, CIPFA had to withdraw from the full range of proposals and in a progress statement (CIPFA 1984c) came to the following main conclusions:

(i) Members, in commenting on the discussion paper, recognized and supported the need for change, particularly to improve consistency and comparability. They also emphasized that any revised basis for capital accounting should be intelligible, relatively simple to operate and the benefits should outweigh the costs.

(ii) Preliminary experiments, carried out in seven authorities, showed that in many areas the discussion paper's proposals were capable of practical implementation but, in general, the results were not conclusive.

(iii) A series of more closely defined experiments would be carried out which would build on the valuable information already obtained. These experiments would concentrate on the costs and benefits of capital charges based, broadly, on rents for land and buildings and deferred charges (or notional debt charges) for infrastructure and other specialized assets. Other forms of capital charge, particularly replacement-cost depreciation, would also be tested.

(iv) The experiments did not imply a commitment to any particular form of capital charge. No recommendations would be made by CIPFA until the responses to a discussion paper were considered. No changes in the form of local authority accounts would be required as a result of this research until the financial year 1986/87 at the earliest.

The review was unable to persuade sufficient CIPFA members of the benefits of change. Much of the criticism of the proposals reflected the simple desire, which is very understandable, to avoid changes at a time when accounting resources are already hard-pressed, not least as a result of a variety of government legislation.

What CIPFA might have considered was an interim solution, which would be based on eliminating the greatest deficiencies in the status quo, even though it might not have met all the objectives set.

Such an interim solution would have to have minimum setting-up and running costs and would preferably be rooted in present practices rather than radical innovation. The interim solution might have contained these elements:

(i) Authorities given two years to set up asset registers. Even if a valuation basis is rejected, there can be little rationale, if only from a pure stewardship viewpoint, in continuing to avoid producing such registers. But a reasonable period of notice needs to be given.

(iii) Wherever legally possible, councils should cycle all non-loan-funded schemes through the council's capital fund, repayments into which should be on an identical basis to loan charges. This could well create a different incidence of revenue charge, particularly where schemes are currently funded directly from capital receipts, but need not alter the overall costs of capital to the ratepayer.

(iii) CIPFA should give consideration to an extended timetable for implementation for smaller councils. It is perhaps increasingly necessary to recognize the genuine difficulties facing the smallest authorities which may have only limited accounting resources.

There is one authority in the country which pioneered a low-cost, innovative method which stands as a good example to all those concerned with the costs (financial and otherwise) of change. This is Suffolk County Council.

It has gathered together all capital transactions except those funded by capital receipts under one committee – the policy committee.

Individual service committees are then charged what is in effect a rent for the use of the asset. Covered by this system are loan charges, revenue contributions, building maintenance and insurances.

The Suffolk method, though by no means theoretically pure, is a significant improvement on the status quo, is low cost and is capable of further development when research evidence and CIPFA permits. If it included schemes funded from capital receipts it would be close to the interim solution above.

Revenue charges for capital expenditure

Capital accounting practice by and large closely relates the revenue charge for a particular capital asset to the actual method of capital finance used to fund that asset. For example, if a capital asset is wholly funded by a direct revenue contribution or by using receipts from the sale of an asset (capital receipt applied) there will usually be no ongoing revenue charge for that particular asset. This is equivalent to writing off the asset completely in its first year of existence and could be of importance in any service where charges are levied, and it makes inter-authority comparisons involving revenue charges for capital expenditure fraught with difficulty. If a trading undertaking such as an airport or market has had significant amounts of capital expenditure written out, the 'surplus' achieved will be higher than it would have been under commercial accounting principles. In another situation (and perhaps even within the same authority) both revenue contributions and capital receipts may be cycled through the capital fund rather than directly to individual schemes. In this case there will usually be a revenue charge, 'repayment to the capital fund', equivalent to loan charges.

It can be seen that, because of the varying forms of financing, the actual incidence of revenue charges falling to be met by services in respect of capital expenditure tends to be very arbitrary. An authority which has made substantial use of revenue contributions to capital on a particular service will have a very different revenue charge for that service from an authority which has exclusively used loan. The accounts will therefore be misleading in respect of the consumption of capital assets even though they will of course correctly reflect the pure financing transactions.

Depreciation

This arbitrary situation transgresses the matching principle that the accounts should be charged only with costs contributing to the units of service provided in the year of account. This is one of the purposes of depreciation accounting. The other purpose is to maintain the real pool of capital at its true value. Even though the principal element of loan charges approximates to a depreciation charge in most cses, the effect of historical depreciation is not actually attained unless debt redemption is deducted from asset values. In this respect, local government practice has not been consistent.

In view of this situation it is perhaps not surprising that in its Exposure Draft on Accounting Principles (CIPFA, 1975) the CIPFA Accounting Panel recommended the introduction of depreciation accounting in local government, with legal constraints in the 1972 Local Government Act being removed to allow this. They argued:

> One of the reasons why we feel the need for depreciation accounting is to enable proper charges to be made in each year's accounts for the annual depreciation of assets and to ensure that the charge is consistent whether the asset be financed out of loans, capital fund, revenue contributions or other sources. This has an importance not only in following the matching principle but also for pricing, for use of resources (both locally and nationally) and for comparability.

This would have involved a final break of the traditional link in local authority accounts between assets and their source of finance. Even without changes in the law it would have been possible to make a substantial move towards depreciation accounting by interim arrangements, particularly making greater use of the capital fund by cycling revenue contributions and capital receipts through it, and by the creation of an appropriation account. (An alternative approach of a community equity account was suggested by Pearson (1978).) The controversy over these proposals and their withdrawal has already been noted but it is unlikely that local authorities can continue to avoid all use of depreciation accounting, if only on trading accounts.

Inflation accounting

Local government's stance in relation to inflation accounting has largely been reactive rather than initiating. CIPFA as a whole took a close interest in all the inflation accounting debates of the 1970s;

but it was the nationalized industries who were directly and particularly affected. A comment by the Chairman of the Accounting Panel (Patrick, 1979) after ED24 had been published showed little support for CCA in the non-trading public sector. He concluded:

> Nothing has happened to alter the conclusion already reached that the adoption of a full scale CCA system by public sector non-trading organisations is inappropriate at this time. If it offers benefits, they are small compared with the cost in introducing it . . . It is therefore unrealistic to expect public sector non-trading bodies to adopt full CCA techniques, at least for a long time to come.

Events moved apace and the 1980 Local Government, Planning and Land Act required direct labour organizations to compute their rates of return on capital employed on a current cost accounting (CCA) basis – the first time that inflation accounting had been directly embodied in statute in either public or the private sector. A CCA basis was also to be used to calculate trading undertakings' profit for the purposes of enhancing capital allocations. Most significantly, CIPFA's own Working Group on CCA in Trading Services had seen the outcome of a one-year experiment on the application of CCA to a wide variety of services. Its broad conclusions (Brooke, 1981) were that:

(a) A fairly narrow definition of 'trading services' should be adopted, excluding areas where the trading nature of the service was at least in doubt.

(b) The capital replacement issue was of central interest. Except for supplies organisations, the cost of sales adjustment and monetary working capital adjustment are not material and can be omitted.

(c) The basic accounts should be kept on principles consistent with local authority accounting practice, with CCA data published as supplementary statements.

(d) There should be a cut-off point for the scale of trading services below which CCA accounts are not recognised as essential.

These conclusions formed the basis of the draft guidance note on SSAP 16 submitted to the ASC. In the non-trading sector, the 'Woodham' report considered a number of alternatives (Woodham, 1981) for meeting the objectives of current cost accounting, viz. opportunity cost accounting, replacement cost accounting, a consolidated capital fund and SSAP 12. All were rejected apart from the consolidated capital fund which fell short of the CCA system itself. Woodham's proposals were to move towards 'true' CCA systems, with the aim being to maintain 'constant equity' of the authority. On the initial indications of the research, which were to be subjected to more intensive testing, the continued revenue cost of CCA would be very close to that of debt-charge finance, thus apparently overcoming one of the major fears – that CCA would put up the rates. Practical details of CCA would require amendment. In particular, the capital gearing adjustment would need to be related to the 'inflation premium' on interest payments, although other adjustments could be possible.

Woodham's proposals were not expected to find universal approval but stimulated the lively discussion on accounting matters that had been found previously in the mid-1970s. Probably few even then would have anticipated the way in which local authority trading services were to espouse private sector accounting methods so quickly, and in which similar pressure was brought to bear on the non-trading services. Certainly there was a feeling within CIPFA, even if not a majority one, that perhaps local authority accounting had developed too far in its own distinctive mould and that this was a barrier to meeting at least some of the user objectives highlighted earlier.

Costs of administration and management

One of the few areas of continuing weakness in local authorities revenue accounts has been the very varying treatments of central and departmental administrative costs between authorities. In an important statement on the topic (CIPFA 1982b) it was admitted that:

> Although the treatment of central administrative expenses has been the subject of discussion and research by the Institute over the years, the diversity of treatment has remained sufficient to diminish seriously the usefulness of local government's published reports and accounts and associated statistics.

Central administration costs are 'that share of the authority's total expenditure which supports the direct provision of services'. It includes central support services and buildings, departmental administration and centre expenses. The 1982 statement which built on a research study (CIPFA 1981) gave clear guidance on appropriate treatment.

> Where the costs of management and administration are accounted for centrally, rather than identified in the first instance with particular services or departments the costs must be fully apportioned to all

services which the authority provides. Allocations should be made to main services (including the services provided directly by central departments); trading accounts; capital accounts; special funds; and services provided for other bodies. Allocations should be made to subdivisions of service if substantial income is involved or if standard accounting practice so requires.

The published final accounts will show the costs of management and administration apportioned to the relevant funds and services. However, the Institute also recommends that these costs be analysed and reported separately in order to provide direct information about the source and nature of these costs. This will assist users of accounts, particularly when they wish to have regard to matters such as overhead costs or a service manager's directly controllable expenditure.

The Institute has considered carefully the arguments for making certain exemptions to the principle that all central administrative expenses must be allocated. In particular it has been suggested that certain costs in local government, such as members expenses, are of a special nature and might therefore be exempted. The overriding test, however, is not how special is the cost but whether the activity which results in these costs can reasonably be defined as part of an authority's management and administration. Where this is so, the principle of full allocation must apply. The separate reporting requirements referred to earlier in this statement will mean that relevant information would be available should separate account of management and administration expenses need to be taken.

This statement was reinforced by further detailed guidance (CIPFA 1982c). However, lack of progress in implementation in the following years budgets brought a strong criticism from an external auditor (Sparrow, 1983) who particularly stressed the need to eliminate unnecessary variations to aid inter-authority comparisons, and advocated comprehensive time recording systems to aid allocations. In a later review of accountancy developments (Rogers, 1985) it was commented that

> The recommendations appeared to have been well received in theory, but on evidence so far available, it seems that the practical application has left something to be desired.

The original 1981 research proposed further studies into 'activity analysis', based on management and administration processes, and the Society of County Treasurers undertook such a study for the costs of support services.

The issue of the costs of administration and management had in fact taken on a new significance since the 1980 Direct Labour Organization legislation. The need to make commercial rates of return meant that items of overhead in the DLO accounts came under new scrutiny. In some authorities this led to revised methods of calculating allocations so that DLO's were not unfairly penalized.

A parallel issue was the question of treatment of administration and management costs when services were potentially or actually privatized. This was given increased momentum by the DOE's proposals (DOE, 1985) to extend competitive tendering and value for money comparisons to a much wider range of services than covered in the 1980 DLO legislation. It became particularly important to distinguish between the relatively fixed overheads that were independent of whether services were provided internally or externally, and those which directly resulted from providing an in-house service. CIPFA was not able directly to resolve these problems, but relied on the clear reporting of costs, before and after allocation, so that the marginal or other types of costing could be undertaken as the need arose.

EXAMINATION QUESTIONS

4.1 Describe the role of the Accounting Standards Committee and discuss its relevance to public sector accounting. (CIPFA. Accounting and Audit. November 1980)

4.2 Describe the purposes and discuss the relevance of UK Statements of Standard Accounting Practice on the reporting of a public sector organization of your choice. (CIPFA. Accounting and Audit. November 1980)

4.3 Comment on the assertion that the wider dissemination of inter-authority comparisons will improve a local authority's accountability to the public. (CIPFA. Policy Making. November 1980)

4.4 What are the short- and long-term implications of public sector organizations financing capital out of revenue? What methods would you consider appropriate? How could more revenue financing be achieved? Do you consider it desirable? Explain in relation to present practices in one such organization.

4.5 Explain what you understand by the term zero base budgeting, giving details of how such a technique would operate and the additional benefits that this technique might give over traditional budgets. (Association of Certified Accountants, draft Public Sector exam)

4.6 'Is the supply of information as a basis for sound decisions on local authority spending adequate and available for those who need it?.' (Layfield Report)

4.7 What do you understand by the term incremental budgeting in the context of the policy making process and resource planning in a public sector authority of your choice? (CIPFA. Policy Making. November 1981)

4.8 The Local Government, Planning and Land Act 1980 requires local authorities to publish an Annual Report.
(a) Outline the essential features of such a report
(b) Comment on its possible influence on policy making. (CIPFA. Policy Making. November 1981)

4.9 As a member of a Local Authority Chief Officers Management Team, outline the considerations which should be taken into account when a policy of privatization is proposed for a section of the Council's work. (CIPFA. Policy Making. December 1982)

4.10 Outline and discuss the function of performance indicators in the policy process of a public sector organization of your choice. (CIPFA. Policy Making. December 1983)

4.11 The Chief Executive has been asked to prepare a strategy dealing with improving value for money (VFM) in your local authority. He has asked you to prepare a paper in the form of a report explaining the concept of VFM and outlining the major policy considerations to be included in a VFM strategy for the authority. (CIPFA. Policy Making. December 1983)

4.12 In 1982 CIPFA issued an Institute Statement on Accounting for the costs of Management and Administration in Local Government.
Set out and briefly discuss the approach taken in the Statement and the associated Notes of Guidance to:
(a) The allocation of central departments' costs;
(b) The treatment of the costs of democracy;
(c) The presentation in final accounts;
(d) The treatment of central departments' costs in estimates. (CIPFA. Public Sector Accounting. December 1983)

4.13 Explain the main functions of an Annual Budget for a public sector organization with which you are familiar. (Association of Certified Accountants. Public Sector Accounting. June 1983)

4.14 Discuss the objectives of, and necessity for, capital budgets in public sector organizations. (Association of Certified Accountants. Public Sector Accounting. June 1984)

APPENDIX 4.1 LOCAL AUTHORITY EXPENDITURE AND JUDICIAL DECISIONS

The block grant system took effect for the 1981-82 financial year, and introduced detailed and specific grant penalties for authorities who were relatively high spenders in relation to targets set by the Government. One unexpected effect of this was that local authority budgets became more vulnerable to challenge in the courts.

There was considerable initial surprise in local government at the House of Lords' judgement in the case brought by Bromley LBC objecting to the GLC cutting fares, thereby increasing the deficit of London Transport, losing £50 million RSG by way of penalty, and passing a supplementary rate: *Bromley LBV* v. *Greater London Council* (1982). The House of Lords in a complex judgement found that the GLC had failed to act in accordance with statutory provisions and had failed to hold the balance between transport fares and ratepayers as it should have done. The supplementary rate was quashed. Lord Diplock used the word 'thriftless' in his judgement:

> As the GLC well knew when it took the decision to reduce the fares, it would entail a loss of rate grant amounting to £50 million, which would have to be made good by ratepayers as a result of the GLC's decision. So the total financial burden to be shared by passengers and the ratepayers was to be increased by an extra £50 million without any equivalent improvement in the efficiency of the system. That would, in my view, clearly be a thriftless use of monies and a deliberate failure to deploy to the best advantage the full financial resources available to it by avoiding any action that would involve forfeiting grants from central government funds.

There was a surge of court actions after the Bromley case but subsequent judgements, admittedly in situations that were not identical with the GLC position, did not lead to rates being quashed. In *R* v. *Merseyside County Council, ex p. Great Universal Stores* (1982), the judge stressed the need for an authority to carefully consider all relevant considerations in budgeting. And in *BL Limited* v. *Birmingham City Council and Coventry City Council* (1982) Sir John Willis, sitting in the High Court, refused to quash a rate because of an allegation that insufficient attention had been paid to 'targets' set by the Secretary of State. He said:

> . . . It is common ground that, in the present state of the law, central government cannot dictate to a local authority any part of the framework within which it should make its annual rate. It can exhort authorities to reduce expenditure, as happened in the two instant

cases, and it can withhold grant if exhortation fails, but in the end, in my view, it is for the authority to decide on the level of expenditure for services which it has considered it should provide, after taking into account all relevant matters, including grant, or any reduction thereof, from central funds, and then fix the rate.

It has become clear that, particularly if a local authority is likely to face grant penalties, careful attention must be paid to the form of advice to the council and the actual way in which expenditure and rating decisions are made. For example, at the committees considering the 1982-83 budgets of the Greater Manchester Council, the following extract from Counsel's written opinion was read out to the committees:

(a) Electoral promises, while deserving some weight and considera- tion, must not govern the council's spending decisions in any instance.

(b) The council enjoy a wide but not unlimited discretion in exercising their statutory powers. The Court's control over the exercise of that discretion is limited to ensuring that the council has acted within the powers conferred on it.

(c) When exercising its discretion the council must take properly into account all relevant matters and must not take into account irrelevant matters. After that, the council's decision might be one that no reasonable authority having regard to its fiduciary duty to the ratepayers in its area could have reached. If that was so, the decision would be unlawful.

(d) One of the relevant matters to which the council must have regard is the guidance or advice offered to it on national policy and in particular government targets. A council would be prudent to regard such guidance or advice as a weighty consideration and to be seen to have so regarded it.

(e) In reaching decisions on passenger transport matters the council must act upon ordinary business principles (in the sense of that term appearing from the Bromley case judgements).

(f) In reaching spending decisions, the council owes a fiduciary duty to the ratepayers in their area and must balance fairly the needs of the service against the costs to be borne by the ratepayers. When that decision may of itself, or in combination with other spending decisions, affect the amount of government grant which the council is likely to receive that effect must be properly assessed and be taken into account in making the decision.

(g) In the case of every decision the terms of the relevant statutory provision in regard to which the decision is made must be complied with.*

* This extract is reproduced by kind permission of the Greater Manchester Council, who took Counsel's opinion when considering these matters.

This is only one counsel's opinion but there can be little doubt that in reaching decisions councils must be *seen* to take into account all relevant matters, and be *seen* to maintain a reasonable balance between ratepayers and the users of its services. Providing this is done and providing there is no actual breach of the law, it would seem that the Bromley decision has not fundamentally altered the legal position of local authorities' budgeting and ratemaking, although it has served to emphasise authorities' fiduciary position.

BIBLIOGRAPHY

Accounting Standards Committee (1983) *Guidance Notes on the Application of SSAP's to Local Authorities in England and Wales.*

Audit Commission (1983) *Code of Local Government Audit Practice for England and Wales.*

Audit Commission (1984a) *Economy, Efficiency and Effectiveness (Volume 2).*

Audit Commission (1984b) *The Impact on Local Authorities Economy, Efficiency and Effectiveness of the Block Grant Distribution System.*

Brooke, P. (1981) 'Current Cost Accounts in Local Authorities', *Public Finance and Accountancy*, October 1982, 15-16.

CBI (1980) *A Businessman's Guide to Local Authority Finance and Expenditure.*

CIPFA (1975) Local Authority Accounting Exposure Draft 1, *Accountancy Principles.*

CIPFA (1976) 'Institute Response to Corporate Report', *Public Finance and Accountacy*, March 1976.

CIPFA (1979) *Cost Reduction in Public Authorities – A View.*

CIPFA (1980a) 'Institute Statement: Applicability of Accountancy Standards to Local Authorities', *Public Finance and Accountancy*, September 1980, 19-21.

CIPFA (1980b) *Value for Money in Local Government.*

CIPFA (1981) *Accounting for the Costs of Management and Administration in Local Government.*

CIPFA (1982a) *The Local Government Value for Money Handbook.*

CIPFA (1982b) 'Accounting for the Costs of Management and Administration in Local Government', *Public Finance and Accountacny*, August 1982, 10.

CIPFA (1982c) *Guidance Notes on Accounting for the Costs of Management and Administration in Local Government.*

CIPFA (1983a) *Capital Accounting.*

CIPFA (1983b) *Published Form of Accounts in Local Authorities and their Standard Detail.*

CIPFA (1984a) *Glossary of Local Authority Accounting Terms.*

CIPFA (1984b) *Guide to Local Authority Finance.*

CIPFA (1984c) Institute Progress Statement: Capital Accounting, *Public Finance and Accountancy*, June 1984, 15.

CIPFA FDP Panel (1980) *Budgetary Control Systems – Financial Systems Review.*

CIPFA FIS Vol. 1(II): *Local Government Accountancy.*

CIPFA FIS Vol. 4: *Budgetary Processes.*

Danziger, J.M. (1978) *Making Budgets*, Sage Publications.

Departmental Committee on Accounts (1907) *Report.*

DOE (1981) *Annual Reports and Financial Statements.*

DOE (1984) *Standardised Statements of Accounts by Local Authorities: A Consultation Paper.*

DOE (1985) *Competition in the Provision of Local Authority Services,* Consultation Paper.

Fletcher, P.J. (1984) *Standardised Statements of Accounts for Local Authorities in England and Wales* – correspondence with local authority associations.

Hatry, H.P., Clarren, S.N., Van Houten, T., Woodward, J.P. and Don Vito, P.A. (1979) *Efficiency Measurement for Local Government Services*, Urban Institute, Washington DC.

Hayes, F.O'R. (1977) *Productivity in Local Government*, Lexington Books.

Hill, J. (1980) 'An Approach to Efficiency and Effectiveness', *Local Government Studies*, September/October 1980, 37-45.

Hollis, G. (1981) 'Changing Internal Reporting Practices', *Public Finance and Accountancy*, January 1981, 19-22.

Holtham, C.W. and Stewart, J.D. (1981) *Value for Money: A Framework for Action*, INLOGOV, Birmingham.

Holtham, C. (1984) 'Financial Planning and Control', in *Issues in Public Sector Accounting* (Eds. A. Hopwood and C. Tomkins).

IMTA (1963) *The Standardisation of Accounts: General Principles.*

IMTA (1967) *Programme Budgeting Concept and Application.*

IMTA (1971) *Programme Budgeting – Practical Problems of Implementation.*

IMTA Output Measurement Working Party (1974). 'Output Measurement', *Public Finance and Accountancy*, October 1974, 339-42.

INLOGOV (1981) *Codes of Practice in the Publication of Information,* Institute of Local Government Studies, Birmingham University.

ICAEW (1976) *The Finance and Audit of Local Government*, TR 202.

ICAEW (1977) *Local Government Finance*, TR 254 (Memorandum submitted in September 1977 to the Secretary of State for the Environment by the Institute of Chartered Accountants in England and Wales).

ICAEW (1979) *Publication of Financial and Other Information by Local*

Authorities, TR 370 (Memorandum submitted in December 1979 to the Minister of State, Department of the Environment, by the Institute of Chartered Accountants in England and Wales).

Jones, R. and Pendlebury, M. (1984) *Public Sector Accounting*. Pitman.

Jönsson, S. (1984) 'Budget Making in Central and Local Government' in *Issues in Public Sector Accounting*. (Eds. A. Hopwood and C. Tompkins).

Layfield Committee (1976) *Local Government Finance: Report of the Committee of Enquiry*, Cmnd. 6453, HMSO.

Long, J. (1981) 'The Publication of Information – Implications of the New Codes of Practice', *Local Government Studies*, September/October 1981, 21-34.

Norton, A. and Wedgwood-Oppenheim, F. (1981) 'The Concept of Corporate Planning in English Local Government – Learning from its History', *Local Government Studies*, September/October 1981, 55-72.

Patrick, J. (1979) 'Does the Public Sector Need Inflation Accounting?', *Public Finance and Accountancy*, September 1979, 34-6.

Pearson, J.V. (1978) 'Relevant Financial Reporting for Local Authorities', *Public Finance and Accountancy*, April 1978, 211-13.

Rockley, L.E. (1978) *Public and Local Authority Accounts*, Heinemann.

Rogers, M. (1985) 'Accounting Developments', *Public Finance and Accountancy*, February 1985, 15-16.

Rutherford, B.A. (1983) *Financial Reporting in the Public Sector*, Butterworth.

Sarant, P.C. (1978) *Zero-Base Budgeting in the Public Sector*, Addison-Wesley.

Sparrow, C. (1983) 'Accounting for Management and Administration Costs', *Public Finance and Accountancy*, August 1983, 16-18.

Stewart, J.D. (1971) *Management in Local Government*, Charles Knight.

Stewart, J. (1983) *Local Government: The Conditions of Local Choice*. George Allen & Unwin.

Sypula, S. and Gray, C. (1981) 'Revising the Standard Form', *Public Finance and Accountancy*, September 1981, 34-35.

Tomkins, C. and Colville, I. (1984) 'The Role of Accounting in Local Government: Some illustrations from practice' in *Issues in Public Sector Accounting* (Eds. A. Hopwood and C. Tomkins).

Walls, T. (1980) 'Consistent, Comprehensive and above all Understandable?', *Public Finance and Accountancy*, October 1980, 15-18.

Wildavsky, A. (1975) *Budgeting: A Comparative Theory of Budgetary Processes*, Little Brown, Boston.

Woodham, J. (1982) 'Depreciation Accounting: Local Government', *Public Finance and Accountancy*, May 1982, 34-36.

Worthley, J.A. and Ludwin, W.G. (1979) *Zero-Based Budgeting in State and Local Government*, Praeger.

Essential Reading

There are a variety of introductory texts to local government in general, and one of the most up-to-date and concise is Byrne (1981).

In terms of general works on local government finance, there are two complementary works which have become the standard texts. Hepworth (1978) looks at local government finance and the general aspects of financial management. Marshall (1974) goes into some depth on the role of the financial manager in a corporate management system. A concise review of local government finance produced from outside local government itself is CBI (1980). The Layfield Report is an authoritative study of many aspects of local government finance.

In relation to the financing of local government, there has been a wide variety of material published, but Foster *et al.* (1980) and the Layfield Report (1976) are the two premier texts.

The SSRC has sponsored a major project on financial control in local government at the University of Bath, and publications produced from this include Tomkins (1981).

There is one book which provides a useful introduction to the bookkeeping aspects of local government accounting: Rockley (1978). FIS Vol. 2 II is a convenient summary which is kept up-to-date on a regular basis.

One of the major problems in an ever-changing field is to keep up to date. One series of publications by CIPFA – the Financial Information Service (colloquially known as FIS) – is of almost unparalleled scope and depth. The volumes covered are indicated below and they are of a loose-leaf format so that they can be more easily kept up to date, although the up-dating process itself is lengthy, so all volumes are not equally up to date. Almost without exception, local authority finance departments subscribe to FIS. So do most college libraries teaching for the CIPFA qualification. It is possible to subscribe to individual volumes and these are being increasingly purchased by service departments.

CIPFA's Financial Information Service (FIS)

Functional Volumes
1. General Reference
2. (I) Accounting Standards
2. (II) Local Government Accounting
3. Audit
4. Budgetary Processes
5. Direct Labour Organizations
6. Capital Expenditure and Finance
7. Central Purchasing
8. (Unallocated)
9. Financial Administration
10. Data Processing
11. Insurance
12. Investments
13. Means Tested Benefits
14. (Unallocated)
15. Management Techniques
16. Financial Resources for Economic Development
17. Personnel Services
18. Revenues

Service Volumes
19. Leisure Services
20. Education
21. Environmental Services
22. Personal Social Services
23. Housing
24. Law and Order
25. Planned Urban Development
26. Planning
27. Transport
28. Water
29. Scotland
30. Health

Information sources

Local government's operations and finance represent an extremely open form of government. It is very easy to find out more about the finances of each and every authority from CIPFA statistics.

The one major document not published by CIPFA is *Local*

Government Financial Statistics in England and Wales, which summarizes actual expenditure figures. These include statistics not easily obtainable elsewhere, but there has been a very long lead time in their production, of up to two years.

Probably the single most useful CIPFA publication is *Financial General and Rating Statistics.* This contains the summarized budgets of each English and Welsh authority, both in cash and per thousand population. It is always timely and illustrates the professionalism of CIPFA's statistical information service.

One innovation has been the publication of *Comparative Statistics.* Again containing figures for each authority of the latest actuals, its aim was to assist authorities in compiling statistics for annual reports. A special service enables the statistics for one authority to be compared with the average statistics for a group of authorities as chosen by the person requesting the comparison.

Useful for a general survey of local government and its environment is *Local Government Trends.* There are additionally two reference volumes: *Statistical Techniques* and *Community Indicators.*

Journals

The two journals which consistently cover the area of local government finance and accounting in greater depth are both published by CIPFA, namely *Public Finance and Accountancy* and *Public Money. Local Government Studies* (8 per year) and *Public Administration* (quarterly) contain regular items on local government finance, particularly the former. For weekly news and analysis in this area, *Local Government Chronicle* provides a wide coverage.

GLOSSARY OF LOCAL GOVERNMENT FINANCE

Balance In general, the surplus or deficit on any account at the end of the year. Often used to refer to the surplus available in aid of the rate or precept, which has accumulated through underspending in past years, or by deliberate policy.

Capital receipts Capital money received from the sale of land or other assets which is available to finance other items of capital (but not revenue) spending, or to repay debt on assets originally financed from loan.

Central Establishment (or Administration) Charges (CEC) The cost of central administrative departments, e.g. Chief Executive, Finance Department, Administration Department, Estates Department, which are apportioned to service committees usually on the basis of time spent on each committee's activities.

Contingencies Money set aside in the estimates to pay for inflation (and sometimes unforeseen events). Usually a lump sum rather than amounts specifically set aside. Because councils normally prepare detailed estimates at a November price base, the inflation contingency for, say, 1986-87 covered inflation from November 1985 to March 1987.

Debt charges The annual revenue charges resulting from the repayment of advances to the consolidated loans and capital funds. These comprise the annual repayment of a specified proportion of the advance together with interest at the fund rate on the balance outstanding during the year. Sometimes referred to as loan charges. Local authorities do not formally depreciate their assets, but the principal repayment is very similar in practice to a historic cost depreciation provision.

Education pooled expenditure The incidence of certain education expenditure, principally training of teachers and advanced further education, is uneven throughout the country and for this reason is pooled. Authorities providing these services are reimbursed their costs, which are then apportioned over all education authorities on a uniform basis – by school population or a combination of school population and rateable value.

Estimate (Estimate Head) The type of item for which an Estimate has been prepared; usually a subjective heading (e.g. salaries or equipment) within a service (e.g. primary education or refuse collection).

 Original Estimate The Estimate for the year approved before the start of the financial year, usually at the previous November's price levels.

 Revised Estimate The Original Estimate for the year updated by price changes since it was prepared, and by Supplementary Estimates and virement.

 Supplementary Estimate An amount which has been approved by the council to be spent in excess of the Original Estimate.

Financial regulations A formal code of procedures to be followed in the financial management of the council.

Fund Local authorities must account for certain types of expenditure in separate funds, e.g. consolidated loans fund. Other funds are created for specific purposes, e.g. repairs and renewals fund. Some of the many types of fund are:

Capital fund An internal fund of the authority created to finance capital expenditure. The fund may be built up by contributions from revenue, repayments by borrowing committees and capital receipts.

Consolidated loans fund (CLF) The proceeds of all loans, stock issues, etc., raised to finance capital spending are paid into the capital account of this fund. Advances are made from the fund to finance the capital spending of the various services and are repaid by annual instalments over fixed periods. Interest and expenses are charged to the fund revenue account and recovered annually from the service revenue accounts at an average rate based on the loan debt outstanding on each service.

County fund The rate-borne expenditure of county councils.

General rate fund (GRF) The rate-borne expenditure of district councils.

Internal funds These are funds created for specific purposes, e.g. capital funds, insurance funds and repair and renewals funds. Some authorities have introduced general funds – earmarked, but not necessarily for a specific purpose.

Repairs and renewals fund A fund created to meet the cost of replacing or making repairs to vehicles, plant, furniture or equipment, with the object of equalizing the cost over a number of years.

Gross expenditure The cost of providing the Council's services before deduction of government grants or other sources of income.

Housing investment programme (HIP) The method by which the government has allocated capital funds to housing authorities, involving submission of a bid, with subsequent notification of approvals.

Housing Revenue Account (HRA) A separate account dealing with expenditure and income arising from the letting of local authority houses. Expenditure includes supervision and management costs, repairs and debt charges. Income includes rent, government subsidies and mandatory rate fund contributions towards the cost of rebates. Councils may also make discretionary contributions from the rate fund towards deficiencies.

Interest on revenue balances (or interest receipts) The day-to-day cash flow of the authority is invested when it is in surplus, and borrowing is required when it is in deficit. The interest gained on the net surplus over the year's cash flow is given one or other of these names.

Loan charges, see Debt charges.

Net expenditure Gross expenditure less specific government grants and service income but before deduction of block grant.

Precept The net rate-borne expenditure of a non-rating authority which a rating authority must provide for in its rate levy and pay over to the non-rating authority. A county council is, of course, a precepting authority.

Price base The pay and price levels of a specified year used for calculating Estimates, forecasts, policy options, etc.

November prices Pay and price levels known in November in a particular year.

Outturn prices The actual price levels at the time the money was spent.

Product of a penny rate (PRP) Rate income available from levying a rate of one penny in the pound on the district's rateable value after allowing for costs and losses on rate collection.

Public Works Loan Board (PWLB) A government agency which provides longer-term loans to public authorities at interest rates slightly higher than those at which the government itself can borrow. Local authorities are able to borrow a proportion of their requirements to finance capital spending from this source.

Rateable value (RV) A value placed on all properties subject to rating, to which rate poundages are applied to arrive at rates payable. The value is based on a notional rent that the property could be expected to yield after deducting the cost of repairs.

Rate levy The number of pence in the pound that the council determines should be applied to the rateable value of properties. This is sometimes referred to as rate poundage. A smaller rate is levied on domestic ratepayers because of the domestic rate relief grant.

Rate support grant (RSG) This has two main elements: domestic rate relief grant and block grant. Detailed terminology of RSG includes:

Block grant This has two separate objectives:

(i) to enable all authorities to levy similar rate poundages for similar standards of service;
(ii) to discourage high spending through tapering grant support for authorities whose expenditure exceeds a predetermined level.

Clawback The amount of grant claimed by councils is unlikely to match exactly the total grant available, and will usually exceed it, at least initially. Because the block grant is cash-limited, all authorities' claims are adjusted (clawed back) to ensure the calculated entitlements are in line with the grant pool.

Domestic Rate Relief Grant A grant paid by the government to reduce domestic rate bills (by 18.5p in recent years).

Grant Related Expenditure (GRE) A centrally determined assessment of an authority's costs in providing average standards of service, taking into account its demographic and other circumstances. It was not intended to be an expenditure target but only a mechanism for distributing grant. The assessment for individual authorities is known as the Grant Related Expenditure Assessment (GREA).

Grant related poundage (GRP) The objective of block grant is that all authorities of the same class (e.g. Outer London boroughs) should face the same rate for spending in line with GRE. They should also face the same change in poundage for equal changes in expenditure per head above and below these levels. The GRP schedule is used to compute GRPs for given levels of expenditure relative to GRE.

Guidance see Target.

Holdback Witholding of grant to individual authorities, or collectively by the Secretary of State for failure to make expenditure reductions in line with some target other than those implied in the basic block grant system, e.g. the current expenditure target in 1981/82.

Multiplier A number (usually less than 1) used mostly to moderate authorities' grant losses due to changes in the formulae.

Relevant expenditure Broadly an authority's total revenue expenditure but excluding expenditure and grant on mandatory student awards and certain 'non-relevant' Home Office expenditure. Reconciled with public expenditure on current account in the Public Expenditure White Paper.

Taper For spending above threshold, authorities receive a tapering amount of support from the government – a form of penalty. For very high resource authorities – mostly in London – the taper can lead to no grant at all being paid for high levels of spending above GRE.

Target An expenditure target other than GRE. In 1981-82 it referred to a reduction of 5.6% off 1978-79 current expenditure. In 1982-83, it was a much more complex figure calculated by reference to 1982-83 GRE *and* 1981-82 current expenditure. Also known as 'guidance'.

Threshold The amount of spending above GRE before the government starts to taper grant. It has been 10% since block grant was introduced.

Revenue contribution to capital outlay (RCCO) The financing of capital spending directly from revenue. The council may determine that certain capital projects should be financed in this way or alternatively may include in the revenue budget a prescribed sum for this purpose.

Specific grants Government grants to local authorities in aid of particular projects or services, paid at a fixed proportion (e.g. 75%) of expenditure actually incurred, e.g. Magistrates Courts grant, police, inner urban aid.

Transport policy and programme (TPP) A statement of transport objectives and policies designed to achieve those objectives, together with a five-year programme of expenditure to implement the stated policies.

Transport supplementary grant (TSG) A grant in respect of accepted spending in connection with public transport, highways, traffic regulations, and the provision of parking spaces. The grant is related to local authorities' programmes contained in their TPP, the level of grant reflecting the TPP spending level accepted by the government. Grant is paid on estimates of accepted spending and not adjusted in the light of actual spending.

5

Nationalized industries

5.1 INTRODUCTION

The nationalized industries covered in this part of the book are, socially and economically, a major part of the British economy. They employ about a million people and are responsible for about 10% of the country's fixed investment. Industries such as British Gas and the Post Office are household names because they deal directly with the public, while others such as the British Airports Authority (which runs many of the country's airports) or the British Waterways Board (which manages many inland waterways) are less familiar.

The industries are often regarded as a group, and are usually treated as such in planning the country's financial and economic policy. But it is important to remember that they vary in many ways:

(a) Some, such as the electricity industry, are monopolies (at least in electricity, though not in energy) while others, such as British Shipbuilders, are subject to national or international competition.
(b) The industries also vary greatly in size. British Waterways employs about 3,000 people, the National Coal Board nearly 200,000.
(c) Some have a record of profitable operation, British Gas for example, while British Steel lost several billion pounds in the 1970s and 1980s.

Table 5.1 lists those industries which have their own identifiable and separate financing from central government. It is from these industries that the examples in this section of the book will be taken. There are a large variety of other publicly owned organizations which are funded by government departments.

These include organizations as diverse as the National Film Finance Corporation and the Royal Mint. A full list is given in Appendix 5.1. There are also organizations which are not formally nationalized, but where the State has a majority shareholding, for example British Leyland and Rolls Royce. These are not included because for most financial purposes they can be treated like private sector organizations which happen to be state funded.

Table 5.1
The main industries

British Airports Authority	London Regional Transport
British Gas Corporation	National Bus Company
British Railways Board	National Coal Board
British Shipbuilders	North of Scotland Hydroelectric Board
British Steel Corporation	Post Office
British Waterways Board	Scottish Transport Group
Civil Aviation Authority	South of Scotland Electricity Board
Electricity Council	Water Authorities (England and Wales)

There have been many changes in these lists of organizations since the late 1940s when most of the larger industries were nationalized. British Steel went out of public ownership once and was then renationalized. British Aerospace was nationalized in 1977 only to have the shares sold back to the private sector in 1981 and 1985. The British National Oil Corporation was created as a new nationalized industry in 1976 but the organization was divided into two in 1982. A majority of the shares in the largest part were sold to the private sector a year later and the rump was closed down in 1985. Indeed in the early 1980s a whole range of industries were privatized (denationalized). So this is a group whose members are liable to change at any time as a result of changes in government policy towards public ownership. The industries covered in this section of the book might therefore be joined at any time by others or may be reduced in number by privatization.

The system of parliamentary and government monitoring and control described in the following sections also varies, so developments need to be watched carefully to make sure that what is described and analysed still applies. In particular, at the time this edition of the book was being prepared, the government indicated that they intended to legislate 'in due course' to tidy up a number of matters not satisfactorily covered by the existing nationalized industry statutes. Matters which were potentially going to be the subject of legislation included borrowing and guarantees; accounts, reports and audit; financial targets, balance sheets and formation of companies and privatization. Appendix 5.4 gives details of these proposals.

The organization of the electricity and water industries needs some additional explanation. The Electricity Council is really only an 'umbrella' policy-making body for the electricity industry in England and Wales. Power is generated by the Central Electricity Generating Board, which then transmits it in bulk to the 12 area Electricity Boards. Industrial and domestic consumers are supplied by these Area Boards through their own networks. Scotland and Northern Ireland have their own arrangements. As for the water industry, the Water Act 1983 replaced the National Water Council with the Water Authorities Association in which the ten Water Authorities are equal shareholders. This Association may discuss national issues but is not an 'umbrella' body like the Electricity Council. The Water Authorities are therefore effectively individual nationalized industries. Again Scotland and Northern Ireland have their own arrangements.

Finally, a note on abbreviations. The industries are often referred to by their initials, but apart from abbreviating some titles (British Railways Board to British Rail, etc.) initials have not been used in the text in order to maintain clarity and avoid jumbles of letters.

5.2 POLICY-MAKING

Government and Parliament

Public ownership means that the basis of all policy is the legislation which covers each industry. The Acts which contain the most important passages as far as finance and accounting policy are concerned are listed in Appendix 5.2 and the main details of what is in the legislation is examined in the section on external reporting.

It is the Minister who is formally responsible to Parliament for implementing the legislation and this responsibility means, for example, that the auditors report not to the management of the industry or to Parliament, but to the Minister.

In practice, this responsibility is not exercised entirely personally. Although the Minister answers certain questions relating to an industry in the House of Commons, the day-to-day work is done under his authority by officials of the government department that 'sponsors' a particular industry. The sponsoring role means that the department is primarily responsible for government policy in relation to the industry and looks after its interests in discussions with the Treasury and other government departments. These discussions will generally be between senior officials from the sponsoring department and senior management of the industry, but for matters concerning financing, capital expenditure monitoring and the accounts, Treasury officials are also likely to be involved. Table 5.2 gives a list of sponsoring government departments.

Table 5.2
Sponsoring Departments

Department of Energy	British Gas, Electricity Council, National Coal Board
Department of the Environment	British Waterways, Water Authorities (England)
Department of Industry	British Shipbuilders, British Steel, Post Office
Department of Transport	British Airports Authority, British Rail, Civil Aviation Authority, London Regional Transport, National Bus
Scottish Office	North of Scotland Hydroelectric Board, Scottish Transport, South of Scotland Electricity Board
Welsh Office	Welsh Water Authority

Parliamentary control is rarely exercised through the House of Commons as a whole, although on occasions there may be problems with an industry of such magnitude that there will be a debate on its position on the 'floor' of the House of Commons. Normally, however, parliamentary control over an industry is exercised through a select committee. Until the 1978-79 parliamentary session, all industries were covered by the Select Committee on Nationalised Industries (SCNI), but in 1980 the SCNI was abolished and a system of select committees was set up so that a committee covered each of the main government departments. The select committee responsible for an industry will be the one covering its sponsoring department.

Select committees are in general more likely to be interested in general policy (including finance) than accountancy issues, though the Transport and Energy Select Committees have undertaken a specific investigation of the reports and accounts of certain industries. The Treasury Select Committee has also taken an interest in financial policy for the nationalised industries as a whole. Otherwise, finance and accounting matters come up at various times when chairmen and other board members of an industry are giving oral or written evidence before select committees. Because they are often spontaneous, some of the answers given in oral evidence are revealing and make fascinating reading. (The more important recent reports are listed in the bibliography.) But these investigations are not conducted primarily to provide entertainment. The select committee draws to the attention of the House of Commons as a whole those matters the committee feels require action. Often, however, a report itself will be enough to produce any changes which the industry's management, or the government may agree to be necessary.

Policy through White Papers

The formal control mechanism through the Minister and Parliament has, since 1961, been supplemented by White Papers outlining government policy towards the industries. The current White Paper *The Nationalised Industries* (Cmnd. 7131) was issued in 1978. Its predecessors were:

(a) *The Financial and Economic Obligations of the Nationalised Industries* (Cmnd. 1337) issued in 1961,
(b) *Nationalised Industries: A Review of Economic and Financial Objectives* (Cmnd. 3437) issued in 1967.

In practice, while some of the policies set out in White Papers have become firmly established, others have been varied by successive governments because of changing ideologies or economic circumstances. So although the White Papers provide important guidelines on government policy, day-to-day decisions will be based more on the needs of the moment. The effect of rapid changes in policy and the resulting conflicts are dealt with in greater detail later in this section.

The 1978 White Paper itself was the government's response to a report issued in 1976 by the National Economic Development Office (NEDO) called *A Study of the UK Nationalised Industries: Their Role in the Economy and Control in the Future*. This criticized some of the ambiguities in government policy, and although the government rejected some of the recommendations of the report, it accepted the need for greater clarity on financial and other objectives. So the White Paper laid down a financial and economic framework within which the industries were to work. Key areas covered by the White Paper were:

Financial Targets. After confirming that each industry would work to a specific financial target, the White Paper stipulated that 'the level of each financial target will be decided industry by industry. It will take account of a wide range of factors. These will include the expected return from effective, cost conscious management of existing and new assets; market prospects; the scope for improved productivity and efficiency; the opportunity cost of capital; the implications for the public sector borrowing requirement; counter-inflation policy; and social or sectoral objectives, for e.g. the Energy and Transport Industries.' For those industries not likely to make a profit, the White Paper said that the target would be set in terms of the amount of grant or deficit. The financial target was also said to be the 'primary expression' of financial performance.

Investment Criterion. The legislation covering an industry generally requires that the Minister approves programmes of major capital expenditure. The White Paper supplemented this by stating that the industries should earn a required rate of return (RRR) on new investment as a whole of 5% in real terms before tax. This figure was based on 'the pre-tax real returns which have been achieved by private companies and the likely trend in the return on private investment. The cost of finance to the private sector has also been taken into account along with considerations of social time preference'. The 5% figure was to be reviewed every three to five years and an appendix in the White Paper gave details of how the link between the financial target and the RRR was to be made.

Non-financial Performance Indicators. To supplement the financial targets, the White Paper also stipulated that each industry should publish non-financial indicators of performance and service standards, to ensure that an industry should not be able to improve its financial performance simply by increasing prices or lowering standards of service. It was explained that the government had 'asked each industry, in consultation with its sponsoring department, to select a number of key performance indicators, including valid international comparisons, and to publish them prominently in their annual reports. They would be supported by an explanation of why they had been chosen and of significant trends . . . There will probably be some indicators common to most including, for example, labour productivity and standards of service where these are readily measurable.

Financial targets, the RRR and non-financial performance indicators were designed to be the three major elements of the control mechanism for nationalized industries. The White Paper also covered many other aspects of the relationship between industries and government of which other important financial and accounting elements included:

Corporate Plans. Financial targets and investment strategies were to be part of the framework of the corporate plan whose importance was underlined by the statement that 'the government considers that the corporate plan, and the examination of strategic options, should have a central place in the relationship between the nationalized industries and their sponsoring departments'.

Audit Committees. The development of audit committees within the industries' own boards was welcomed, and their role in looking at efficiency and performance was emphasised.

Pricing Policy. Prices were to be the result of the level at which the financial targets were set rather than of following the principle in the 1967 White Paper that the nationalized industries should price to cover their long-run marginal costs.

Inflation Accounting. The importance of inflation accounting was emphasized and the White Paper stated that financial targets 'should be put on some suitable inflation-adjusted basis'.

Cash Limits. Flexibility was to be allowed on cash limits in view of the fact that, 'like private sector companies, their revenues and expenditures depend on trading conditions'. But while acknowledging that there might be conditions in which the cash limits should be increased, the White Paper also emphasised there was no guarantee that this would be automatic.

Disclosure. The White Paper provided that a large amount of information should be published in the annual report and accounts including
(a) the main points in the corporate plan and any government response to them,
(b) the financial target and the accompanying parliamentary statement explaining it, including any sectoral and social objectives set for the industry as well as how financial performance compared against target,
(c) the cash limit set and how well the industry had performed against it,
(d) the performance indicators and how well the industry had done against them.

It can be seen from this list that the White Paper was an attempt to provide a comprehensive financial and economic framework, and to ensure that the public was informed about what was going on through disclosure in the annual report and accounts.

Financing the industries

Almost all the funds provided for the industries by the government are in the form of loans from the National Loans Fund administered by the Treasury. Interest is payable on these loans at the rate prevailing when the loan is taken out. The industries are also able to borrow on the home or overseas capital markets if they consider the terms more favourable and if government policy allows them to do so. These loans are usually guaranteed by the government and therefore count as part of government financing, even though the money may not come directly from public funds. In the case of overseas borrowing, the Treasury has a scheme whereby the industries are insured against losses that might arise for them if the pound depreciates against the currency in which the loan has been taken out. The industry pays the Treasury a premium for this service, exactly as it would do on any insurance policy.

A few industries are partly financed by a form of share capital known as public dividend capital (PDC). Dividends are payable on PDC on a basis which reflects trading profits, so PDC has generally been made available only to industries which were thought to have a reasonable chance of paying dividends in good trading years. Two which have PDC are British Steel and the Giro part of the Post Office.

The total of grants, net borrowing, leasing and PDC make up the industry's cash limit (known since 1979 as the external financing limit or EFL). This limit is determined each year, taking into account the capital requirements of the industry and the internal resources which it can generate. Table 5.3 gives an example of how an EFL is built up for the Water Authorities. Some points to note from the table are:

(a) 'Other capital requirements' means mainly working capital,
(b) The capital value of leases is included both under 'capital requirements' and also under 'net borrowing, etc.' This treatment of leases is an attempt to stop industries leasing assets in order to get round the government's cash constraints.

EFLs are first published before the beginning of the financial

Table 5.3
Water Authorities' EFL for 1985-86

	£ million	Total
Capital requirements		
Fixed assets in the UK	852	
Other	(9)	843
Financed by		
Internal resources		
— current cost operating profit	353	
— interest, dividends, tax	(547)	
— depreciation	781	
— other receipts and payments	54	
	640	
External finance		
— government grant, net borrowing and leasing	203	843

Source: 1985 Public Expenditure White Paper. Reproduced by permission of the Controller, Her Majesty's Stationery Office. Crown copyright.

year, usually in November, and the full table can be found in the *Financial Statement and Budget Report* (FSBR) published each year at the time of the Budget. Details of cash actually provided in the year are published with the following year's FSBR, in the Public Expenditure White Paper and also in the reports and accounts of each industry.

EFLs are by no means as severe a constraint as an overdraft limit for a private sector organization at a commercial bank. This is because the government does not have statutory powers to force the industry to keep within its EFL for the year, so the limit can only be maintained by agreement. In practice the government has a great deal more muscle, since ministers can withhold agreement for major investment decisions or borrowing. Nevertheless, in recognition of the fact that it is often difficult for an industry to keep within a fixed target set up months before the beginning of the financial year, there is some flexibility built into the system based on an agreement reached in 1980 by a study group of members of the Nationalised Industries Chairmen's Group and the Treasury. Under this agreement, some flexibility is allowed for EFLs if, on the basis of discussions, there is a danger of a major departure from the industries' medium-term commercial interests or damage to explicit government objectives (announcement in *Hansard*, Cols. 41-42, 4 August 1981). An additional 'fine-tuning' formula was also agreed so that additional borrowing of 1% of the total of the turnover and capital expenditure for the year over and above the EFL would be allowed. The sting in the tail is that this amount is deducted from the limit for the next year.

The level at which the EFL is set will be determined by a large number of factors but will usually be a compromise between the claims of the industry for the cash to finance its current programme and the needs of governments to balance the needs of individual spending programmes, as well as keeping public expenditure as a whole under control. Starting from those two bargaining positions, there will be a great deal of discussion about the 'appropriate' level to be set for the coming year.

Policy issues

Conflicts between objectives

In theory there ought to be no difficulty in reconciling the objectives set out in the White Paper. The corporate plan should be the mechanism by which financial targets, non-financial performance indicators and the RRR are reconciled. In theory, too, the corporate plan ought to include sufficient provision of cash to ensure that the plan can be carried out. However, there are both theoretical as well as practical difficulties in reconciling the objectives.

Taking the relationship between the RRR and the financial target first, the White Paper suggests that an industry's revenue requirement should be the link between the two, the financial target on all assets being set to reflect the need to earn the 5% RRR on new investment. But one difficulty in linking them is the difference in the time scales involved. The financial target is supposed to last three to five years. The RRR, on the other hand, is assessed over the life of the project as a whole and indeed may be altered by the time a project with a long lead time comes on stream. With a regular ordering pattern, timing may not be such a problem, but if there is 'lumpy' investment, it is likely to be difficult in practice to match the two year by year. The calculation will be made even more difficult because estimates have to be made for the rates of return on 'old assets' and because the RRR is an average of 5%, so that in any one year the return is unlikely to correspond to the average even if it is exactly as planned.

To take an example, a new nuclear power station, costing hundreds of millions of pounds, may be planned. If it takes, say, 7 years to build and has a life of 25 years, the average rate of return may be calculated at 10%. But the return may never be 10% in any one year and may have to be very high in the first few years of operation to balance out lower returns in its life, when maintenance costs are likely to increase.

Meanwhile, the financial target will be calculated taking into account not only this new station, but all existing stations. It can be seen that there will be difficulties in combining, in any one year, the return from the new station with the returns from all other stations to reconcile to a financial target figure. These difficulties will be compounded in practice because of the uncertainties surrounding the construction times and costs of each station, the relative costs of coal, oil and nuclear fuel as well as many of the other factors involved in energy planning.

A further problem is the reconciliation of financial and non-financial performance measures, and there may well be difficulty in succeeding both financially and against non-financial perform-ance measures, particularly those on standards of service. For example, projects to improve the financial return may cause a deterioration in standards of service, so that running down the maintenance staff may save money, but may also result in more planes or trains being cancelled. A similar conflict may arise between better performance against non-financial performance indicators and achieving a 5% RRR. It may be necessary to improve standards of service, but only by accepting projects that cause the industry to fail to meet the 5% target.

In theory, too, the primary position of the financial target should mean that, in case of any conflict, the non-financial performance criteria will have to take second place. In practice, the problem has not turned out to be reconciling the three targets, but reconciling all three with a target not given any prominence within the White Paper – keeping within the EFL. This was originally seen as a constraint rather than a target, but has become more important than financial and non-financial targets. That this is so continues to provoke debate. For example in 1984 the Select Committee on Energy in their report on electricity and gas prices was highly critical of the Electricity Council's EFL which, it said, was imposed without due consultation and was not consistent with the other elements of its guidelines.

In its 1983/4 Annual Report the Electricity Council set out (no doubt in an attempt to influence future discussions with the government) that:

The Industry was disappointed that the EFL repayment was given precedence over the financial target and is pleased to note that the Treasury and the Department of Energy have, in this reply to the Select Committee on Energy, reaffirmed the principles of the 1978 White Paper 'The Nationalised Industries' which stated that the financial target was to be the primary expression of the financial performance which the Government expects of the Industry.

The North of Scotland Hydroelectric Board was equally blunt in its 1983/4 report:

In common with other nationalised industries the Board is concerned at the tendency to set, in the short term, external financing limits which are not consistent with the longer term financial targets, far less with the needs of the Board.

It appears that the government itself has not been able to reconcile these objectives because the need to limit the total of public borrowing has overridden the need to give the industries a satisfactory financial policy framework.

The use of the 5% RRR

The idea of taking a standard rate of 5% RRR on new investment as a whole for all industries is conceptually difficult to justify. It is also difficult to apply in practice. Financial targets are supposed to be set in a way which mirrors the differences in the circumstances of each industry. But, curiously, the White Paper fails to follow the logic through and gives a standard RRR, no matter how risky each of the projects might be. It would seem more appropriate, at a time when capital is rationed, to take different rates of return depending on the risk. The idea behind taking a standard rate may well have been that capital should be rationed across all the industries using the same rate of return, to enable comparisons to be made between competing projects from every source. But without more information on the reasons it seems very difficult to justify the use of a standard rate on these grounds, and more probably the standard rate was included to avoid the difficult and embarrassing job of quantifying risk.

Methods of financing

The industries have often argued that using loan capital financing through the National Loans Fund as virtually the only way of providing funds is far too inflexible, and that the industries should be allowed to borrow directly from the market. On the face of it, this argument would seem to be very reasonable, bearing in mind the very different circumstances of each industry, but there are some powerful arguments against a greater variety of financing methods. First, loan capital may be the only way by which a return can be assured on the money provided by the government. PDC has on the whole fallen into disrepute because industries financed in this way have often not been able to pay dividends. And even those able to pay have generally been unwilling to do so because, with controls on external borrowing, they needed the cash for the internal financing of investment. Second, the justification for borrowing through the National Loans Fund (which means that the source is the money raised by the government for all its purposes) rather than letting the industries go straight to the market to borrow, is that the industries with no independent credit standing would then be competing with central government. It is argued that it is therefore more economic to go through a central mechanism to ensure that rates are not bid up as public sector institutions compete with each other to raise funds. Third, the argument has also been that since an industry's borrowings are guaranteed by the government, it would be wrong for them to go separately to the market and commit the government in such a way that it might break its overall financial limits.

A separate argument on financing has been whether interest should be payable when the project being financed has not yet come 'on stream'. Certain industries, notably the National Coal Board, have argued that with very long projects the interest ought to be deferred until the projects being financed are ready to generate revenue and thereby pay off the accumulated interest charges. Successive governments have rejected these arguments, mainly on the grounds that to give in to them would mean less financial discipline and a loss of control over their ability to get any return on the money which has been provided. Over the years the government has made some concessions, such as allowing the industries to borrow for varying periods of time, but the central arguments against greater flexibility have been upheld.

Flexibility in the control mechanism

Industries have also regularly complained that the system by which they are financially controlled is far too inflexible. This has applied both to the setting of financial targets and to EFLs.

In the case of financial targets, it has never been clear what the appropriate circumstances are for changing them. For example, will the target be adjusted if any industry consistently beats it or consistently fails to beat it? And what circumstances (domestic recession, world trade recession, bad weather) mean that the industry has to adjust to the target or that the target has to be adjusted? This is obviously an important issue in the way in which an industry responds to changing circumstances. After all, if the financial target has got to be maintained at all costs, this may mean that big savings have to be made and services may be cut with severe consequences for the consumer and maybe the economy. On the other hand, if it is entirely flexible, it could be argued that, once again, discipline is lost. In practice, the financial targets have rarely been adjusted in order to take account of changed circumstances, and there seems to be an 'unofficial' adjusted target for any year, which operates on the basis of an agreement between the industry and its sponsoring department, but which is not published.

The second major area where the issue of flexibility has arisen is in the operation of EFLs. The nationalized industries have regularly complained about the difficulty of aiming at a precise target figure for financing which is a very small difference between large amounts of income and expenditure (both on current purchases and on capital expenditure). The chairman of one industry likened it to trying to land a jumbo jet on a postage stamp. The agreement reached in 1980 on increased flexibility for the industries means that they have at least some margin of safety for financing. But even this formula has not satisfied many industries on the grounds that EFLs are not really a suitable method for controlling the industries anyway. Indeed, it has been argued that it is beyond the capability of any industry to forecast its capital requirements with such precision, bearing in mind not only the normal commercial uncertainties of the market place, such as an unexpectedly steep recession, but also many factors outside their control, such as political turmoil in a key market or major currency fluctuations. The industries' difficulties are increased because even if they want to increase prices to meet the EFL, they often have to go through a lengthy enquiry procedure before they can do so.

In practice, EFLs have really not turned out to be such a harsh discipline because successive governments have either allowed the industries to overspend their EFL or have raised it when it has become clear that commercial circumstances have dramatically changed. So the system has been operated on the basis of an implicit ambiguity. The government has not officially been willing to be seen to give much away to the industries, because they have not wanted it to be seen that the control mechanism has become slack. On the other hand, they have acknowledged by their action in raising limits that industries cannot in reality be controlled down to a very small amount.

Control using EFLs as the main instrument

The system of cash control through EFLs has been condemned for a number of reasons. First, it has been argued that EFLs unjustifiably push up prices; second, that they are simply a means of implementing pay policy; and third that they burden today's consumers with the cost of investment which is for the benefit of the consumers of tomorrow.

None of these arguments carry much weight. Taking them in turn, EFLs of themselves do not necessarily mean increased prices for the consumer – an argument which can anyway only apply to those industries which are monopoly suppliers, since the effect of the others raising prices to a level which is higher than private sector competitors will be that they lose business. But even monopoly suppliers do not have complete freedom of action. If British Rail's prices are too high, consumers can and indeed do switch to bus, car or air transport. There are also a number of mechanisms to ensure that the industries do not automatically pass on the full burden to the consumer. These include statutory consumers' councils and the government's power to refer an industry to the Monopolies and Mergers Commission to investigate their efficiency. The fact that EFLs have sometimes been set at a low level because of the need to keep down the call on government funds does not mean the system itself is to blame. Any mechanism of cash control, whether called EFL or not, would have exactly the same effect.

As to whether EFLs constitute an unofficial incomes policy for an industry, when an EFL is set, an industry will make an assumption about the level of wage settlements for a coming year. This means that if an industry exceeds the assumed level of wage increase for a year, it has a number of options, including raising prices, or making a trade-off between wages paid and the numbers of people employed. The government itself may respond by increasing the EFL, or by acquiescing in overspending. This means that although EFLs are a *guide* to wage settlements, there is enough flexibility for the system of itself not to constitute a pay policy.

Finally, the argument that, if EFLs are set at a level which means that the industries have got to raise money to finance capital investment from charging their customers more, this will mean that today's customers are paying for the benefits which will be enjoyed by customers in future years, confuses cause and effect. EFLs do not in themselves shift the burden. They are simply one means of carrying out a policy decision about how public expenditure should be controlled. Indeed, there is no guarantee that an industry will not cut its capital expenditure, thereby depriving future consumers of their coal, electricity or airline seats.

What all three arguments have in common is that the mechanism for controlling expenditure is taken as the cause of a lack of funds, a continuation of the long and honourable tradition of executing the messenger bringing bad news.

5.3 INTERNAL CONTROL AND PERFORMANCE MEASUREMENT

This section concentrates on performance measurement rather than internal control because the details of how to operate the control mechanism, including budgeting, financial management, capital investment and internal reporting, are left very much to the individual industry. So there is no common system covering internal control, and practice varies between industries as much as it does between private sector organizations. This means that there is a fundamental distinction between the well established rules and constraints for external reporting which are common to all industries and internal mechanisms which are a matter of individual management style.

The measurement of performance links what the organization decides to do internally with how other people measure it. So while each industry has its own way of deciding how well or badly it is doing, in general it will tend to watch most closely those performance measures which the outside world is using. This section therefore deals with those measures of performance that are commonly used to assess the industries.

Determining performance measures

The legislation

The legislation which set up each of the industries contains some statement about a financial objective. Often that objective is to break even, taking one year with another, although some are set profit targets. Table 5.4 summarizes the financial objectives of the 17 industries as set out in the legislation.

In most cases, the legislation also gives the industries a variety of non-financial tasks. These may be expressed as obligations or duties and some examples are:

Table 5.4
Financial objectives in the legislation

British Airports Authority
  Revenue is not less than sufficient for making provision for the meeting of charges properly chargeable to revenue taking one year with another.

British Gas
  The combined revenue of the corporation and its subsidiaries is to be enough to meet the charges to revenue and to enable them to make adequate allocation to reserve.

British Rail
  The combined revenues of the Board and its subsidiaries must be sufficient to meet the combined charges to revenue taking one year with another.

British Shipbuilders
  The financial duties . . . shall be such as may from time to time be determined by the Secretary of State with the approval of the Treasury and after consultation with the Corporation.

British Steel
  The combined revenues of the corporation must be sufficient to meet the combined charges to revenue taking one year with another.

  Secretary of State can also determine a reasonable rate of return on net assets as a target.

British Waterways
  As for British Rail.

Electricity Council
  Combined revenues must be sufficient to meet combined charges taking one year with another.

London Regional Transport
  So far as practicable the combined revenues of London Regional Transport and any subsidiaries of theirs are not less than sufficient to meet their combined charges properly chargeable to revenue account, taking one accounting year with another.

National Bus
  As for British Rail.

National Coal Board
  The revenues of the board shall be not less than sufficient for meeting all their outgoings properly chargeable to revenue account . . . on an average of good and bad years.

North of Scotland Hydroelectric Board
  Revenues not less than sufficient to meet their outgoings properly chargeable to revenue account taking one year with another.

Civil Aviation Authority
  As for British Airports Authority.

Scottish Transport
  As for British Rail.

South of Scotland Electricity Board
  As for North of Scotland Hydroelectric Board.

Water Authorities
  As for North of Scotland Hydroelectric Board.

It shall be the duty of the Railways Board . . . to provide railway services in Great Britain . . . and to provide such other services and facilities as appear to the Board to be expedient and to have due regard . . . to efficiency, economy and safety of operation. (British Rail: Transport Act 1962)

To have full regard to the requirements of national defence [and] to promote industrial democracy in a strong and organic form. (British Shipbuilders: Aircraft and Shipbuilding Act 1977)

Such statements are of course only very vague and do not provide clear indications about what constitutes a good performance for an industry. Nevertheless they are important in establishing the background against which an industry's decisions are taken. It is also easy to see how these general objectives might clash with financial objectives, and it is not unusual to find an industry required to break even but also to provide loss-making services.

The corporate plan

An industry's corporate plan, which will be seen and approved by the minister and the sponsoring department, usually contains a statement of broad objectives as well as a variety of specific objectives, some financial and some non-financial.

For example, the requirements for the British Airports Authority are couched in very unspecific terms

. . . to respond to the present and future needs of air transport in an efficient and profitable way by operating, planning and developing its airports so that air travellers and cargo may pass through safely, swiftly and as conveniently as possible. (Annual Report for 1983-84)

while that for British Shipbuilders is more down to earth:

The Plan . . . . . . emphasises the action required and in hand to reverse the trend of escalating losses. (Annual Report for 1983-84)

Performance targets and aims

Almost all industries have a financial performance target, set by the minister in one of three main forms:

Return on assets,
Profit as a percentage of turnover,
Target profitability or loss.

Most of the targets have been set as a percentage return on net assets, as set out in the 1978 White Paper.

In addition to the financial targets, non-financial performance aims may also be set by the minister. Two examples are:

British Gas 12% reduction in real unit costs 1982-83 to 1986-87
Scottish Transport Group – hold constant or reduce in real terms operating costs per vehicle mile.

These aims are in addition to the performance measures described in the section on policy making. Both the performance aims and the performance measures will be published in the report and accounts. Table 5.5 gives an illustration.

Internally set targets

Most of the industries also set themselves targets as a means of measuring their performance. These are sometimes made public in the annual report and accounts and include a wide variety of different measures. One which appears again and again and is certainly regarded as important inside each industry is the self-financing ratio defined as either

(a) that proportion of capital expenditure over a period which is financed from internal resources, or

(b) that proportion of the total funds required for a period financed internally.

The 1978 White Paper specifically rejected this means of measuring performance, perhaps because there are so many different ways of defining it and of interpreting what the ratio means (see *Self financing ratio*). But there is no doubt that most of the industries see their ability to generate their own funds as an important indication of how well they are doing. It is also a measurement of how dependent they are on public funds and therefore the amount of pressure they perceive the Treasury will be able to exert on them.

Types of financial performance measure

In interpreting the figures for some of the more common measures, a number of factors need to be carefully considered, including not only items normally taken into account when considering results in the private sector, such as the treatment of exceptional or extraordinary items, but also

Table 5.5
Railways performance indicators 1979-1983

	Total Rail Business		1979	1980	1981	1982	1983
1.	Total receipts per train mile	£	7.41	6.97	6.89	6.62	6.83
2.	Train service (operating) expenses per train mile	£		2.30	2.36	2.39	2.31
3.	Train service (maintenance) expenses per train mile	£		1.97	1.94	2.13	1.90
4.	Terminal expenses per train mile	£		1.17	1.10	1.12	1.06
5.	Infrastructure expenses per train mile	£		2.60	2.58	2.82	2.72
6.	Administration costs per train mile	£	1.36	1.33	1.41	1.49	1.35
7.	Train miles per member of staff (Total staff productivity)	no.	1,521	1,570	1,597	1,686	
8.	Revenue per £1,000 gross paybill costs	£	1,537	1,459	1,394	1,256	1,400
9.	Train miles per train crew member (Train crew productivity)	no.					
10.	Track maintenance costs per single track mile	£	7,099	7,244	7,478	6,947	7,898
11.	Signal renewal and maintenance costs per single track mile	£	9,621	9,539	9,523	9,475	10,010
12.	Signal operating costs per single track mile	£	6,379	6,342	6,284	5,982	6,000
13.	Train miles per single track mile	000s	4,625	4,547	4,655	4,463	4,506
14.	Train miles per locomotive/HST set	000s	12.6	12.8	12.6	11.3	12.5
			51.7	53.4	55.2	51.1	57.1

Notes:
(1) Monetary items have been converted to 1983 price levels using GDP deflator, (1979 = 67.5, 1980 = 80.4, 1981 = 88.6, 1982 = 94.3, 1983 = 100).

(2) Receipts include miscellaneous receipts but exclude PSO grants.

(3) Indicators 7 and 8 – staff numbers and paybill costs exclude British Rail Engineering Limited.

(4) Indicator 9 includes train miles for the Board's internal use. It does *not* represent the average mileage per driver, since most trains have a minimum crew of two.

(5) Indicator 11 includes expenditure of a capital nature chargeable to revenue account.
Source: British Railways Board Annual Report and Accounts.

(a) the precise method of calculating the current cost adjustments, since these are on the whole more complex for the public sector,

(b) major write-offs of fixed assets (for example British Rail and British Steel),

(c) whether the book values of assets reflect particular historical circumstances,

(d) 'relifing' of assets, when because of technological developments or other circumstances, asset lives are altered,

(e) special grants paid for various reasons, which may well be included as part of the industry's revenue.

The impact of these adjustments is often very large for the nationalized industries, because changes in policy or trading circumstances can have very large effects on the results.

Return on net assets

The 1978 White Paper confirmed that this would be the 'main form' of target for profitable industries. The target level is set to reflect the different circumstances of each industry and is normally calculated on a current cost basis. In general the return is calculated before interest and tax since the management is not responsible for the way in which the industry is financed and therefore for the proportion of finance provided by interest-bearing loans. Table 5.6 shows the calculation for the South of Scotland Electricity Board, together with the calculation of two of the other measures.

Profit margin

The 'profit' figure may be the same as that used in calculating the 'return' for return on net assets, or may be variations of it. Such variations might exclude income from investments, or include interest.

Profit margin is much more rarely used as a financial target by the government than return on net assets, but it is almost always used within an industry as a measure of performance.

Self-financing ratio

Although not acknowledged by the government as a proper measure of performance, there is no doubt about its importance

Table 5.6
Profit margin, return on net assets and self-financing ratio:
South of Scotland Electricity Board

		£ million
1.	Income	782.5
2.	Expenditure	611.4
3.	Profit before interest	171.0
4.	Interest	154.9
5.	Profit after interest	16.1

Profit margin $\dfrac{16.1}{782.5} \times 100 = 2.1\%$

6.	Fixed assets less depreciation	1577.4
7.	Net current assets	201.9
8.	Net assets employed at year end	1779.3
9.	Average net assets during year	1598.8

Return on net assets $\dfrac{171.0}{1598.8} \times 100 = 10.7\%$[1]

10.	Financing from internal resources	187.3
11.	Net external borrowing	248.6
12.	Capital requirements during the year	435.8

Self-financing ratio $\dfrac{187.3}{435.8} \times 100 = 43.0\%$

[1]*Note*: This ratio differs from that published in the accounts (12.4%) because the Board deducts supplementary depreciation from expenditure to arrive at the profit before interest.
Derived from South of Scotland Electricity Board Report and Accounts 1983-84 pp. 60-61.

to the industries, and examining a series of ratios over a few years helps to build up a useful picture of an industry's ability to finance itself. Industries themselves vary in the way in which they use the ratio, referring sometimes to the proportion of its capital expenditure which it is financing internally and sometimes whether it is the proportion of funds as a whole. The South of Scotland Electricity Board in Table 5.6 used the former.

In assessing the ratio, it is necessary to take into account many factors, including the capital expenditure required to fulfill the industry's plans and the government's financing constraints, as well as their policy on prices and the level of the financial target set for the industry. These factors may mean that a high self-financing ratio is not necessarily 'good' and a low ratio not necessarily 'bad'.

Achieving a target of profit or loss

The requirement to achieve a certain level of profit or to contain loss to a certain figure is often though not always, given to industries which are loss-making.

In assessing what an industry with this kind of target has achieved, once again changes in government policy and trading conditions since the target was set need to be taken into account. Either may change very rapidly and make it easier or more difficult for an industry to achieve the planned performance level.

Operating within the EFL

The importance of the EFLs and the problems surrounding their operation have already been discussed in the context of policy making, and Table 5.3 has given an example of how the EFL is built up.

Measuring performance – an assessment

It can be seen that it is likely to be difficult to avoid conflict between different types of performance measures. The problem of reconciling non-financial with financial objectives in the legislation has already been mentioned. Combining these with the targets set by the minister, an industry may well have a set of objectives which are not reconcilable with each other. In this respect, the industries are very different from private sector organizations even though most private companies rarely have a single, 'profit maximizing', target and have other targets, as well as acknowledging their obligations as a member of the community and employer. Nevertheless, in terms of the sheer diversity of the measures, public sector enterprises generally have a more complex job to achieve satisfactory performance than the private sector. And it is because different groups in the community perceive success for the industries in very different ways that many of the industries' managers complain that they are being asked to do a task in which they cannot possibly succeed in everything required of them. This almost certainly has an adverse effect on their morale and may make it more difficult to attract capable managers into the industry.

Another problem in measuring performance is that many of the industries are unique inside the UK in that there are no organizations with which they can be closely compared. In this respect also, therefore, nationalized industries differ from private sector organizations where comparisons between similar organizations are often regarded as the key indicator of success and failure. So the emphasis almost certainly has to be on the analysis of trends over time, or international comparisons and performance against target. But analysis of each of these has to be handled with great care.

(a) Trends need to be interpreted in the light of changing commercial circumstances and government policies.

(b) International comparisons are fraught with difficulty because of circumstances particular to each country and the fact that the organizations are rarely comparable in what they do, so adjustments have to be made to the figures.

(c) Targets may not be a good guideline because the level is to some extent the result of bargaining between the industry and the sponsoring department.

Of the three, the comparison between target and actual performance is probably the least complicated to interpret, and international comparisons are the most complicated.

5.4 EXTERNAL REPORTING

Accounting and external reporting in nationalized industries is much closer to private sector practice than for most of the other parts of the public sector.

The rules governing external reporting

The starting point for nationalized industry accounting is that it should follow best commercial accounting practice, and indeed this is sometimes included in the legislation. For the Electricity Council the relevant passage reads

> The central authority and each Area Board shall keep proper accounts and other records . . . being a form which shall conform with the best commercial standards. (Electricity Act 1947)

This means taking into consideration (though not necessarily being bound by) four types of regulation.

(a) The 1948, 1967 and 1980 Companies Acts.

(b) Stock Exchange requirements. Even though the industries

are not quoted on the Stock Exchange, they will normally be expected to follow the disclosure requirements for quoted companies.

(c) Professional regulation. The industries are covered by the work of the Accounting Standards Committee (ASC) and will be expected to follow Standard Statements of Accounting Practice (SSAPs). Only in the case of SSAP 16 (inflation accounting) have the nationalized industries been specifically mentioned in any standard, but with the setting up of a sub-committee to deal with the public sector, the ASC may become more directly active in the area of nationalized industry accounts.

(d) General accounting practice. The industries are covered by normal accounting conventions and will generally follow the principles of private practice.

But in addition, the accounting rules will be more specific as a result of legislation and ministerial direction, and a self-regulatory mechanism.

Legislation

There is no standard wording in the legislation covering each industry, but a number of items are always included, such as the appointment of auditors, the need to present information to the minister, and the power of the minister to give directions on the form of the accounts, with the approval of the Treasury. The proposed legislation (see Appendix 5.4) may 'tidy up' some of the variations, but Appendix 5.2 gives the original legislation where relevant passages on the accounts can be found. Some examples are:

British Steel
The Corporation shall keep proper accounts and other records and shall prepare in such a form as the Secretary of State may, with the approval of the Treasury, direct
   (a) in respect of each financial year, a statement of the accounts of the corporation;
   (b) in respect of each financial year, a consolidated statement of accounts dealing with the state of affairs and profit or loss of the corporation and their subsidiaries . . .
(Iron and Steel (Amendments) Act 1976)

British Rail, National Bus, British Transport Docks, British Waterways, Scottish Transport
Each Board
   (a) shall cause proper accounts and other records in relation thereto be kept and

(b) shall prepare an annual statement of accounts in such form and containing such particulars compiled in such manner as the minister may from time to time direct with the approval of the Treasury.

(Transport Act 1962)

British Airports Authority

The report for any accounting year shall include such information relating to the plans, and past and present activities of the Authority and the financial position of the Authority, as the Secretary of State may from time to time direct.

(Airports Authority Act 1975)

Water authorities

(a) At each audit of the accounts of a water authority under this schedule any local government elector for any area to which the accounts to be audited relate may inspect those accounts and all books, deeds, contracts, bills, vouchers and receipts relating to them and make copies of all or any part of the accounts and those other documents.

(b) At the request of any such local government elector, the auditor shall give the elector, or any representative of his, an opportunity to question the auditor about these accounts or to draw the auditor's attention to any matter on which he could make a report. . .

(Local Government Finance Act, 1982.)

Some passages in the legislation are open to differing interpretations, and this has led to trouble on occasions between the board of an industry and its sponsoring department. For example, some industries are required to set aside reserves – for British Gas, the Gas Act 1972 states

It shall be the duty of the corporation . . . to secure that taking one year with another, the combined revenues of the corporation and their subsidiaries are not less than sufficient.

(a) to meet the total outgoings of the corporation and their subsidiaries properly chargeable to revenue account, and

(b) to enable the corporation and their subsidiaries to make such allocations to reserve as the corporation considers adequate . . .

(Section 14)

If the legislation being discussed when this edition of the book went to press (Appendix 5.4) is enacted there will be a much greater degree of control not only over the form of nationalized industry accounts but also what they can put into their reserves.

Meanwhile an example of the type of direction issued in recent years is given in Appendix 5.3. It can be seen that this example, for the Civil Aviation Authority, covers a large number of items.

Self-regulation

A mechanism peculiar to the nationalized industries has grown up over the past few years using the Nationalised Industries' Chairmen's Group (NICG). The NICG has acted as a forum for discussion on a number of important policy issues which concern the industries collectively, and financial matters are dealt with by their Finance Panel. The Panel has been particularly active in the field of inflation accounting and was responsible for compiling both an Interim Code of Practice published in 1979 and a Final Code published in 1981. Looking at this system of regulation, it might be thought that the industries would be very constrained in what they could do. But one of the major problems in developing a framework of regulation for the industries as a whole is the sheer diversity of their activities. This means that the industries themselves are not likely to be agreed about what constitutes best practice, and it is clear from their reporting practices that there is much more flexibility than might at first appear possible. While ministers might seem to have almost total power over the industries in this area through their ability to issue directions, in practice there is a good deal of negotiation between the industry and the sponsoring department before directions are issued.

Differences between the accounts of nationalized industries and of private sector organizations

There are two kinds of difference; the first in the underlying purpose of producing a report and accounts document, the second the more detailed differences in the financial information shown.

The most obvious difference in the purpose of producing accounts is that while private sector organizations do so to conform with the Companies Acts, each nationalized industry has to conform with the legislation specific to that industry. This is not merely a technical difference, since it means that responsibility in the private sector is to the shareholders, while for the industries it is through the minister to Parliament. But behind these formal differences are the differences in the practical needs of users. Taking the framework of *The Corporate Report*, a 1976 discussion document from the Accounting Standards Committee on the 'fundamental aims of published financial reports and the means by which these aims can be achieved', the authors took the view that reports, including those for nationalized industries, should be based on satisfying the information needs of users identified as

the equity investor group
the loan-creditor group
the employee group
the analyst-advisor group
the business contact group
the government
the public

Using this classification, it is clear that there are important differences between the user needs of the private sector, where the seven groups represent seven different interests, and the nationalized industries. Parliament can be said to be ultimately both the equity investor group and the loan creditor group through its power to control funds, as well as having an important role to play as a watchdog over the interests of the public. But the government's role also spans these three functions as part of day-to-day management. Moreover, through the sponsoring department the government is also to a large extent acting in the role of the analyst-advisor.

Apart from Parliament and the government, the public's interests are served by bodies set up specifically to look after consumers of a particular industry such as the Transport Users' Consultative Committee on behalf of the transport industries' customers and the Post Office Users' National Council for those of the Post Office. But it is the media which probably act as the most influential watchdogs, though their influence is generally more idiosyncratic than systematic.

It can be seen that the relative importance of groups using the accounts is very different compared to those concerned with the accounts of large private sector organizations. There are also great differences in how much information is available to the users. Unlike the private sector, where the report and accounts document is virtually the only source of information to all except the loan-creditor group (who need to have detailed financial projections directly from the organization to which they lend in order to safeguard their own funds), the sponsoring government department already has very detailed information. This includes not only information on past performance but also short and longer term projections, both financial and non-financial. The report and accounts document, therefore, may provide some additional useful information to the government but in practice it is Parliament, the media, consumer and employee organizations and the public at large for whom the document is crucial. Apart from answers to parliamentary questions, select committee investigations and other ad hoc reports, it will be their only public source of financial information. For this reason alone, the industries tend to regard a major purpose of the document to be to give their views about current problems and achievements, partly for public relations purposes, partly as a means of exercising indirect pressure on the government.

The difficulty of combining a campaigning and opinion-forming document with one which also provides a clear and dispassionate view of the industry to enable users to make up their own minds, is obvious enough. Some of these more dispassionate purposes include helping the reader to

(a) evaluate an industry's performance over time;
(b) establish its liquidity and possible future requirements for funds;
(c) assess future prospects and the vulnerability of the industries to outside forces;
(d) have a basis for comparing it with other organisations;
(e) act as a starting point to assess the effectiveness of the management;
(f) find facts and figures about the industry.

The user group having rather different requirements is that represented by the employees who may well want the document for any of the purposes outlined above, but are likely to be primarily interested in the information as a means of establishing a wage-bargaining position.

Turning to the specific accounting differences between private sector organizations and nationalized industries, anyone comparing the main financial statements will find most of the items covered, and the way they are presented, to be very similar. But there are differences, and these are outlined below.

Profit and loss accounts

The major differences from the private sector is the way the current cost accounts are compiled, though there is no doubt that the continuing controversy over the future of accounting for inflation will mean that the position may change in future years. The position at the time of writing is that the rules had been

determined by a mish-mash of sometimes contradictory requirements. Paragraph 51 of SSAP 16 stated that

> No gearing adjustment should be made in the profit and loss accounts
> of nationalised industries in view of the special nature of their capital
> structure. Accordingly, in such cases interest on their net borrowing
> should be shown after taxation and extraordinary items.

The rules for the format of the current cost profit and loss
account were amplified in the Code of Practice on Inflation
Accounting issued by the Finance Panel of the NICG. This
provided a specific format for the profit and loss account. But the
code also went further than SSAP 16. After quoting Paragraph 51,
it went on to say

> However, the Government has requested the Corporations (with
> certain exceptions) to show what the effect of the gearing adjustment
> would be if it were included in the accounts. Accordingly, this
> information should be given in the explanatory notes forming part of
> each Corporation's accounts. (Paragrah 4.4)

In fact, the Finance Panel were not breaking new ground, since
a ministerial statement two months before had already indicated
that a note showing the effect of a gearing adjustment should be
included (statement by Mr. John Biffen, *Hansard*, Col. 454, 21
December 1979).

The other main differences from private sector practice are in
the amount of detail available in the profit and loss account and
the treatment of grants.

In general, because of the importance of accountability, the
amount of detail given by the nationalized industries to support
the profit and loss account is much greater than that available in
private sector accounts. Many industries provide details of
profitability by types of activity or even by location, and the
amount of supporting information is often extensive, covering the
breakdown between different types of expenditure and other
information not normally provided in the private sector. This
information may not necessarily be attached to the profit and loss
account, and may be in separate statements elsewhere in the
report and accounts document.

Balance sheets

There are no major differences here, though the balance sheets
will reflect differences in the form of capital structure, with loans
as the permanent financing for most nationalized industries.

Even though individual loans will be repaid on the due dates, they will usually be replaced by new ones.

Auditors' Report

The form of statement reflects the fact that while auditors in the private sector report to the shareholders, nationalized industry auditors report to the Minister. Assuming that the auditors have not qualified the accounts, their report will confirm to the Minister that the accounts comply with the relevant legislation and any directions given. The complexity of the rules as a whole means that qualifications are more common for nationalized industries than for private sector organizations (see p. 151).

Other statements and notes

As made clear above, in general far more information is available in the statements supplementary to the accounts than is shown in the accounts of private sector companies. The greater detail may be not only the result of initiatives by the industries or ministerial direction but also the product of encouragement by a parliamentary select committee or discussions with the sponsoring department. This requirement for greater public disclosure has not gone unchallenged. Some industries operating in competitive markets have in fact objected to the amount of information they have to disclose.

Other items

In almost all other respects, the structure of the report and accounts document is similar to the private sector and items other than statistical material in the report and accounts will include

(a) the letter signed by the chairman formally submitting the report and accounts to the minister,
(b) the chairman's statement, the length, style and content of which varies as much as similar statements for private sector organizations,
(c) a summary of key figures or highlights at the beginning of the report – in some cases this may be purely statistical and financial, in other cases it may cover all aspects of the year's operations,

(d) a review of the past year, usually covering finance, organization, technical aspects, marketing and sales,

(e) performance, the economic and social environment and recent research developments,

(f) prospects for the year ahead, either as part of the chairman's statement or as a summary of the corporate plan,

(g) members of the board and some details of the organization of senior management.

Most of this information is provided in a form which is at the discretion of the industry though, as already described, the 1978 White Paper required publication of certain information including the financial target for the year and the outturn, the cash limit and outturn, performance indicators and the main points of the corporate plan.

Issues in external reporting

Uniformity of presentation and accounting treatment

There have been calls at various times to standardize the terminology used by the industries, the format of their accounts or the way in which items are treated within the accounts. The three cannot be treated entirely separately since in each case there is a question of whether the industries *ought* to be similar to each other as a matter of principle, rather than following the private sector practice of leaving it to the individual organization to decide, together with the auditors, on 'best accounting practice'.

Taking terminology first, the industries use a large number of different terms, particularly to describe profit or loss. The words surplus, revenue, income and profit are used to cover various terms, no doubt in part reflecting different views about the objectives for a nationalized industry, bearing in mind that they are not generally trying to maximize their profits. Indeed, the objective may just be to break even over a number of years.

The question of these differences in the use of terminology is probably only important because profit is most often used to describe how well an industry is doing, and a large variety of terms may well confuse the reader. On the other hand it could be argued that it is for the industries themselves to decide what terms they should use and terminology is not a proper matter for anyone else.

But terminology is not nearly as significant as questions of whether there should be uniformity in format and accounting treatment. Following evidence to the Treasury and Civil Service Select Committee in the 1980/1 session, the Treasury submitted a memorandum on nationalized industry accounts. The Treasury stated that 'it has been the policy of successive governments . . . to reduce, so far as practicable, unnecessary diversity in the accounts of different industries'. It is clear that this is not going nearly as far as suggesting uniformity, and such a softly-softly approach seems appropriate, since accounting rules covering not only the nationalized industries but also private sector organizations are essentially a compromise between the desire to show uniformity where possible and the need to show diversity where essential. It is then up to the analyst to make adjustments when comparing organizations for particular purposes. The danger in a common format is that it would result in a distorted picture being presented because the diversity of the industries' activities could not be reflected in the financial information. The industries have also pointed out that since it is normal to allow differences for private sector organizations, there is no reason why they should be treated any differently.

There have also been calls for uniform treatment of similar items, for example for the industries to depreciate similar items at the same rate. The fear that lies behind some of these calls is that accounting differences will distort policy decisions or that the industries will try to use accounting manipulation to meet a financial target. These fears should not be taken too seriously. The differences in accounting treatment are clear from the report and accounts, even though expertise may be needed to find and interpret all the relevant figures, and in general the figures are subject to far more public scrutiny than those of a private sector organization. The sponsoring department obviously also plays an important role in ensuring that accounting differences do not lead to distortions of policy, but as a more practical point it is doubtful in any case whether the government or Parliament has the right under existing regulations to impose strict uniformity for the accounts.

Auditing and the value for money audit

Public sector audit as a subject is covered elsewhere in this book, but two auditing issues are worth noting here: first, the difficulties faced by some auditors in being able to show that the accounts present a 'true and fair view'; second, the need for a value-for-money audit.

A far higher proportion of nationalized accounts are qualified than is common in the private sector. This does not mean that the industries do not adhere to the rules but it illustrates the complexity of their commercial circumstances and the difficulties of fitting them into some parts of the framework of accounting rules.

An extreme example is the Auditor's Report on the 1983/4 accounts of British Shipbuilders which states:

We are unable to express an opinion as to whether the accounts, which have been prepared under the historical cost convention, give a true and fair view of:
(i) the state of affairs of the Corporation and of the Group at 31 March 1984.
(ii) the loss of the Corporation and of the Group for the year to 31 March 1984.
(iii) the source and application of funds of the Group for the year to 31 March 1984.

Two other examples give an indication of the kinds of difficulties faced by auditors in giving an unqualified audit report:

Uncertainty exists about the value of the net tangible fixed assets shown in the balance sheet [and] the future level and nature of claims for surface damage caused by mining up to the balance sheet data. (National Coal Board, Annual Report for 1983/4)

The British Railways Board consider it impracticable to estimate the amount that will be received from the sale of Sealink UK Ltd. This investment is stated at an historical cost of £103m in these accounts (excluding sub-leases from Parent Body. (British Rail Annual Report for 1983)

In recent years there have been considerable discussions of value for money audit. The argument is that the financial audit does not go far enough in establishing whether the industries are efficient and how well they have used the assets under their control. With this in mind, it has been argued that a value for money audit is needed to monitor their use of resources and efficiency in providing goods or services. The main issues to be decided for such an audit are the choice of the body to carry out the investigation, the frequency with which it should be done, the nature of the investigation to be carried out and the body to whom the report should be submitted.

Nationalized industries are specifically excluded from investigation by the National Audit Office under Section 7 of the National Audit Act 1983, which covers examination into the economy, efficiency and effectiveness with which bodies mainly supported by public funds use their resources. However there are two other mechanisms for conducting audits of efficiency. The Monopolies and Mergers Commission has an annual programme of investigations, including a major reference to each nationalized industry every four years. These investigations can also cover formal accounting procedures; the 1983 report on the London Electricity Board, for example, recommended a more detailed breakdown of the Board's financing of retail showrooms to be shown in the Annual Report. In addition the Government uses consultants to conduct efficiency audits. One of the first was conducted by Deloitte, Haskins & Sells at British Gas in 1983. Chapter 7 discusses some of the issues in this area in relation to the role of the National Audit Office.

Inflation accounting

No subject has aroused more controversy in the field of accounting in the nationalized industries than the introduction of accounting for inflation. There have been a large variety of methods used over the years, including:

(a) current cost accounts on a CCA basis as the only accounts,
(b) current cost accounts as the main accounts, with supplementary historic cost accounts,
(c) historic cost accounts as the main accounts with supplementary current cost accounts,
(d) historic cost accounts incorporating additional depreciation as a form of inflation adjustment.

These variations have included some industries providing only partial cost accounts (a profit and loss account or statement) and some including – and others not – a gearing adjustment in the current cost accounts. The list is so varied because until 1981 there was no agreement on what form of inflation adjustment should be made by the industries. But in the NICG code of practice they were given three presentation options:

(a) historic cost accounts as the main accounts with prominent supplementary current cost accounts,
(b) current cost accounts as the main accounts with supplementary historic cost accounts,
(c) current cost accounts as the only accounts accompanied by adequate historic cost information,

although there is a general provision allowing the industries additional flexibility.

One major controversy on inflation accounting has been the treatment of the gearing adjustment. The arguments have probably been more strongly rooted in differences about policy than principle – industries tended to advocate whichever course of action would put their results in the best possible light. The main argument for having a gearing adjustment was that the industries benefited from the falling real value of their loan capital in exactly the same way as private sector organizations and that this should be reflected in an allowance for that proportion of their net operating assets financed by borrowing. The main argument against was that although the industries are financed by a combination of loans and equity, the relationship between the two was much less clear than for private sector organizations because all the funds were derived from a single central source. Since these loans were the normal form of finance, treatment should not be the same as for the private sector where finance was through a combination of equity and loans, so a gearing adjustment was not appropriate. The compromise struck in a statement issued by the government in 1979 was that the gearing adjustment should go in a note, so that the information was available to make a calculation of profit including the adjustment while the profit would be declared without it. This decision meant in practice that industries were indeed treated differently from the private sector.

Another major issue arising from the adoption of current cost accounting is the implication it has for the industries' ability to fulfill their statutory obligations. The financial requirements in the legislation were generally drawn up at a time when historic cost accounting was the accepted form of financial reporting. It is unclear whether these obligations should be restated in current cost terms, quite apart from any financial target stipulated by the government. This may not be as simple as substituting one figure for another – there are complex technical problems involved in the calculation. Power stations, railway lines, and airport runways are just some examples for which difficult decisions have to be made. Two key decisions are on the length of life of the assets and whether they will be replaced by assets of a similar kind. The importance of the technical decisions is magnified because many of the industries which have these 'difficult' assets are highly capital intensive, and the results of the decisions will have a major effect on profitability through the valuation of the asset base and the determination of current cost depreciation.

What are acknowledged to be unrealistic assumptions are built into the calculations of several industries, often because there is no more realistic valuation method. The Electricity Council for example values power stations on the basis of modern equivalent assets, but uses the convention that stations will be replaced by stations with a similar fuel source (coal by coal, nuclear by nuclear, and so on). The industries deserve a good deal of sympathy in having to grapple with these difficult technical problems and while they do so, readers of the accounts need to look carefully at the basis which has been used, to make sure they understand the implications of the decisions which have been made.

Deciding the framework of accounting rules

The framework of rules, incorporating legislation and ministerial direction, accounting practice and self-regulation ought to mean that the industries have a clear basis for compiling their accounts. But over the years there has been a great deal of controversy about whether the framework is too loose and whether they should not be more closely controlled, as well as what the answers should be to some of the more contentious accounting issues. What is clear from looking at the way in which the industries have presented their accounts over the years is that they have used a great deal of discretion in applying the rules, and compliance with the requirements either of White Papers or of the self regulation mechanism has been frankly patchy. It has also become apparent that there are no effective sanctions for non-compliance.

The proposals for legislation (Appendix 5.4) to cover such items as the form of the accounts may well provide the basis of a framework satisfactory to both the government and the industries. Other suggestions on how to achieve closer control have involved using Parliament, the sponsoring departments or the Accounting Standards Committee. But simply setting rules is not enough, as the history of the debate on inflation accounting shows, and agreement may not ensure compliance unless the industries enter into the spirit of any new arrangements. Here, progress will probably be determined by developments in the whole relationship between nationalised industries and the government. Seen in the perspective of this wider picture, problems over accounting rules are just one manifestation of a difficult and often ambiguous relationship. It may well be that clarity in the framework of accounting rules will only come with less ambiguity in the relationship as a whole.

EXAMINATION QUESTIONS

5.1   How would policy making in a public corporation be changed if equity capital were introduced? (CIPFA. Policy Making in the Public Sector)

5.2   Under the 1978 White Paper, nationalised industries like gas and electricity were asked to aim for a required return on their investment programme. Examine the rationale. (CIPFA. Public Finance)

5.3   Explain the strong opposition of nationalized industries to the use of EFLs as the most important element in financial control by government.

5.4   Explain the reasoning behind the suggestion in the 1978 White Paper on nationalised industries (Cmnd. 7131) that they should earn a required rate of return. (CIPFA. Policy Making in the Public Sector)

5.5   'It is unrealistic to have multiple targets for nationalised industries of the kind set out in the 1978 White Paper. They are difficult to calculate, impossible to reconcile and not understood by managers.' Discuss.

5.6   Outline the objectives of nationalised industries and discuss the methods available for determining whether or not the objectives are being achieved. (ACCA Pilot Question for Public Sector Accounting)

5.7   Is there any point in having risk capital for nationalized industries?

5.8   'Cash flow is the key to nationalized industries performance since the calculation of profit and loss is too subjective.' Discuss.

5.9   Discuss ways in which financial control of nationalized industries might be improved.

5.10 'The private sector has a simple measure of performance – profit. While this is inappropriate for the public sector some indication of performance must be prepared if only in response to public pressure.' (Public Finance and Accountancy. March 1980) Critically review the validity of this statement in a public sector organization of your choice and appraise developments in the performance measurement. (CIPFA. Accounting and Audit in the Public Sector)

5.11 Is there a case for using only non-financial indicators to measure the performance of nationalized industries?

5.12 'Historic cost figures are misleading but current cost figures are wrong.' Discuss this statement in relation to one particular nationalized industry or nationalized industries as a whole.

5.13 If financial targets for nationalized industries are set independently of accounting practice, does it matter which accounting practices are used?

5.14 Discuss the case for setting accounting standards for nationalized industries in a different way to those for the private sector.

5.15 'The accounts of nationalized industries are just like those of private sector organisations except that the Government is the sole shareholder.' Discuss.

5.16 Summarize the arguments for and against a value for money audit of the nationalized industries. Who might carry it out and to whom should reports be made?

APPENDIX 5.1   OTHER PUBLIC CORPORATIONS

Audit Commission
Bank of England
British Broadcasting Corporation (Home)
British Technology Group
Cable Authority
Commonwealth Development Corporation
Covent Garden Market Authority
Crown Agents
Crown Agents Holding and Realisation Board
Development Board for Rural Wales
Development Board for Rural Wales (New Town activities)
General Practice Finance Corporation
Government Trading Funds
Highlands and Islands Development Board
Housing Corporation
Independent Broadcasting Authority
National Dock Labour Board
National Film Finance Corporation
New Town Development Corporations and the Commission for the New Towns
Northern Ireland Electricity Services
Northern Ireland Housing Executive
Northern Ireland Public Trust Port Authorities
Northern Ireland Transport Holding Company
Pilotage Commission
Public Trust Ports
Scottish Development Agency
Scottish Special Housing Association

Urban Development Corporations
Welsh Development Agency

Note: The way these corporations are treated for public expenditure purposes varies. In some cases all finance is included, in
others only capital expenditure. The latest Public Expenditure
White Paper gives full details.
Source: Public Expenditure White Paper 1985 Vol. 2 p. 296.

APPENDIX 5.2   IMPORTANT LEGISLATION COVERING EACH INDUSTRY

British Airports Authority
  Airports Authority Act 1975
British Gas
  Gas Act 1972
British Rail
  Transport Act 1962
  Transport Act 1968
  Railways Act 1974
British Shipbuilders
  Aircraft and Shipbuilding Industries Act 1977
  British Shipbuilders Act 1983
British Steel
  Iron and Steel Act 1975
  Iron and Steel (Amendment) Act 1976
  Iron and Steel Act 1981
British Waterways
  Transport Act 1962
  Transport Act 1968
Civil Aviation Authority
  Civil Aviation Act 1971
  Civil Aviation Act 1982
Electricity Council
  Electricity Act 1947
  Electricity Act 1968
  Energy Act 1983
London Regional Transport
  London Regional Transport Act 1984
National Bus
  Transport Act 1962
  Transport Act 1968

National Coal Board
   Coal Industry Nationalisation Act 1946
   Coal Industry Act 1980
   Coal Industry Act 1983
North of Scotland Hydroelectric Board
   Hydro Electric Development (Scotland) Act 1954
   Electricity Act 1947
   Electricity Reorganisation (Scotland) Act 1954
   Electricity (Scotland) Act 1979
   Energy Act 1983
Post Office
   Post Office Act 1969
   Post Office (Banking Services) Act 1976
   British Telecommunications Act 1981
Scottish Transport
   Transport Act 1962
   Transport Act 1968
South of Scotland Electricity Board
   Hydro-Electric Development (Scotland) Act 1943
   Electricity Act 1947
   Electricity Reorganisation (Scotland) Act 1954
   Electricity (Scotland) Act 1979
   Energy Act 1983
Water Authorities
   Water Act 1973
   Water Charges Equalization Act 1977
   Local Government Finance Act 1982
   Water Act 1983

APPENDIX 5.3   DIRECTION BY A MINISTER

CIVIL AVIATION AUTHORITY (ACCOUNTS) DIRECTION 1984

The Secretary of State, with the approval of the Treasury, in pursuance of Section 15(1) of the Civil Aviation Act 1982, hereby gives the following Direction:

1   The statement of accounts which it is the duty of the Authority to prepare in respect of their financial year ended 31 March 1984 and in respect of any subsequent accounting year shall comprise:-
   (i)   a profit and loss account,
   (ii)   a balance sheet,
   (iii)   a source and application of funds statement,
including in each case such notes as may be necessary for the purposes referred to in paragraph 2 below.

2   The accounts referred to above shall give a true and fair view of the profit or loss, state of affairs and source and application of funds of the Authority. Subject to the foregoing requirement, the statement of accounts shall also, without limiting the information given, accord, insofar as they are appropriate to the Authority, with:

(a)   the accounts requirements of the Companies Acts for the time being in force save as described in Schedule 1 of this Direction, and with the limitations imposed in that Schedule;

(b)   the accounts disclosure requirements of paragraph 10 of the Stock Exchange Listing Agreement; and

(c)   the best commercial practices including Statements of Standard Accounting Practice issued by the member bodies of the Consultative Committee of Accountancy bodies.

3   The statement mentioned in paragraph 1 above shall also include the supplementary information set out in Schedule 2 to this Direction.

4   The Direction issued to the Authority dated 10 May 1982 and supplementary Schedule is hereby revoked.

19 June 1984   H J BLANKS
                                          Under Secretary
                                          Department of Transport

Schedule 1

1   The choice made by the Authority and approved by the Secretary of State and the Treasury in respect of the formats available under Section B of Part I to the Companies Act 1981 is:
(i)   balance sheet format 1
(ii)   profit and loss account format 2.

2   The balance sheet totals will be struck at total assets less current liabilities, and after deducting provisions which are of a short term and/or fluctuating nature.

3   In the balance sheet of the Authority loan capital will be grouped together in Capital Loans and Reserves. The element of long-term debt due for repayment in the following year should be included as part of loan capital unless the Authority is expected to be a net repayer of debt, in which case it should be included within 'creditors due within one year'.

4   The profit and loss account or notes thereto shall include:

(a)   Analyses of turnover, expenditure and profit and loss on ordinary activities before interest and tax for each of the main elements of the Authority's activities comprising:

Airport air traffic services
North Atlantic air traffic services
UK airspace traffic services

CAA Scottish aerodromes
Economic services
Air safety services
Miscellaneous services:
(i) Turnover shall be analysed as appropriate from navigation services charges, traffic operations, statutory and scheme charges, grant and other income. Expenditure shall be analysed with staff costs, services and materials, repairs and maintenance, research and development, depreciation and amortisation, and other operating and general expenditure.
(ii) Airport air traffic services shall be analysed by individual airports, distinguishing British Airports Authority airports and other airports. Turnover from UK airspace traffic services shall be analysed, from Eurocontrol, North Sea helicopter, Ministry of Defence and other services. Scottish aerodromes shall be analysed by individual airports. Air safety services shall be analysed over airworthiness and operational safety.

(b) in turnover separately identified the amount of Government revenue grants received and a statement of the basis and calculation thereof.

(c) intererst on capital loans stated separately.

5 In the profit and loss account, provision for income equalisation shall be shown after line 16 of format 2, 'Profit or loss on ordinary activities after taxation'.

Schedule 2

Supplementary information
1 The balance sheet or a note thereto shall show:
(i) the Authority's maximum borrowing powers,
(ii) all sums borrowed showing separately amounts borrowed from the National Loans Fund (NLF) and other borrowings and showing when repayment is due.

2 The statement of accounts or notes thereto shall include a statement of the Authority's financial target showing the rate of return on capital employed for:
(i) operations where charges are controlled by the CAA,
(ii) operations where charges are not controlled by the CAA,
together with an explanation of the manner in which the returns have been computed and, where applicable, comparisons with any performance aims which have been agreed with the Authority.

CIVIL AVIATION AUTHORITY (REPORT) DIRECTION

The Secretary of State in exercise of his powers under Section 20(2)(c) of the Civil Aviation Act 1971 hereby specifies that the Annual Report of the Civil Aviation Authority ("The Authority") for the year ended 31

March 1982 and for each subsequent accounting year shall include:-

(i)   the performance and service aims, which have been agreed with the Authority, and the outturn against these,

(ii)   the main features of the latest Corporate Plan of the Authority,

(iii) the External Financial Limit (EFL) of the Authority compared with the outturn,

(iv) a 5-year summary of the financial results, and

(v)   this Direction and the Accounts Direction.

10 May 1982   H J BLANKS
                                                Under Secretary
                                                Department of Trade

Reproduced by permission of the Controller, Her Majesty's Stationery Office. Crown copyright.

APPENDIX 5.4   EXTRACTS OF PROPOSALS ON NATIONALIZED INDUSTRY STATUTES

The Government intends to legislate in due course to update various aspects of nationalised industry statutes. This note sets out the background to the proposed changes and indicates what areas might be covered. It has been prepared so that the Government can take account of comments on these proposals received by end-February 1985. There will be subsequent opportunities for nationalised industries to review detailed legislative proposals.

The Treasury is coordinating this consultation on behalf of the various Departments which sponsor nationalised industries. Departments will be discussing the proposals with individual industries.

1.   The Government has reviewed the existing statutes of nationalised industries and has concluded that they need to be updated. Although the differing nature of industries clearly needs to be recognised a number of policies are applied consistently to all industries. Present statutes do not reflect this and vary greatly depending in part on when they were enacted. Some statutes are nearly forty years old and have not been kept in line with policies developed by successive Governments.

2.   Private sector companies are regulated by a common set of statutory provisions and the Government considers that it would be advantageous if a single Act set out the core framework to be applied to nationalised industries. This would incorporate many provisions from existing statutes and would also reflect developments in the relationship between industries and the Government since statutes were originally enacted. The legislation that would result would provide clear guidelines within which those industries remaining in the public sector would have freedom to operate as successful commercial businesses. Parliament, industries and the Government would know more clearly where they stand.

3.   The proposed legislation would set out standard provisions and

also insert them appropriately into existing Acts. The powers would generally be permissive, allowing the use made of them to be tailored to the specific circumstances of each industry. In applying the new Act to individual industries, the Government would intend to use its powers only after proper consultation with the boards concerned.

4. Nearly all the proposals have precedents in existing legislation. There is an outstanding commitment to legislate to establish a more uniform legal basis for Nationalised Industry Consumer Councils operations and the Government is considering whether to extend its proposals to cover this. If so, the Government will consult separately about this.

5. In a number of cases, implementation of the proposed powers in respect of individual industries would involve supplementary legal procedures. The possible alternatives are notices in writing, formal directions, or statutory instruments which may or may not involve a Parliamentary procedure. The proposed method of implementation is shown where appropriate. Powers over industries' reserves, privatisation and financial targets would all be exercised via statutory instruments.

Borrowing and guarantees

6. The Government considers that all nationalised industries should have comprehensive powers to borrow with the approval of Ministers either within the UK or overseas. At present, some industries' statutes bar them from certain sources of finance and it is proposed that these restrictions should be removed. It is generally advantageous for industries to borrow from the National Loans Fund but removal of the restrictions would, for example, permit the introduction of market finance into any industry, if this was thought desirable.

7. The Public Accounts Committee (PAC) has recommended that statutory borrowing limits of public bodies should include borrowings by subsidiaries and guarantees made by an industry or its subsidiaries in order to ensure Parliament's overall financial control of public bodies. Although borrowing limits might need to be substantially higher in recognition of the change, this would be no more than a recognition of the realities of the situation of which Parliament should be made fully aware. It is therefore proposed that the coverage of industries' borrowing limits should be adjusted to include borrowing by wholly-owned subsidiaries and all borrowing by third parties which is guaranteed by an industry or its wholly-owned subsidiaries.

8. Occasionally, new forms of raising finance are devised which legally are not defined as 'borrowing' although they are closely akin. In order that borrowing limits can properly ensure overall financial control, it is proposed that there should be a mechanism for bringing such liabilities within the scope of borrowing limits. This power would be exercised via statutory instruments.

9. Some industries borrow in overseas currencies which may or may

not be covered by the Public Sector Exchange Cover Scheme. In order to be included in an industry's statutory borrowing limit, such loans must be converted into sterling. It is proposed that the principles by which such loans are valued should be legally determined with the presumption that normal accounting principles would generally be followed (e.g. as set out in SSAP20) unless the Secretary of State specifies otherwise.

10.   In order that a comprehensive set of provisions can be drafted, it is proposed also to include standard provisions relating to the issuing of Treasury guarantees, the purposes for which money can be borrowed, the setting of statutory borrowing limits (subject as now to Parliamentary procedure), the powers of the Secretary of State to lend to an industry, and some ancillary provisions.

Accounts, report and audit

11.   Individual industries' accounts are produced to a high standard and are often commended both for their content and manner of presentation. It would however assist those outside the industries who use the accounts, including Parliament and Government, if there were greater consistency in presentation and in the accounting principles that are applied. To supplement the overriding requirement that the accounts give a true and fair view, it is proposed to bring the differing statutory requirements governing the accounts into a common form in line with recent legislative precedents. There would be powers for the Secretary of State with the approval of the Treasury to direct:

(i)   the information to be contained in the accounts,
(ii)   the manner in which the information is to be presented, and
(iii) the methods and principles by which the accounts are to be prepared.

Given the overriding requirement that all industries' accounts give a true and fair view, the accounting rules and presentation set by the Secretary of State would have to be appropriate to the particular industry.

12.   Industries' annual accounts should be audited to the highest standards comparable to those found in the private sector. Auditors should have generally the same rights and duties as those appointed under the Companies Acts. Although present audit provisions are comprehensive, they have certain technical deficiencies compared to analogous Companies Acts requirements (e.g. there is no statutory access to information) and it is proposed to remedy this.

13.   Although what is said in an industry's annual report is essentially a matter for the industry, the Government thinks it right to be able to require that specified topics are included. These topics might include, for example, performance against targets and an industry's response to any MMC study that has been carried out during the year. Annual

reports are all laid before Parliament and it is open to Parliament to examine industries on what is said. The reports are an important aspect of accountability and the inclusion of specified topics would strengthen this.

Financial targets

14.   It is Government policy that financial targets, normally expressed as a specified rate of return on assets, should be set for nationalised industries. These targets provide an incentive for industries to operate efficiently and are a proxy for the financial disciplines found in the private sector. The targets which are set after consultation with the industry concerned, normally span a 3–5 year period, and are notified to Parliament or subject to a Parliamentary procedure.

15.   In the case of nearly half the nationalised industries, it is already possible to give financial targets statutory backing. Because of their central place in the financial framework, the Government considers it right to give all targets this backing. It is proposed that Ministers should set targets for each industry after full consultation with its board and that boards should be required to conduct their affairs with a view to achieving whatever targets are currently in force. The target would thus not be cast in the form of an absolute duty. It is not intended that the proposed legislation should put performance aims or external financing limits (EFLs) onto a statutory basis.

16.   Unlike the traditional break-even requirement, targets can be tailored to fit the circumstances of individual industries. The Government is therefore considering repealing existing break-even duties which in their present statutory form are no longer a satisfactory form of control. If this is done, it would be necessary to place a duty on the Secretary of State to set a financial target in order to ensure that a vacuum is not created.

Balance sheets

17.   Nationalised industry balance sheets are very different from those of private sector companies. When they were set up, most of the industries were given debt liabilities equal to their net assets, in the expectation that debt interest would adequately reflect the cost of capital employed. However, with time, the real value of this debt has been progressively eroded. There have also been substantial repayments and rising internal financing ratios. Overall, debt financing is now, on average, around 20 per cent of real capital employed, and interest payments amount to only 2 per cent per annum of capital employed. In the private sector, the impact of inflation in reducing the real cost of conventional debt has led to higher earnings and dividends on equity capital. A number of nationalised industries are approaching

or have reached a debt free position and in the absence of an equivalent to equity capital in their balance sheets have little or no external liabilities.

18. As the cost of capital has progressively disappeared from the accounts of some industries, their apparent profits have increased. More importantly, funds, which in the private sector would have gone into higher dividend payments to maintain or increase the worth of shareholders' capital have been entirely ploughed back into the business. The overall effect is to relax financial disciplines.

19. The PAC has considered the position of industries which generate surpluses. It concluded that 'there should not be a strong presumption that surpluses in excess of interest commitments should all be retained by an industry'. It thought that 'an industry should not be allowed to amass reserves to such an extent that there is a danger of blunting the edge of the discipline that should operate on future investment decisions'.

20. Separately, the PAC has concluded that the creation and maintenance of a suitable capital structure has an important role in promoting financial discipline. It recommended that the creation of liabilities to pay to the Exchequer out of surpluses 'a pre-determined sum related to the target set could be seen as equivalent to servicing the publicly-owned "equity" in the industries; and payments required in this way should be less of a disincentive to the management than claw-back arrangements'. The Government agrees with this.

21. The Government considers therefore that powers should be taken which would allow industries' balance sheets to be restructured. The powers, the exercise of which would require a Statutory Instrument to be laid before Parliament, would allow all or part of reserves to be capitalised as debt and public dividend capital. Restructuring would only be carried out after consultation with the industry affected and would be required to have due regard to the interests of creditors. The intention would be to create balance sheets that properly reflected a medium term view of industries' commerical circumstances and prospects taking account of financial targets.

22. Additionally, the Government intends to take powers which would allow the introduction of new public dividend capital into industries in appropriate circumstances and is considering allowing lending on indexed-terms to the industries from the National Loans Fund.

23. In order that all matters relating to balance sheets can be brought together, the Government is considering consolidating existing powers over reserves which allow the Secretary of State to direct allocation and reallocations and permit control, if necessary, over the application of reserves within an industry.

ormation of companies and privatization

27. The Government considers as a general principle that activities of

state-owned businesses should be transferred to the private sector where this makes commercial and practical sense. This enables market influences to operate to the benefit of the activities themselves, customers, employees, and the economy as a whole. For a number of industries, enabling legislation already exists that allows privatisation to take place. It is intended to extend this and apply general enabling legislation to all industries which would allow private capital to be introduced and activities and assets sold. However, complete privatisation of a whole corporation would continue to require primary legislation.

28.   All industries would be given power to set up subsidiaries under the Companies Acts and transfer property, rights and liabilities to them. This would enable industries to carry out their activities through Companies Acts companies where this seems sensible and to structure their operations in accordance with normal commercial practice. This restructuring may or may not be a prelude to privatisation.

29.   Powers, involving a Parliamentary procedure, would also be taken allowing Ministers to require that assets and activities are privatised in accordance with their instructions.

30.   As a corollary to the above powers, Ministers would be able by order to require industries to discontinue specified activities and direct them not to extend their interests. This power is already found in some existing statutes. It is proposed that its exercise should require a Parliamentary procedure.

Source: National Industrial Legislation Consultation Proposals, H.M. Treasury Reproduced by permission of the Controller, Her Majesty's Stationery Office Crown copyright.

BIBLIOGRAPHY

Basic reading

To get a 'feel' for the subject, it is essential to look at some examples of the reports and accounts. A selection of the most important books, articles and other sources are marked with an asterisk in the relevant section of the bibliography.

Information sources

Annual reports and accounts

Invaluable as source documents for facts about the industries as well as indications about government policy and the industries response. Most industries make a small charge for the document. Although most of these documents must be ordered from HMSO or through bookshops, some are obtainable directly from the head office of the industry.

Most of the transport industries have a year-end in December. Their Report and Accounts normally appear the following April or May. The other industries have a March year-end and publish the Report and Accounts in July or August.

Official reports

Listed below are some important recent reports. Almost all are obtainable through HMSO. Additional material will be found in other reports of House of Commons Select Committees, the Monopolies and Mergers Commission and other relevant official bodies such as statutory Users Councils.

HM Treasury, *The Test Discount Rate and the Required Rate of Return on Investment*. Government Economic Service Working Paper, No. 22, 1979.

House of Commons Committee of Public Accounts, 15th Report, Session 1980/1. Appendix on 'Nationalised Industry Accounts', HC 349.

House of Commons Public Accounts Committee, Session 1983/4, *The monitoring and control activities of sponsoring departments – Departments of Industry, Transport and Energy*, HC 139.

House of Commons Select Committee on Energy, Session 1983/4, *Electricity and Gas prices*. JC 276.

House of Commons Select Committee on Nationalised Industries, 6th Special Report, Session 1977/8, *Comments by Nationalised Industries and Others on the Government White Paper on the Nationalised Industries*, HC 638.

House of Commons Select Committee on Nationalised Industries, 2nd Special Report, Session 1978/9, *Further Comments on the Government White Paper on the Nationalised Industries*, HC 48.

House of Commons Select Committee on Nationalised Industries, 3rd Report, Session 1978/9, *Reports and Accounts on the Nationalised Industries*, HC 335.

House of Commons Select Committee on Transport 3rd Report, Session 1981/2, *The Form of Nationalised Industries' Reports and Accounts*, HC 390.

House of Commons Treasury and Civil Service Select Committee, 8th Report, Session 1980/1, *Financing of the Nationalised Industries*, HC 348.

Monopolies and Mergers Commission, 'London Electricity Board', Cmnd. 8812, 1983.

National Audit Office, *Departments of Energy, Trade and Industry and Transport: Monitoring and control of nationalised industries*, HC 553, 1983.

*National Economic Development Office, *A Study of the UK Nationalised Industries: Their Role in the Economy and Control in the Future*, NEDO, 1976.

*National Economic Development Office, Appendices to Vol. 2, *A Study of UK Nationalised Industries* (especially Appendix D 'Review of Pricing Policies, Investment Criteria and Financial Objectives of Four Nationalised Industries', Coopers and Lybrand Associates), NEDO, 1976.

Price Commission, *South of Scotland Electricity Board – Price Increases in the Supply of Electricity*, HC 535, 1978.

Recent publications

Accounting Standards Committee (1975) *The Corporate Report* ASC.

Accounting Standards Committee (1980) Statement of Standard Accounting Practice No. 16, *Current Cost Accounting*.

Carsberg, B. and Lumby, S. (1983) 'Current cost accounting in the water industry', *Public Finance and Accountancy*, September.

Collins, B. and Wharton, B. (1984) 'Investigating Public Industries: how has the Monopolies & Mergers Commission performed?' *Public Money*, Vol. 4, No. 2, September.

Davies, J.R. and McInnes, W.K. (1982) 'The valuation of fixed assets in the financial accounts of UK nationalised industries and the implications for monitoring performance: a comment' *Journal of Business Finance and Accounting*, Summer.

Davies, J.R. and McInnes, W.M. (1982) 'The efficiency and accountability of UK nationalised industries', *Accounting and Business Research*, Winter.

Gibbs, M. and Taylor, B. (1979) *Nationalised Industries Accounting Policies*, Consumers Association.

Glendinning, R. (1982) 'Accounting in the nationalised industries', *Management Accounting*, April.

*Hatch, J. and Redwood, J. (1981) *Value for Money Audits*, Centre for Policy Studies.

*Heald, D. (1980) 'The economic and financial control of UK nationalised industries', *Economic Journal*, 90.

Heald, D. and Steel, D. (1981) 'Nationalised industries: the search for control', *Public Money*, Vol. 1, No. 1, June.

Heath, J.B. (1980) *Management in Nationalised Industries*, Nationalised Industries Chairmen's Group, NICG Occasional Paper No. 2

Jones, R. and Pendlebury, M. (1984) *Public Sector Accounting* Pitman.

Kay, J.A. (1976; 'Accountants, too, could be happy in a golden age: the accountant's rate of profit and the internal rate of return', *Oxford Economic Papers, 28.*

Lee, T.A. and Stark, A.W. (1984) 'A cash flow disclosure of government supported enterprises' results', *Journal of Business Finance and Accounting,* Spring.

Likierman, J.A. (1981) *Cash Limits and External Financing Limits,* Civil Service College Handbook No. 22, HMSO.

*Likierman, J.A.L (1981) 'Nationalised industries: accounting for inflation', *Public Money,* Vol. 1 No. 3, December.

Likierman, J.A. (1983) 'Evidence on accusation of manipulating profitability: adjustments for inflation by the nationalised industries 1976-81', *Accounting and Business Research,* Winter.

Likierman, J.A. (1983) 'Setting accounting standards for nationalised industries', *Public Finance and Accountancy,* November.

Lumby, S. (1981) 'A method of financing nationalised industries', *Lloyds Bank Review,* July.

MacArthur, J.B. (1980) 'Valuation of fixed assets in the financial accounts of UK nationalised industries and the implications for monitoring performance', *Journal of Business Finance and Accounting,* Spring.

MacArthur, J.B. (1982) 'The valuation of fixed assets in the financial accounts of UK nationalised industries and the implications for monitoring performance: a reply', *Journal of Business Finance and Accounting,* Summer.

Morgan, C. (1983) 'Accounting standards and the public sector', *Public Finance and Accountancy,* January.

Nationalised Industries Chairmen's Group (1979) *Accounting in the Nationalised Industries,* NICG.

*Nationalised Industries Chairmen's Group (1981) *Code of Practice for Current Cost Accounting in the Public Sector Corporations,* NICG.

Perks, R.W. and Glendinning, R. (1981) 'Performance indicators applied to the nationalised industries', *Management Accounting,* October 1981; and 'Little progress seen in published performance indicators', *Management Accounting,* December.

*Pryke, R. (1981) *The Nationalised Industries, Policies and Performance since 1968,* Martin Robertson.

Rees, R. (1979) 'The pricing policies of nationalised industries', *Three Banks' Review,* 122.

Rutherford, B.A. (1983) *Financial reporting in the public sector,* Butterworths.

Vernon, R. and Aharonyi, Y. (1981) *State-owned enterprise in the Western economies,* Croom Helm.

Williams, G. (1983) 'Planning for British Rail', *Public Finance and Accountancy,* August.

Wright, F.K. (1978) 'Accounting Rate of Profit and Internal Rate of return', *Oxford Economic Papers*, 30.

Wright, D.M. (1979) 'Inflation accounts in the nationalised industries: a survey and appraisal', *Accounting and Business Research*, Winter.

Wright, D.M. (1980) 'Real rates of return on capital: some estimates for British Gas', *Journal of Business Finance and Accounting*, 7, 1, Spring.

Wright, M. (1984) 'Auditing the efficiency of the nationalised industries: exit the Comptroller and Auditor General?', *Public Administration*, Spring.

GLOSSARY

Cash limit The limit on the amount of cash that can be spent on certain specified services during one financial year.

External Financing Limit (EFL) A form of cash limit for a nationalised industry used as a means of controlling the amount of finance (grants and borrowing) which an industry can raise in any financial year from external sources. The limit is the difference between an industry's capital requirements and its internally generated funds.

Public Dividend Capital (PDC) Capital provided as permanent finance on which a dividend is expected to be paid to the Exchequer. This dividend will normally be related to the industry's profitability in that year, though on average dividends are expected to be not less than the interest which would be payable on government loans.

Self-financing ratio Used to mean, often without specifying which, *either* the proportion of the capital expenditure which is financed internally over a period, *or* the proportion of the funds required for a period which are financed internally.

NOTE ADDED IN PROOF

At the beginning of this chapter, it was said that policy was constantly evolving. Since the chapter was written

— there have been delays to the privatization of British Airways which had not been included among the industries covered in the chapter, since privatization was supposed to have been before publication.

— the government has announced its intention to privatize British Airports, British Gas and National Bus in whole or in part.

These changes reinforce the message that this is a constantly evolving area and developments need to be monitored.

6

The National Health Service

6.1 INTRODUCTION

There are a number of public services which, for reasons of history or of policy are administered under the ownership or ultimate control of central government, and yet which have substantial degrees of autonomy in the interpretation of policy and in day-to-day administration. These include public corporations such as the British Broadcasting Corporation (BBC) with a partly independent source of funds through licence fees; the universities, with some operational independence ensured through the medium of the University Grants Committee, yet with major funding firmly controlled by government policy from central tax revenues; and the National Health Service (NHS) which, although funded almost totally by central government, retains a degree of autonomy in the use of funds at the regional and local levels, through the medium of appointed authorities (boards) which determine how available funds should be expended. This chapter will deal with the National Health Service, the largest and most costly public service not directly managed by central government or local government.

The NHS is administered by the Department of Health and Social Security (DHSS). The NHS encompasses primary care (the family doctor, dentistry and ophthalmic services, subsidized prescriptions, etc.), hospital care (the most costly part of the service), and community care (public health, clinics, visiting nursing services, etc.). The community health part of the NHS was administered by local authorities prior to the 1974 reorganization, while linked activities in personal social services (e.g. social workers, including those working in hospitals, and home helps) are indeed still administered by local authorities (except in Northern Ireland where they are integrated with the health services). Expenditure on the NHS, for the UK in total, may exceed 16 billion pounds in 1986/7. Of this, almost three-quarters is expended on the hospital and community health services, and the remainder on the family doctor, dentistry and prescription services, and on central services provided by the government health departments.

Salary costs (including superannuation and social security oncosts) constitute nearly 75% of the total costs of th NHS, so real growth in the NHS is most easily illustrated by staffing numbers: recent growth in NHS staffing in England is shown in Table 6.1. For the UK as a whole, and if we include the general practitioners, who are self-employed contractors rather than employees of the NHS, and their staffs, the total employment funded by the NHS exceeds one million, which represents about 4% of the employed population.

Table 6.1
NHS employed staff and general practitioners

Directly Employed Staff[1]	1978	1983	% increase
Nursing and Midwifery[2] [3]	351,000	397,100	13.0
Medical and dental[4]	35,900	40,200	11.9
Ancillary	172,200	166,200	−3.5
Administrative and clerical	100,300	110,000	9.6
Professional and technical	57,200	68,700	20.0
Maintenance	19,900	20,800	4.9
Works	5,600	6,000	7.0
Ambulance (including officers)	17,500	18,400	5.0
All staff (directly employed)	**759,700**	**827,400**	**8.9**
General medical and dental practitioners[5]	33,100	37,000	11.8

[1]Includes staff at the Dental Estimates Board and Prescription Pricing Authority.
[2]Not adjusted for reduction in working hours in 1980 (from 40 to 37½ hours per week). On an adjusted basis the figure for 1978 for these staff is 374,400 and the increase 1978-1983 is 6.1 per cent; and for all directly employed staff the increase over this period is then 5.7 per cent.
[3]Includes agency staff and health visitor students.
[4]Includes permanent paid, honorary and locum staff in hospitals and community health services but excludes hospital practitioners and part-time medical officers.
[5]Excludes medical trainees and dental assistants.
Figures are expressed as 'whole-time equivalents'. (Reproduced from *The Health Service in England Annual Report 1983*, p. 8, by permission of the Controller, Her Majesty's Stationery Office. Crown copyright.)

Figure 6.1 illustrates how some key indicators of NHS activity (or workload) and use of resources have altered over ten years from 1973. Broadly, advances in drugs and in medical and surgical skills and technology, have enabled the average length of stay (LOS) in hospital to be reduced for in-patients. This has made it possible to reduce the total number of NHS hospital beds

n spite of treating an increased number of patients. But the
eduction in number of beds (through closing many smaller
hospitals and some large, long-stay hospitals) has not made
possible an equivalent reduction in NHS manpower. On the
contrary, the reduction in LOS has involved increasingly intensive treatment and thus the expansion of medical, nursing, and
professional and technical manpower. In addition, during the ten
years covered by the chart there was a substantial reduction in the
over-long hours of work especially of nursing staff, and also a
significant expansion in the number of administrative and clerical
staff. This is reflected in Table 6.1, as also is the fact that the only
major reductions in NHS staffing, more or less paralleling the
reductions in beds and hospitals, have been in ancillary staff (i.e.,
mainly in catering, cleaning and laundry services).

We can obtain some approximation of the cost-effectiveness of
the NHS by reference to international comparisons. The NHS,
together with Britain's small private health sector, consumes only
some 6% of gross domestic product (GDP), whereas health care
in other developed countries (except Japan) costs between 7%

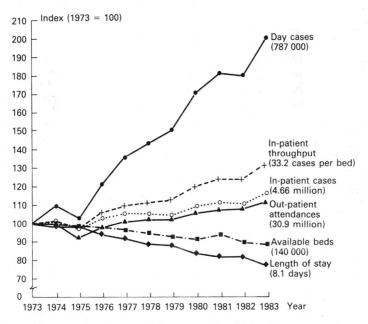

Fig. 6.1 Acute hospital services 1973–1983, England. Figures for 1983 are
given in parentheses. (Reproduced from *The Health Service in England
Annual Report 1984*, p. 45 by permission of the Controller, Her Majesty's
Stationery Office. Crown copyright.)

and 10% of total GDP. Discussions of international comparative costliness and cost-effectiveness of health services may be found in Bevan et al (1980) and Maxwell (1981). The most probable reason why health care costs less in Britain is not that standards here are uniformly lower than the average of other developed countries, but rather that the British system of financial allocation to hospitals, and of remuneration to the medical profession discourages unnecessary medical intervention or hospitalization in a way that does not happen in systems funded on a basis of health insurance, or which otherwise give financial inducements to doctors to provide medical treatment even when the expected benefits therefrom are only marginal or problematic.

There is no space here for any detailed history of the back ground to the NHS, and of how central government in Britain became (almost uniquely among free nations) the provider of finance for a national health system, universal of access and generally free of charge at the time of use, certainly as regards major and 'catastrophic' health conditions. For this background see Levitt and Wall (1984) and Bevan et al (1980) for summaries of key factors and guidance to further reading. The Beveridge Report of 1942 was a watershed. Inter alia it expounded the idea that a comprehensive system of health care was essential to any expectation of improving living standards. Thus the National Health Service came into being on 5 July 1948 (CIPFA's FIS Vol 30, *Health* – 1980 with updates – summarizes the legislative history of the NHS).

6.2 FINANCE AND RESOURCE ALLOCATION

Financing the NHS nationally and regionally

Funding the NHS centrally

While the NHS locally may be able to obtain modest amounts of funds from donations, voluntary fund-raising and charges for private patients and for services to the private sector (e.g. diagnostic back-up services for private hospitals), in practice nearly the whole of NHS funds are provided by the government following cabinet agreement on total public spending and the relative resource needs of the numerous branches of the public sector. The decision on the total funding allocation to the NHS is independent of how much is raised in income from prescription charges and other fees, or from that small portion of National nsurance charges that is notionally designated as a National Health Insurance charge. Strictly, these apparently health-related sources of income have no more direct impact on determining total expenditure on the NHS than do vehicle and petrol taxes on the level of highway construction and maintenance. Currently about 4% of total NHS expenditure is met by income from health-service charges and some 8% is provided by notional health insurance levied with National Insurance contributions. The remaining 88% of expenditure is provided from the general pool of government taxation revenues.

It appears that the funding of the NHS has been the most successfully protected from economic crises, with continuous growth in real terms, even though at rates varying through time, of all the major public services (see Bevan et al, 1980). Indeed this is only rational, since health care for the sick is perhaps the least postponable of services. And as the environment has improved (better education, water, sewerage, control of pollution, and improved housing and health care for at least the large majority of the population) people live longer. Thus the numbers of the elderly increase, and the increase of those over 75 years of age is especially prominent. But the longer people live, the more prone they are to diseases which are not immediately life-threatening, but debilitating, crippling or otherwise destructive of the quality of life. About half the total resources of the NHS are expended on persons aged 65 and over, and it is estimated that the rising population of the elderly requires expansion of NHS resources by about 1% per year just to cope with this demographic change in the population.

But there are also other pressures for sharing in any growth moneys the NHS may secure. Technological progress in curative medicine is costly: new 'wonder drugs' are typically expensive, as are many of the newer surgical techniques, including not just the well-publicized heart and kidney transplants, but also the more numerous and much-needed interventions such as artificial joints for those crippled by arthritis but otherwise in good health and able to look after themselves.

Criteria for funding allocations to regions (RAWP).

Until the Crossman formula of 1970 and its first major reorganizaion in 1974, the NHS simply grew organically and incrementally. That is, generally speaking, it grew on an unplanned basis, roughly proportional in each locality to its pre-existing size, and with little coherent guidance for equalizing the

scale and accessibility of health-care resources across the regions
Historically the poorer and industrial parts of the country had
fewer beds, doctors and support resources, and this historical
pattern was little altered in the first quarter-century of the NHS
But the matter caused increasing dissatisfaction, culminating in
'equal access to health care' as a main objective of the 197
reorganization, and in the establishment of the Resource Alloca
tion Working Party (RAWP). RAWP reported in 1976 and
proposed that health-care funds should be allocated to the region
of England according to equitable criteria of need, as measured by
objective formulae (and rather similar proposals were brough
forward separately for Wales, Scotland and Northern Ireland)
Accordingly, it became accepted that the practical policy was to
progress to RAWP equalization of resources regionally by increas
ing the funding allocations of the best-provided regions only
slowly, while using the bulk of the annual growth in funding to
accelerate the expansion of health-care resources in the under
provided regions at a faster rate. At the time (in the mid
seventies) it was hoped that resource equalization might be
achieved nationally by the 1990s or even earlier. But as economic
depression settled on Britain, and the annual rate of growth in
real terms of NHS funding was cut back, the horizon date for
expected equalization receded.

The RAWP formulae are based on population, adjusted for the
age, sex and marital status of the resident population, for the
Standard Mortality Ratios (SMRs) locally as surrogate for the
morbidity rate (i.e. measure of sickness and health need) for
which no reliable information is currently available, and for the
cross-boundary flows of inpatients. This RAWP approach recog
nizes that needs for health care are not a constant function of
population, but are indeed affected strongly by social and
economic factors. Analysis has shown (see Holland et al, 1980
that the RAWP formula for revenue allocation is reasonabl
robust (i.e. little affected by possible errors in the parameters)
and as a basis for resource allocation to Regional Health
Authorities the RAWP approach is now generally accepted a
both equitable and efficient. RAWP and the link with planning
are discussed in some detail in Bevan et al (1980), Butts et a
(1981), Jones & Prowle (1984) and Rigden (1983).

Revenue RAWP

RAWP revenue allocations are calculated from the previous
year's approved expenditure, plus a percentage growth deter

mined by *relative* under/over funding as against the RAWP targets. The allocations are then uplifted for the degree of 'pay and prices' inflation the Government is prepared to fund in the NHS cash limits in the year ahead. Assuming actual pay and prices increase at the allowed rate, the allocations would result in an average increase of about 1.5% in NHS purchasing power, after allowing for savings obtained from the required annual 'cost improvement programmes'. But as it is widely accepted that the NHS needs spending growth of about 1% per year simply to maintain existing standards of care for the rising population of the elderly, the supposedly 'real' increase in the cash-planning expenditure limit could become wholly absorbed in inflation above that allowed for. However, that is a statement relating to the national average, whereas the situation can have a very different impact as between regions with differing rates of percentage growth. For example, East Anglia and Trent can hold back some growth money in reserves until it is known if it will be required for inflation. But the Thames regions (London and the Home Counties) do not receive a large enough allocation to cope even with a modest amount of excess inflation. Their financial reserves will be negligible, unless they actually initiate cuts in existing services for which the rising population of the elderly is inevitably causing a gradual but continuous rise in demand. Where funds are held back until late in the year against the contingency of a rising rate of inflation, it may be difficult to spend any residue not needed for inflation, except by a hasty programme of non-recurrent spending late in the year on supplies, equipment, maintenance, etc., or by using the funds for virement and carry-forward (discussed later in the chapter).

The Service Increment for Teaching

Within the regional revenue allocations is included, additional to the main block of funding determined by existing expenditure and progress to the RAWP target, a smaller amount of revenue identified as the Service Increment for Teaching (SIFT). The need for this arises because, for historical reasons, the distribution of medical schools and teaching hospitals in Britain is nowhere near proportional to the distribution of the weighted populations used in calculating RAWP targets. While in the longer term there may be some geographical redistribution of medical schools and teaching hospitals more evenly across the country, in the shorter term it would clearly be harmful to medical teaching, and to the care of patients in teaching hospitals, if some financial protection could not be given to regions carrying above-average financial burdens of teaching hospitals. These hospitals not only provide the clinical teaching of medical under-graduates, but also carry out research, innovational and developmental medicine, the training of other professions ancillary to medicine – and, in general, they provide high-quality, high-cost centres of advanced medicine.

The clearest explanation of the calculation of SIFT is contained in the *Report of the Advisory Group on Resource Allocation* (the AGRA Report, 1980). First is determined which hospitals have a significant teaching role in association with each medical school. Their actual costs for the base year are then ascertained. From these are deducted what those hospitals' costs notionally would have been had the hospitals been typical non-teaching district general hospitals (DGHs) (based on costs from a '45-hospitals' sample of modern DGHs, with adjustment for differences in the mix of specialties treated, given data from a DHSS index of specialty costs). The resultant differences, after further adjustments for the higher salaries and wages paid in London, where over 40% of medical education is concentrated, are termed the 'excess costs' of teaching hospitals. Then for the teaching hospitals associated with each medical school the 'excess cost per student' is determined by dividing by the number of clinical students expected to be in those hospitals at a date two years later.

Studies carried out by Professor Culyer and others for RAWP had concluded by regression analysis and supporting calculations that the proportion of the excess costs of teaching hospitals that might be explained by their teaching function, broadly defined, was of the order of 75%. The balance of excess cost was probably attributable mainly to a high-cost case mix arising from a concentration of regional and subregional specialties, such as would be properly fundable from within the normal RAWP revenue allocation, as distinct from SIFT. On this background the DHSS held that the SIFT allocation should cover 75% of the median excess costs of teaching hospitals.

Capital RAWP

NHS capital allocations do not correlate well with the order of revenue allocations, revenue percentage growth, or distance from RAWP revenue targets between Regions. In the NHS, capital expenditure is defined to include spending on new buildings and reconstructions; on the original quota of plant, equipment and furnishings installed therein; and on the replacement of certain designated categories of equipment, e.g. computers and ambulances. Otherwise the ongoing replacement and upgrading of most furnishings, equipment, and plant and fabric must be funded from revenue. Thus capital expenditure in the NHS is primarily for major construction/reconstruction of hospitals, health centres, and facilities such as ambulance stations and laundries. The RAWP policy for capital allocation is to move towards equity of distribution of *capital stock*, on a basis of relative need related to forecasts of future population. Regions with growing population or population redeployments away from inner cities will need new hospitals in terms of locational need and of absolute level of demand. That aside, the quality (age, environment, condition, ease of access, etc.) of existing hospitals need not correlate closely with the scale of revenue-RAWP funding, and hence the overall lack of correlation between the levels of capital and revenue funding. Owen (1978) examines the problems of NHS capital stock and capital expenditure.

Financing the NHS subregionally

Alternative approaches to funding within regions

Regional Health Authorities (RHAs) have responsibilities for allocating financial resources within their regions. Their discretion is considerable: for example, they are not obliged to pass on to District Health Authorities (DHAs) containing teaching hospitals the exact amount of revenue allocation they themselves have received through the SIFT adjustment. Also, after deduction ('top slicing') for the funding of their own administration and for common services supplied to, or managed on behalf of, health districts (e.g. blood-donor services, computer and supplies-procurement services, and professional works services in support of major capital developments), they have discretion to allocate the remaining funds to District Health Authorities broadly on the same basis of gradually adjusting funding year by year towards resource equalization targets on the basis of the national RAWP formula (or some amended formula). Or there may be substantial additional top slicing to create earmarked reserves before the residual funds are distributed on a basis of movement towards RAWP targets.

It is widely agreed that it is not wise for RHAs to hold reserves in respect of inflation or other contingencies which might arise at the DHA level – this may leave district treasurers in uncertainty or tempt them to behave irresponsibly. But it is legitimate for RHAs to hold reserves to release as needed to DHAs as the latter bring on stream new developments as part of approved service programmes. This especially applies where new developments are linked to major capital schemes (controlled by region, with 'lumpy' expenditure, and with incremental recurrent-revenue implications for DHAs when new capital assets are actually commissioned), or where districts are developing a service (e.g. a subregional clinical specialty) where costs will be met from the funds of one district, but whose benefits may be shared with the populations of adjoining districts. To take the example of the West Midlands region, at least three main types of earmarked reserves have been used. RCCS reserves (Revenue Consequences of Capital Schemes) provide funding for the incremental revenue-expenditure effects following capital development, mentioned above. RCMA (Revenue Consequences of Medical Appointments) and RCCD (Revenue Consequences of Clinical Developments) cope with the incremental cost arising from the appointment of additional consultants, or from bringing new services or facilities into use. Constructive use of reserves in these ways depends on effective strategic planning, looking some way ahead and operating wise and acceptable criteria for determining relative need, and applying these rationally and fairly to determine the relative priority of major new capital and revenue developments, so that these can be assembled into a costed and timetabled programme. But all this is easier to describe than to achieve, and certainly from the DHA level in some regions there is much criticism of regional top slicing and the use of regionally controlled revenue-reserve programmes.

Supporters of minimizing top slicing and reserves managed at regional level, and of maximizing the distribution of funds to DHAs in consistency with RAWP equalization believe their method to be better because it is consistent with policy to encourage devolution and decision-making at the local level, and because the consequential motivation combined with local knowledge could lead to better decisions and more effective implementation. This may be true, but there are questions of possible disadvantage which need to be considered. If districts obtain all revenue on a RAWP trend-line of revenue growth, how will they cope with meeting the incremental revenue needs of major new capital installations when commissioned? If they cope with this by marking time on recurrent-revenue expenditure before each new major capital (or other) development, will the resultant temporary surge of non-recurrent revenue be spent wisely, and with a better return of benefit than if it were being distributed from earmarked regional reserves only to meet the recurrent-revenue consequences of some other major development that thus might be funded to come into service sooner than otherwise? Lastly, if initiative for controlling nearly all district-level spending is passed to DHAs through RAWP-type funding allocations, will natural district preferences for providing comprehensive health care locally cause a number of low-volume and/or high-cost services which are only economic when provided at a limited number of centres in each region, as subregional specialties, to be replicated in too many locations, with a low return in cost-benefit terms?

Regional and subregional specialties

Those who are concerned about the risk of excessive replication of low-volume and/or high-cost specialties and facilities may tend to conclude that development-led revenue and capital funding, closely monitored from regions, is most likely to maximize health-service benefit to the public from the limited funds and resources available at any one point in time. There are a very few 'national' specialties with separately assessed allocations analogous to SIFT, but their cost is minute beside the total NHS budget. Also there are 'regional' specialties that may be located in only one or two hospitals within a region, e.g. for haemophilia or renal transplantation. And there are 'subregional', sometimes termed 'supradistrict', specialties that may be designated at several locations within a region. But study of this problem is difficult, as the criteria for determining regional and subregional specialties are not fully consistent across regions, lower-level work in most specialties is anyway done in many district general hospitals and may develop to quite a sophisticated level without formal designation as a specialty centre, and the available methods for measuring the complexity/severity of cases treated in specialties, and for matching cost thereto, are still primitive and inadequate for rational comparison and the setting of definitive criteria. Quite aside from the cost-effectiveness of particular frequencies of replication of high-cost and/or low-volume specialties, there is a further, important problem. There is always a shortage of highly skilled staff (nursing and other support-staff, as well as medical). A high volume of complex work increases skill. Research in the USA suggests that the success rates for advanced medicine are far higher in high-volume centres than in hospitals with a low volume and frequently lower levels of skill available. All these aspects of the problem need further research in order to establish the optimal balance between quality of service, local access and cost efficiency.

This section on financing the NHS has examined a process very different from the financing of nationalized industries, most other public corporations, or local government. The Government decides the NHS's total share of the national public-sector cake, the DHSS allocates wedges of the cake among regions, and the regions cut it into thin slices, keeping a slice for their own costs and the services they provide to DHAs, e.g. computers and supplies, and reallocate to districts. The mechanics of the process are simple, but optimizing public benefit in the choice among alternative policies is complex. Each district ends up on average with about ½% of the NHS cake. A typical health district will receive almost £50m from this allocation process, and will have approaching 4000 employees (note that this excludes personnel paid by the Family Practitioner Committee, funded separately). So a DHA is indeed a large organization, although not so large that it is impossible to treat it as a cohesive management entity in which decisions on the division of resources can be taken on a managerial budgeting basis, rather than a bureaucratic allocation. But as most of the activities of a DHA are ongoing and regarded as essential, there has been a tradition until quite recently of 'incremental' budgeting, whereby it was generally assumed that individual budgets were seldom challenged or cut, and where the main financial interest lay in the process of budgetary control *ex post*, rather than in the possibililties of using the budget-making process *ex ante* as a method of switching resources to more beneficial uses at the margin. Reflecting this, detailed consideration of the budgetary system within the NHS will be left until the next main section.

Joint finance between health and local authorities

There is a need for a close relationship between health and local authorities, particularly in respect of services for the elderly, handicapped and mentally ill client groups. The 1974 reorganization set up a formal system of 'joint planning' and also brought in *joint financing* whereby a small element of health service funds was allocated to health authorities to be spent on local authority projects. In some areas joint finance has led to the stimulation of better joint planning and the introduction of innovative and imaginative projects. In other areas it has in effect served to offset the general lack of availability of funds for social services.

The whole issue of joint finance became of even greater

significance with the publication of *Care in the Community* (1981). This envisaged the transfer of handicapped patients from hospitals to the community – which meant, by and large, out of the NHS and into the care of local authorities. The question of how resources were to be transferred then became of key significance and provided an interesting example of the problems of transferring cash resources between different parts of the public sector.

Policy issues in finance

It should not be surprising that for a public service of the unique character of the NHS, the most important policy issues are not explicitly financial, although, if particular viewpoints were adopted, either massive injections of new finance or redistribution of resources among existing services would be needed. I refer to issues of Parliamentary or public interest such as concern for the relative role, size and funding of the acute hospital services as compared to the primary and community sectors of care, as well as health education or preventive medicine. But here we shall consider only the more important issues in which the financial aspects are a major or dominant part. The paragraphs that follow will consider the problems of cross-boundary flows and shared services; the problems of London and of protecting centres of excellence; the difficulties raised by the virtual independence of Family Practitioner Services; the possibilities for altering the funding of NHS capital and charging for the use of capital; and the contentious question of how far private-sector medicine might be encouraged to develop in cooperation or in competition with the NHS.

Cross-boundary flows of patients and services, and the London problem

'Cross-boundery flows' in the NHS refers to the movements of patients across boundaries between districts or between regions, to obtain treatment elsewhere. Information on these flows is collected and used as the basis for adjustments to regional and district resource allocations. The adjustments are based on specialty costs obtained by the DHSS from a very large number of hospitals, including many small hospitals supplying mainly fairly basic, low-cost treatments. Yet many of the cross-boundary flows, especially to districts containing teaching hospitals and between districts in the London area more generally, are of patients with conditions more severe or complex than average, and thus of above-average cost to treat. Districts receiving such patients to their regional specialties or other centres of advanced medicine resent the underfunding they receive for this in their adjusted revenue allocations. One solution would be to use a more relevant (up-rated) set of specialty costs in making these adjustments. An alternative solution would be to 'recharge' for patients treated from other authorities, as is done already in respect of various common services supplied from one district or, occasionally, region to another.

For major cross-boundary flows of services one might consider applying 'transfer pricing' methods developed for inter-divisional trading in industry. In particular the 'two-part tariff' system first extensively publicized by David Solomons (1965) could be relevant. This system requires the parties sharing in a service to agree on their respective shares of the likely throughput of a shared facility each year, and to meet these shares of the total fixed costs of the facility. Then, during the year, the actual variable costs are shared out among the receiving organizations in exact proportion to the actual volume of throughput realized. Or agreed standard variable costs may be charged instead, to impose greater cost-control discipline on the supplying authority. Rather similarly, transfer prices could be used as an alternative method of reimbursing health authorities for cross-boundary flows of patients between authorities. This could be achieved either on the basis of an improved national system of variable specialty costs, or through local bargaining processes between authorities dispatching and receiving patients. A proper concern here would be the risk that a bargaining process might introduce gamesmanship into the behaviour of the authorities and their attitudes to cross-boundary flows, with effects not in the best interests of patients.

The problems of health services in London and of protecting centres of excellence are partially interconnected, since so many teaching hospitals and centres of advanced medicine are located in London. These involve high (excess) costs, with the SIFT allowance covering only about half the 'excess' costs of many London teaching hospitals, and cross-boundary flow adjustments allegedly being quite inadequate to cover the costs of inpatients and outpatients who include visitors and also persons working in London districts but resident and being counted for RAWP in commuter-belt districts. But this is only one part of the London problem, which is too complex to explain fully here. Briefly, however, Inner London suffers extra need because of social deprivation and its particular demographic mix, yet its primary care and community care services are arguably inadequate. This imposes extra strain on the London health districts, which are constrained because the Thames regions are over-provided on the basis of RAWP criteria, therefore receive low or even negative growth increments, and therefore have little flexibility at the margin to develop additional services. Although probably in lesser degree, similar problems face other large cities with combinations of teaching hospitals and acute inner-city problems. No final resolution to this problem is in sight, with RAWP principles overriding other considerations in national and regional policies – but fairer methods of reimbursing for cross-boundary flows of hospital patients (see preceding paragraph) might help considerably. Many of these problems were examined in the Le Quesne Report (1977).

The financial independence of family practitioners

District Health Authorities finance and manage the hospital services and also the community health services, most of the latter having been administered by local government prior to the 1974 reorganizations of both the NHS and local government. But although there have been previous references to primary care, this is not financed, managed or controlled by the district health authorities. Primary care is provided by family doctors (GPs), dentists, opticians and chemists, all of whom are self-employed persons under contract to the NHS to provide services in return for capitation and other fees (GPs), and piece-rate payments for services rendered (other practitioners). The family practitioner services do not comprise a planned health-care system except to the extent that there are controls over the number and location of the practitioners. They do not have financial allocations or budgets imposed on them. Their financial relationships with the NHS are conducted through Family Practitioner Committees, which now have status comparable with health authorities but which have no significant managerial roles. The Committees' financial officers have no major budgetary control or other financial-management roles, but simply ensure that family practitioners (and pharmacists) are reimbursed properly within the rules and regulations. There are no cash planning limits imposed on the fees of family practitioners or the cost of the various prescriptions they dispense. This is because of their 'independent contractor' status and the freedom of action that involves. In spite of this seemingly open-ended commitment, the proportion of total NHS spending on the family practitioner services has actually fallen significantly over the life of the NHS.

But what has given cause for concern is the continuing rise in the real cost of the prescriptions dispensed by family practitioners, especially drugs, together with the absence of effective machinery for coordinating planning of the family, community and hospital services.

Accountability and financing of capital in the NHS

The NHS obtains its capital as a 'free good'. That is, the NHS does not have to pay any interest on its capital funds, let alone repay the principal. This lack of financial discipline on capital arguably makes the NHS lax in extracting best value for money from capital funding, especially in those years when governments have been keen to encourage extra capital spending as a means of stimulating the construction industry and economic demand in the economy more generally. This is not to deny that the NHS's hospital stock has not been in need of renewal, much of it being of Victorian origin. Rather, the problem in which the DHSS centrally must take its share of the blame, has been that rigorous review of the cost-effectiveness of designs, and the cost and quality of construction, was not maintained. Leslie Chapman made much of this in his book (1979), even if he may have overstated the scale of financial waste. In recent years the DHSS has pressed health authorities to be more economical in the use of capital, and DHSS guidelines on evaluating capital options have been issued. Economists such as Drummond (1980) also have advised the NHS on better methods of capital appraisal.

During recent years of reduced growth in the (real-terms) funding of the NHS there has been rising interest in (a) releasing any financial resources unproductively tied up in fixed assets surplus to operational needs, (b) measuring the costs of capital consumption and relating these to the accountability of Districts, Units and even individual budget holders, and (c) introducing greater flexibility and rational choice into decisions at the margin on the spending of capital versus revenue funds. We will review these briefly in turn.

In 1982 an Enquiry was established to review NHS arrangements for identifying under-used and surplus property, and to make recommendations for improvements. This resulted in the Ceri Davies Report (1983). The report concluded that there was significant surplus land and under-utilized space within buildings in the NHS, and that motivation needed to be provided for Districts to dispose of this. Districts should normally retain the proceeds of sale, as encouragement. Districts were handicapped in applying for planning permission in their own right, and this needed amendment both in the interpretation of regulations, and in future legislation, so that the NHS could secure maximum return for its disposals of property. Districts should be held accountable for their capital estates, and especially for holding estate surplus to operational requirements. Estate assets, and their use, would need to be recorded and assessed, and 'notional rents' could be reported after appropriate valuations of both land and buildings. If Districts continued for some years to have notional rents (and therefore asset values) which were markedly above the normal experience, then this could form the basis for penalties in funding, so as to stimulate cash realization even in those authorities reluctant to sell surplus land, or to sell or demolish surplus building space.

Charging for the use of capital

Turning to the costs of capital consumption, and accountability for these, the definitive debate has been published in the Association of Health Service Treasurers' (AHST's) Report from its Capital and Asset Accounting Working Party (1984). Part of this Report dealt with problems of optimizing the use of capital funding in the NHS, as summarized below. The other part of the Report was concerned with the risk that wrong judgements on efficiency and on accountability might be taken in the NHS if the costs of capital consumption (i.e. the wearing out of capital resources – see Perrin (1984) were not included in accounting information and performance indicators. After discussing the principles involved, and noting also the work which would be involved in establishing accurate 'registers' of fixed assets, the AHST Report made a number of recommendations. Full asset registers should be established, to contain at least a minimum standard set of data on each asset.

Annual NHS revenue accounts should include a charge for the use of capital, and the disaggregation of this should be shown in the budgets and reports supplied to budget holders within the NHS. This would involve the preparation of proper balance sheets, and implicitly it would also involve the adoption of full accrual accounting augmenting the current income and expenditure accounting system. Pilot trials should be carried out in individual health districts to compare the options of (a) 'asset depreciation charges as used by the private sector', (b) 'a system where RHAs would lease all major items of equipment, land and buildings to DHAs', or (c) 'a leasing system for land and buildings, and depreciation charges for equipment'. In this context 'leasing' implies the determination of a reasonable yet market-sensitive annual charge for the use of particular assets during the year in question. It should be remembered that lease charges comprise (in one total figure), (a) recovery of the original (historical) capital outlay over the life of the asset, (b) interest at market rates (including the effects of expected inflation) on the unrecovered portions of the capital outlay, and (c) some profit margin and premium or discount depending upon market conditions. Following successful trials, new standard capital asset accounting methods might be adopted in all health districts by 1988-89.

The Report from the AHST (1984), in search of greater flexibility and rational – or optimal – choice in the use of resources, suggested that in future RHAs should receive a single funding allocation from the DHSS, determined after taking account of both the RAWP revenue and capital allocation formulae. It could then be practicable for Regions more flexibly to take account of the existing levels of capital provision and consumption, as indicated by lease and/or depreciation cost calculations, so as to introduce a stronger discipline into the use of capital by health districts. For example, the use of greater amounts of capital would be reflected in increased capital use charges, which would result in reduced revenue funding – thus concentrating the minds of NHS decision-makers on obtaining the most service-effective balance of use of available funding between capital and revenue applications.

Cooperation or competition with the private sector

For the first time since the formation of the NHS, there has recently arisen seriously the question of whether or not part of the work of the NHS could usefully be redirected to the private sector. At one level, this is manifested in concern for whether or not private contractors might provide non-medical services such as laundry, catering, transport, cleaning, etc., more cheaply than those services could be provided by NHS employees; and for whether or not there was mutual benefit to be obtained by greater exchange of work between public and private health facilities. For example, the NHS might place more of its convalescent or geriatric patients in private nursing homes to release costly acute beds in NHS hospitals, or sell spare capacity in its diagnostic services or the use of convalescent beds, to assist small private hospitals to cope with increasing demand for elective surgery covered by private health insurance. The Government has encouraged developments of these kinds. At a more fundamental level, it has been suggested that the people of Britain (via their Parliamentary representatives) may no longer be willing to pay the high taxes needed to support a universal national health system of high standards, so that the total volume of health care must be stimulated by encouraging those who can afford it, or whose employers will pay, to use private medicine to the maximum extent. All this is very controversial and very political, and largely outside the direct influence of finance personnel in the NHS. But at least NHS finance staff should take care to check that any subcontracting of NHS activities to private contractors is based on acurate and complete, comparative costs, and that contracts and service performance are carefully monitored and controlled.

To assist in providing accurate information, fair play, and the comparing of like with like, individual health districts have prepared manuals of guidance on the preparation of tender specifications and the management of contracts for subcontracting cleaning, laundry or catering services. For example, on the fair-play aspect, the member of finance staff who is advising on the preparation and costing of an in-house tender should not be the same person who prepared the tender specification or who is receiving and evaluating the internal and external tenders. For aid in organizing fair, efficient, competitive tendering, an excellent manual has been prepared by Thornton Baker (1984), and a group of NHS Treasurers have been working through the CIPFA to design and implement standard computer systems for preparing and controlling competitive tenders. To date only a small fraction of NHS ancillary services have been put out to tender. Some of the contracts awarded, especially in cleaning, have proved highly controversial with allegations of poor training of contract staff, and poor standards of cleaning. Contractors have not always reduced previous Whitley Council hourly rates of pay, but it appears that benefits for sickness, holiday and pensions have often been curtailed, and that part of the efficiency savings have been achieved by greater use of part-time staff working short shifts not requiring paid breaks. The one thing that seems certain, which is not to imply any judgement on the overall balance of (social) cost/benefit, is that most authorities which have put ancillary services to tender have realized substantial savings in expenditure, even when the contracts have in the end been awarded to the in-house tender group.

6.3 BUDGETING, INTERNAL CONTROL AND PERFORMANCE MEASUREMENT

The financial planning system

Strategic planning

Naturally planning is not exclusively a financial process. Before the 1974 reorganization in the NHS the planning function was badly organized, and was largely concentrated on the planning of new hospital schemes and programmes. The 1974 reorganization created Regional, Area and District tiers with formal planning obligations, and it encouraged the appointment of staff with better professional skills in health service planning, including epidemiologists and specialists in community medicine. But unfortunately the latter skills have been in very short supply. Also, planning was organized outside the finance function, and the early attempts at strategic plans after the 1974 reorganization were often not fully costed: that is, they were expressed in real resource-unit terms not translated into money values. Thus the strategic plans were not fully testable for practicality against the predicted flow of financial resources for growth (see Bevan et al for more detailed discussion). In recent years the strategic plans have been improved in quality, with an increased financial input, but the economic depression has inevitably increased the uncertainty regarding whether or not sufficient finance for health services will be forthcoming to keep the planned new developments on schedule. New guidelines on the NHS Planning System were issued for the 1982 reorganization (see HC (82)6).

Operational planning

Operational planning in the NHS is an annual exercise, involving an 'operational programme' for the first year, linking firm development proposals to the latest resource assumptions. These first-year plans must merge into the budget-setting process. For the second year DHAs will prepare 'forward programmes', based on provisional development plans and resource assumptions: these will be the basis for consultation with interested parties, including the RHA and relevant local authorities. But the whole planning process is iterative. Ministers indicate through the DHSS to RHAs what are the guidelines on national policies and priorities (e.g. *Care in Action*, 1981) and the resources likely to be available. RHAs amplify and interpret these to DHAs in the light of the circumstances of each region. Districts will have regular annual planning reviews with their RHAs, covering strategy, plans, performance and key issues for the year ahead, and RHAs will have similar annual reviews with the DHSS. But the 1982 reorganization was based on the thesis that the devolution of greater authority and initiative to the DHA-level (and below) will improve the efficiency and effectiveness of health care, and this may assist districts to follow a consistent planning line with more confidence.

For planning purposes the services provided by the NHS are subdivided as follows: general and acute hospital services; primary care (i.e. family practitioner services); services mainly for the elderly and the physically handicapped; services for the mentally ill; services for the mentally handicapped; services mainly for children; and other. In recent years particular priority has been given to the needs of the mentally ill and the handicapped, and the desirability of removing as many as possible of them from long-stay institutions to sheltered accommodation within the local community; and similarly to the benefits of assisting the elderly, by rehabilitation and support services, to live in their own homes or in sheltered accommodation to a greater age than was formerly expected. But there are difficulties in using the above planning categories. For example, the elderly are the main consumers of general and acute hospital services, quite aside from the separate programmes of geriatric care and community accommodation developed exclusively for them, and aside from their representation in the mental illness category. Children similarly appear in several of the categories. In other words the categories are not mutually exclusive. Nor do the categories match well with the organizational structure and responsibilities within the NHS at district level. And since budgetary and costing systems tend naturally to reflect closely the organizational structure and responsibilities, they do not match up with the care groups chosen as the basis for the planning system and the determination of priorities. While these categories, in spite of the overlaps, may appear to provide a suitable basis for a system of programme budgeting, little progress has been made in that direction in costed plans, and it has so far appeared to be impracticable for use in budgetary allocation and control at the operational level.

Budgeting in the NHS

Previously we have considered how the share of total public

sector resources allocated to the NHS by government is successively subdivided by RAWP formulae or other criteria, first to regions, and then again to districts. Aside from regional earmarking for medical education (SIFT), regional specialties/ services, and the regional programme for major capital projects, the balance of the allocation to each District Health Authority has always been in two lump sums, one for revenue and the other for capital. The revenue allocations give no instruction on how expenditure should be broken down between the various categories of cost – for labour, supplies and services, equipment etc. This process is for local determination, through the annual budgetary cycle in each authority. Budgets for minor capital are tied closely to particular approved projects, coordinated at district level, and these are not controlled financially in the NHS in any way especially distinctive from other organizations. But the budgeting of revenue funds is distinctive, and so the paragraphs below relate only to revenue unless otherwise stated.

Functional budgeting

The normal form of budgeting and budgetary control in the NHS is based on what is termed 'functional budgeting'. The term derives from the 'functional' form of organization adopted by the NHS at the time of the 1974 reorganization (see the 'Grey Book', 1972), which laid great stress on the organization and management of the service by functions, i.e. disciplines of professional specialization. Prior to 1974, budgets and accounts had been mainly on a subjective basis for an entire hospital or other organizational unit. After 1974 the subjective data had to be recast across a matrix to relate to the authority and accountability of individual senior managers of functions, for the resources they authorized to be used across the whole of each health district; e.g. the salaries, training costs and certain other expenses of nurses in a district, for the accountability of the district nursing officer. Each senior functional officer could in turn delegate specified parts of his or her overall budget to particular managers within the function, while of course still retaining overall responsibility for the budgetary performance of that function as a whole. The strengths and weaknesses of the functional budgeting system were explored in some depth in Research Paper No. 2 for the Royal Commission on the NHS (1978): that research examined the position in 1977-78 and since then there have been improvements in the use of functional budgets and in their integration with operational planning.

Unit management and budgets

The 1982 reorganization of the NHS had two main objectives; namely, the simplification of management structure and some reduction in management costs, and secondly, the devolution of greater decision-making authority to the operational levels of the service. Thus, the old Area Health Authorities were abolished and their constituent health districts, singly or in combination, were raised to the status of authorities, i.e. they acquired direct statutory responsibilities to RHAs and to the Secretary of State, exercised through boards of health authority members appointed by the parent RHA. Authority previously held at the area level was thus pushed down to the district level. The 1982 reorganization required also that within the new district health authorities as much functional authority as possible should be delegated to lower tiers of organization. The DHSS's Health Circular HC (80) 8 outlined the general framework for this new 'unit' level of management. Each unit would have its own administrator and its own nursing officer, together with a clinician chosen by his peers. A unit could be a single large hospital, or a group of smaller hospitals, or the community services for a geographical area, or some combination of community and hospital services related either to a geographical area or to the integration of service provision for one or more of the main care groups, e.g. the elderly.

It was intended that as many functional areas of management as practicable should be delegated to the units, with the unit administrator controlling budgets for departments for which he is managerially responsible, and coordinating other unit budgets. But even now it is not clear how much can be delegated to unit level without loss of economies of scale (e.g. in organizing the rostering of building and plant maintenance), or without significant loss of district-level control of policy and of initiative for the redistribution of resources needful to meet priorities. For example, it would seem almost essential that DHAs should have well-developed policies on industrial relations and other personnel matters that are consistent across the entire district, and this would appear to call for having a manager of the personnel function based at the DHA headquarters and serving as the principal budget holder for that function, although subdivisions of the budget and staff for conducting routine personnel work might well be outposted to the unit level. And as regards the overall control of resources it is important that units do not become so self-contained or powerful as vested interests, as to be able to block resource redistribution. In most parts of Britain much remains to be done to rationalize and modernize the provision of acute hospital resources, and to transfer a growing proportion of resources into community care and other priority developments. Too-powerful unit managements could frustrate the rate of change to fulfil nationally agreed priorities. Henceforth the district finance function will have to learn to recast its functional expenditure allocations across a further matrix of allocation and monitoring based on the new unit arrangements. Standing financial instructions and the specification of authority limits and accountability requirements will need to be closely reviewed if the new arrangements are to be made to work efficiently and responsibly. These and other problems of the financial managements of units have been discussed by Bland (1981), and in various publications of the Association of Health Service Treasurers (also, see Wickings, 1983).

Clinicians in planning and budgeting

A distinctive feature of financial control in the NHS is the limited role played by its 'production managers'. These are the clinical consultants, and although a few of them double as department managers (e.g. for diagnostic and medical services), the majority of them who treat patients directly, and who determine the workload throughput of the hospitals, do not yet hold budgets for the expenditure they cause. This situation has arisen from the historical background of the development of the role and status of consultants, relative to the hospital management structure. It is defended on the doctrine of clinical autonomy whereby the consultant is personally responsible for the care of all of his patients, so that he argues that he must have the right to call out whatever *available* treatment (i.e. resources) he feels needful for those patients. This doctrine is not in dispute at the level of care for the *individual* patient, but as the growth of the NHS has slowed down and additionally has become constrained at the margin on a cash-limit basis of firm control against any expenditure beyond original authorizations, a growing number of clinicians have come to realize that in order to obtain the best outcome for all patients it is indeed necessary to pay heed to the costs of resources, the comparative costs and benefits of alternative modes of patient management, and the trade-offs of benefit at the margin from using scarce resources in different combinations.

Probably the most interesting initiative to involve clinicians has been the set of projects initiated by CASPE (Clinical Accountability, Service Planning and Evaluation) (see Wickings, 1983). With varying detail, these projects are testing ways in which to involve clinicians, and sometimes nurses and other resource-providers as well, in consultation on choices for the best uses of scarce resources which can be varied in amount by careful planning, but are restricted in their total cost by the cash-limit system. This will often involve making clinicians budget holders, although this is not an essential requirement, and a variety of responsibility-sharing arrangements is possible. Where clinicians do become budget holders, it is essential to segregate the variable costs of services which they can control, from the fixed and indirect costs that remain under the decision-making and control of function (and unit) budgetholders.

Specialty costing

There have been a number of projects developing methods of specialty costing, but only two of the new methods have been tested in several locations, with publication of the methods and results. These are the method of specialty costing by traditional cost accounting and allocation developed by Professor C.C. Magee, and the method of specialty costing by statistical regression analysis developed by Professor J.R. Ashford of Exeter University. Each method has its strengths and weaknesses. A basic question to be considered for any method of specialty costing (or budgeting) is how far support costs and overheads should be allocated to the specialty in addition to the direct costs of nursing, drugs, diagnostic tests, etc. directly controllable by the clinician or the clinically accountable team, including nurses. It appears that regions and the DHSS want *average* specialty costs inclusive of *all* costs, for monitoring and service-planning purposes, but it is not clear that costs other than those which are variable and controllable by management action within the budget period have any real value for routine monthly reporting and analysis. Perhaps this oversimplifies the matter, however. For example, if an individual clinician reduces the number of X-ray tests ordered, all that will be saved is the variable cost of X-ray film, etc. But if he and his colleagues jointly reduced the number of X-ray tests by some larger amount, then eventually the cutback in use of radiological services would reach the point where a staff vacancy need not be refilled, or a machine could be taken out of service and not replaced. In other words, there are step-type semi-fixed costs which become relevant to reporting and decision-making when major changes in resource-use patterns are considered, and the finance function must learn to identify and report on such opportunities for resource saving, so that resources can be diverted to expedite other developments of high priority.

Specialty costing is one of the financial information systems closely examined by the Körner programme on NHS information. The history of the development of specialty costing is reviewed in Carter (1983), and the most recent view of the history and state of the art is by an NHS Treasurer, Ray Hillman (1984). But both of these publications relate mainly to experience with the Magee system of specialty costing. This system was devised to provide information for planning. Some Magee cost components were based on infrequent samplings of workloads and rates of resource consumption. These were approximate costs, and approximation is sufficient for planning purposes. However, once it was suggested that specialty costs, or costs for individual clinicians within specialties, should be used as the basis for budgets and budgetary control, the systems requirements became very different. Budgets are a form of financial discipline upon the budget holders, and most budget holders naturally respond to budgetary discipline by challenging the accuracy and overall credibility of their budgetary expenditure reports, at least when those reports indicate overspending.

Clinical management budgets

In February 1983 the Secretary of State for Social Services commissioned an NHS Management Inquiry under the chairmanship of Mr. Roy Griffiths. The Inquiry reported in October of that year (the Griffiths Report, 1983). The Report dealt particularly with the need for the NHS to develop the 'general management' style and structure of management (i.e. the designation of 'general managers' at every level who would integrate across functions and expedite decision-making when the traditional search for consensus or unanimity might otherwise delay action). But also there were two main recommendations in the Report which were specifically financial. One was that all health authorities should be required to develop formal 'cost improvement' programmes and that progress on these should be monitored through the annual performance review process. The second was that NHS clinicians, as the natural managers of health care delivery, should be made financially accountable for the resources consumed in treating their patients. This should extend to clinical budgets which include not just the costs clinicians control, but also the indirect costs they can influence (e.g. the scale of testing activity in laboratories) and even their share of the overheads of the health district.

Before the Griffiths Inquiry Report had even been published, four health districts had been identified to take part in 'demonstrations' of how clinical management budgets should be made to work. These demonstrations began late in 1983 with assistance from management consultants. The first operational budgets for hospital consultants commenced on 1st April 1985. The preliminary work over some eighteen months in each district cost typically about £300,000. It appears that about 80% of this cost was expended on fees, software, hardware and staff time in upgrading the 'feeder systems'; while only about 20% of the cost was needed for developing the computerized processing of the budgets themselves, and the progress reports of cost against budgets. The problem was that, while expenditure costs anyway already had to be accurately recorded in order to produce the existing functional budgets and cost reports, the feeder systems for recording and reporting the use of resources (e.g. tests, X-rays, etc.) had not previously been used for financial control and often were inaccurate, incomplete, or at least too slow in their compilation and analysis to meet the requirements of prompt budgetary reporting. Therefore major work in systems development and computerization of feeder systems had to be carried out, especially for patient administration, pathology, radiology and pharmacy. Once this work was done, including the coding of all X-ray, laboratory, operating theatre and ward usage to the accountability of individual clinicians, it became possible to collect and report costs classified by clinician. After some months of collecting and assessing costs classified by clinical accountability, it then became possible to forecast and allocate realistic clinical budgets for 1985-86.

A report on progress in the demonstration districts was circulated by the DHSS as HN(85)3, early in 1985. This report did not indicate when clinical management budgeting might become compulsory for implementation throughout the NHS, but such implementation has to be gradual if it is to make best use of scarce resources in skilled manpower for systems development, and if it is to obtain the cooperation of clinicians in each district, as the new financial controls are introduced. It seems unlikely that clinical management budgeting will become mandatory within the NHS earlier than about 1990.

If clinical budgets are introduced in the NHS before the activity-information feeder systems are fully developed and tested, then there is a risk of alienation among the clinicians, and of a backlash of non-cooperation. In particular, if the underlying workload data costed to produce charges against budgets is frequently inaccurate, then the intended discipline of the clinical management budgeting process will break down, as clinicians would regularly challenge the validity of the budgetary-control reports rather than admit excessive use of clinical resources.

An example of the kind of monthly budgetary-control report which can be used in clinical management budgeting is reproduced as Table 6.2. Current-month and cumulative year-to-date expenditure is shown, together with budgeted amounts and variances. The report, which is simulated and does not itemize as many categories of cost as may in practice come to be used regularly in clinical budgets, begins with two sections detailing costs directly controlled by the head of the surgical team. The next section lists budgetary costs influenced by the team (i.e. costs of resources administered by nurses and other department heads, but which are dependent on the admission and treatment policies of clinical consultants). These include both the variable costs of wards and clinics, i.e. the consumables, and also the service department overheads which are fixed costs in the short run but may be altered by policy decisions on the form and volume of treatment over the longer run. The final two sections show the share of general overheads (over which the consultant has no direct influence) apportioned, plus a set of memorandum statistics which comprise selected indicators of both the surgical team's workload or throughput, and its volume consumption of key resources controllable by the team's decisions.

Savings incentives, virement and carry-forward

Some NHS treasurers have consciously sought to encourage their budget holders to identify and carry out planned savings. It is well established in the literature that 'budgetary slack' exists in almost all organizations. That is, budget holders typically claim somewhat more resources than they really expect to need, in order to have some safety margin against unexpected events, and also they recognize that certain activities may be of marginal benefit and could be cut to release funds if needful. It follows that treasurers can assist in the redeployment of resources if they make it worthwhile for budget holders to identify where savings or cuts could be made, and to trade these savings for authority to spend on other and more important facilities to which they attach priority. This approach can be formalized into written rules which can be publicized to budget holders to encourage their coopera tion. Different treasurers have developed different rules, although most approaches attempt to exclude purely fortuitous savings, e.g. those caused by falling demand, mild weather, accidental staff vacancies, etc., from recognition under the incentive schemes. A typical rule for the incentive element in the schemes is to provide that budget holders may vire (i.e. transfer) 50-100% of any savings of *recurrent* expenditure realized in the current year, into spending on any other reasonable *non-recurrent* expenditure in the current year, with most or all of the benefit of consequential savings in future years reverting to the authority as a whole.

The previous paragraph explained a specialized type of virement directly linked to planned savings. But budget holders may seek to transfer resources from one expenditure heading to another during the budget-setting process, or during the year when the budget is in force, either temporarily or under conditions where no long-term savings are in prospect. Treasurers vary in their willingness to approve such virement, and in what their rules allow. Certainly at the time of the financial management research for the Royal Commission, a major criticism from budget holders was regarding the limited discretion allowed to them to effect virement as of right. Even more restricted normally, are the opportunities for budget holders to carry forward any unspent funds from year to year. Treasurers commonly hold that they need to claw back unspent budget allocations when these arise, in order to balance the books overall against other budget holders who have overspent their budgets, often for reasons of meeting approved service needs and the demands of medical staff.

Financial control in the NHS

Budgetary control, flexibility and cash control

Budgetary control is obviously the prime vehicle by which NHS treasurers exercise financial control. But budgets and all other accounting systems in the health authorities, except accounting for capital expenditure, are based on income and expenditure accounting. That is, accruals are brought into account for debtors, creditors and stocks, but not for capital consumption, whereas the government's primary financial control concern is with actual cash payments, receipts and balances under the cash-limit control system. Generally this does not cause too much of a problem. For example, the invoiced expenditure can be charged properly to the

Table 6.2
Budget Variance Report for Surgical Team

| | Current month | | Expense codes | | Year to date | |
	Budget	Actual	Variance		Budget	Actual	Variance
				Staff costs controlled by team			
800	10998	10697	−301	Medical staff costs	54990	53166	−1024
				Other exp controlled by team			
809	12499	12014	−485	Prescribed drugs	62495	58712	−3783
811	290	248	−42	Histopathology – consumables	1450	1193	−257
820	7697	9016	1319	Radiology – consumables	40837	44808	3971
821	7283	7892	609	Operating theatre consumables	36415	38878	2463
	38767	39867	1100	Total costs controlled by team	197187	196757	570
				Costs influenced by team			
840	4166	5152	986	Ward – consumables	20830	22584	1754
841	83	149	66	Outpatient – consumables	415	495	80
845	11572	10983	−589	Ward – overheads	57860	58592	732
846	41	193	152	Outpatient – overheads	205	452	247
849	1565	1782	217	Pharmacy – overheads	7825	8571	746
851	833	814	−19	Histopathology – overheads	4165	4046	−119
861	8208	7932	−276	Operating theatre – overheads	41040	40643	−397
868	4107	4182	75	ECG – overheads	20535	21916	1381
880	15485	15654	169	Physiotherapy-hydrotherapy	77425	75296	−2129
	46060	46841	781	Total costs influenced by team	230300	232595	2295

General services overheads

Code							
890	Unit administration	2499	2261	-238	12495	11236	-1259
891	Catering	973	1028	55	4865	5386	521
892	Domestic	1219	817	-402	6095	3932	-2163
894	Linen/laundry	832	946	114	4160	4701	541
896	Estate management	7499	6753	-746	37495	35388	-2107
	Total general serv. overheads	13022	11805	-1217	65110	60643	-4467
	Total costs for team	97849	98513	664	491597	489995	-1602

Memorandum statistics

Code							
900	Inpatients – days	857	878	21	4285	4382	97
903	Outpatients – attendances	148	193	45	740	849	109
914	Histopathology – tests	499	296	-203	2495	2650	155
937	Radiology – tests	473	682	209	2801	3690	889
940	Operating theatre – hours	599	634	35	2995	3286	291

Preliminary draft for a report, with simulated cost figures, reproduced from the CASPE Project at Lewisham and N. Southwark Health Authority, by permission.

internal accounts and budgets, for accuracy of measurement and of controlling budget holders, while the cash payments owing to suppliers can be paid early or late within the authorized period as best meets balancing-out to cash limits. It is possible for over and underspending to be balanced out between districts within a region, or even between regions, so long as the total authorized spending of the NHS as a whole is not exceeded. It is recognized after all, that there is unmet need for the services of the NHS, and that there is no inherent virtue in the service failing to spend the full moneys voted by Parliament.

The NHS is unique among major services directly managed or controlled by central government in having the facility for the carry-forward of unspent funds from one year to the next (up to 1% of combined revenue and capital allocations), and also the facility for virement between capital and revenue (up to 1% from revenue to capital, and up to 10% from capital to revenue). The higher percentage allowed for capital arises because of its smaller magnitude, but also perhaps mainly because weather and other problems make it much more difficult to control the progress of capital projects and the timing of payment obligations. All the arrangements described here combine to give NHS treasurers an unusual amount of flexibility in organising their end-of-year finances to the best advantage of their authorities, or in dealing with such vagaries as the rate of pay-and-prices inflation turning out to be significantly different from that anticipated when the NHS cash planning limits were set before the beginning of the financial year.

Within each Health Authority financial control is exercised primarily by the monitoring and control of budgets. This is supported by other conventional forms of internal control over purchasing, contracts and cash disbursements, etc. But formal systems of commitment accounting are not widely used. NHS authorities are not allowed to invest any savings or surplus funds (except trust funds), or any end-of-year balances. Rather these must be netted-in with the cash balance at bank, and this is never supposed to exceed a modest working balance. The latter is regulated by control of the timing of drawing further funds from Government against the authorized cash limits (see CIPFA, 198 and updates). These regulations reflect the fact that NHS finance is an integral part of Exchequer financing.

Clinician or specialty budgets are still only developmental. So the main focus of internal financial control is on expenditure against funtional budgets at unit level. This involves keeping the expenditure accounts up to date, and reporting on progress at least monthly. The best form of control is self-control – in this case the control exercised by budget holders over their own budget balances and expenditure commitments. A guideline rule in good budgetary reporting is that performance reports on the preceding period should be supplied to budget holders before the midpoint of the succeeding period, so that budget holders will feel able and motivated to correct their performance in time to improve the next reports they receive on progress to budget.

Internal audit

Internal audit in the NHS has received some criticism (e.g. Royal Commission Research Paper No. 2, 1978). NHS finance offices tend to be understaffed, both absolutely and as regards the proportion of senior, professionally qualified staff, by comparison with local authorities and other large institutions. Priority in the use of staff after the 1974 reorganization was given to the development of new budgetary and management information systems. In general, internal audit was not awarded a high priority. Given the low priority, and the low status deriving from that, it appeared that most of the more able young accountants sought to avoid working in the internal audit section. This was not a desirable state, as internal audit should be of good quality in every organization, and arguably every qualified accountant should have training and work experience in at least one of internal or external audit. But there is evidence that the status and grading of internal audit posts was raised during the management restructuring following the 1982 reorganization.

Performance measurement

The NHS is making increasing use of performance measures for assessing or comparing efficiency or effectiveness, in spite of the difficulty of measuring the ultimate output, or the enhancement of health state in the work of the NHS. Moreover the mix of specialties and conditions treated allegedly varies substantially between different hospitals, partly because consultants practising nominally in the same specialty often develop sub-specialty interests and attract a preponderance of cases meeting that interest, by referral from outside the immediate catchment area of their own hospital. And hospitals as diverse as small general hospitals, modern district general hospitals and major teaching hospitals will obviously differ greatly in the case mix treated, and in the sophistication and costliness of the back-up resources needed. To date the performance measures available have been mainly straightforward measures of the overall costs of whole hospitals; e.g. cost per inpatient-day, cost per inpatient-case, cost per outpatient-attendance. Combined with these are physical measures such as average length of inpatient-stay, average percentage of beds occupied, etc. The information allowing performance comparisons of these kinds to be made between different hospitals and health districts is published only annually, and after some delay, and so does not appear to be used greatly for internal performance review purposes. The alleged large differences in the clinical workload between one hospital and another moreover reduce the moral impact of using these measures to prove any scope and need for greater efficiency. Even to the extent that this allegation is valid, however, it does not negate the benefit of using these and perhaps further measures of cost and resource utilization on a continuing basis *within* each individual institution. That is, trend performance *over time* within a single institution can often give information as useful for spotting performance problems and for initiating investigation into the facts, leading to pressure for remedial action if needed, as can information that is purely comparative *between* institutions (see DHSS, 1983).

6.4 EXTERNAL REPORTING IN THE NATIONAL HEALTH SERVICE

NHS external reporting

Statutory reporting

Individual health authorities are not required by statute or regulation to publish annual accounts in the manner that is expected of local authorities, water authorities or public corporations. However, district health authorities are required to submit a range of reports to the RHAs and the DHSS. These include Health Activity Analysis statistics on patients treated and workload, annual census returns on all manpower employed in the NHS at a particular date in the year, data for the Financial Information System operated by the Treasury to monitor public spending (termed FIS (HA) in its NHS format – see CIPFA (1980) for details), and statutory returns of both financial accounting and cost accounting data. However, the latter are not in the form of conventional accounts, but instead comprise detailed and lengthy schedules reporting expenditure by functional category and by detailed subjective analysis of all expenditure in the case of the financial accounts, and by institution and functional category in the case of the cost accounts. In both instances the accounting data are supplied on an income and expenditure basis, rather than on the cash receipts and payments basis involved in the monitoring and control of expenditure to cash limits; however, additionally a statement reconciling income and expenditure with the cash allocations provided is supplied for the DHSS. From April 1987 the reporting of specialty costs will be required additionally (see NHS/DHSS, 1984.)

Voluntary local reporting

At the local level the progress of expenditure against budget is reported to the monthly Health Authority meetings, at least in most authorities. These meetings are open to the public and are attended by the press, and certainly if there is any serious overspending or other identified problem of major import, one would expect this to be widely reported and critically assessed, locally at least and very probably nationally as well if there are any major issues of probity, or of policy affecting patient care. But some health service treasurers have not been content to rely solely on this form of public reporting and accountability. They have gone further and voluntarily produced annual financial accounts and costing reports, supported by statistical and other information often including illustrative charts and graphs. Extracts from the annual report of the Treasurer of the Coventry Health Authority are reproduced in Figs. 6.2 and 6.3. Fig. 6.2 shows expenditure on a cash (limits) basis, while 6.3 shows hospital and community spending on an income-and-expenditure accounting basis.

It is of course a moot point how far there is need for, or benefit from, detailed reporting of financial performance at the local level. Given that NHS expenditure is funded centrally, with no burden on the rates, it is a reasonable supposition that the degree of local interest in the details of NHS expenditure is relatively limited. It also seems likely that many members of health authorities are unable to evaluate the detail of financial reports. Few of them have any training or experience in management, and even fewer of them have any detailed comprehension of the niceties of finance or of accounting measurement and disclosure. This might suggest that local financial reporting is a waste of time. Alternatively, it may suggest that the challenge to the local

The diagram below shows the sources of finance available to the Authority during 1983-84 and the way in which this finance was used.

There are four main sources of funds:

(a) Central Funding –
cash drawings approved by the DHSS and payments made centrally (e.g. income tax and national insurance contributions).

(b) Income –
the amount the Authority raises itself through the provision of facilities for private treatment, supply of drugs at hospitals and prescription charges raised by the FPS.

(c) Balances –
the change in the Authority's net current assets and liabilities during the year.

(d) Payments by other authorities –
the supply of goods and services by other authorities.

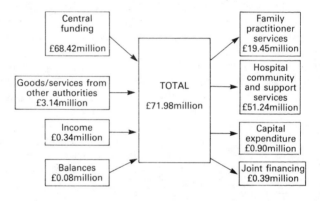

The balances held at the end of the year were as follows:

1982-83	Current Assets/Liabilities	1983-84	Change
£000s		£000s	£000s
1,859	Stocks	1,922	+63
245	Debtors	1,110	+865
1,069	Cash	27	−1,042
3,850	Creditors	3,817	+33
	NET MOVEMENT IN BALANCES		−81

Thus £81,000 of the Authority's balances was used during the year to finance expenditure.

Fig. 6.2 Sources and application of funds 1983-84. (Reproduced from the Coventry Health Authority *Financial Report and Accounts 1983-84*, p. 35.)

Coventry Health Authority spent £50,966,000 during 1983-84 (excluding Joint Finance and the Family Practitioner service).

What did this money provide?

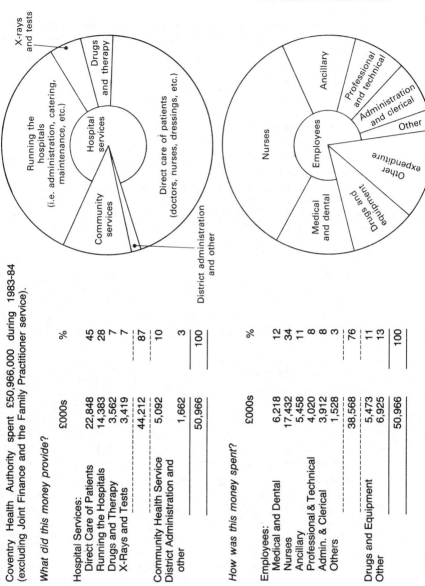

	£000s	%
Hospital Services:		
Direct Care of Patients	22,848	45
Running the Hospitals	14,383	28
Drugs and Therapy	3,562	7
X-Rays and Tests	3,419	7
	44,212	87
Community Health Service	5,092	10
District Administration and other	1,662	3
	50,966	100

How was this money spent?

	£000s	%
Employees:		
Medical and Dental	6,218	12
Nurses	17,432	34
Ancillary	5,458	11
Professional & Technical	4,020	8
Admin. & Clerical	3,912	8
Others	1,528	3
	38,568	76
Drugs and Equipment	5,473	11
Other	6,925	13
	50,966	100

Fig. 6.3 Summary of net revenue expenditure 1983-84. (Reproduced from the Coventry Health Authority *Financial Report and Accounts 1983-84*, p. 32.)

treasurer is all the greater – to produce financial, accounting and activity information in a form, with appropriate visual aids, that even members without previous financial experience can begin to understand. Surely this alternative approach is worth developing further.

Accounting standards and NHS reporting

All professional accountants have a natural interest in how far the Statements of Standard Accounting Practice (SSAPs) adopted by the accountancy profession are relevant to financial disclosure in their own industry or sector. Clearly there is some instinctive feeling that all organizations ought to be able to conform to a common set of accounting measurement and reporting standards, and yet it is clear that many organizational and operational characteristics are very different as between trading (and especially profit-seeking) organizations and those organizations whose whole raison d'etre is the provision of public services, as in the NHS, where an unspent surplus at the end of the year would be interpreted as failure to provide maximum service, rather than as evidence of economic efficiency. This problem was examined, as it affects the NHS, by the Association of Health Service Treasurers (Final Report, 1982). Their conclusions were as follows: SSAP 2 (Accounting Policies) 'is of fundamental importance'; certain other standards 'may be relevant' (i.e. SSAP 5 (VAT), SSAP 9 (Stocks and Work in Progress), SSAP 10 (Source and Application of Funds), and SSAP 18 (Accounting for Contingencies)); and other standards 'may have limited application' (i.e. SSAP 6 (Extraordinary and Prior-Year Adjustments), SSAP 13 (R&D), and SSAP 17 (Post Balance-Sheet Events)). The remaining SSAPs were considered to be 'not applicable' to the NHS, at least in present circumstances (e.g. where capital assets are neither capitalized nor depreciated). The foregoing is not of great importance to the extent that the existing forms of statutory reporting take no account of standard accounting practices. But this could change within a few years, and anyway, to the extent that DHAs seek to prepare voluntary local reports for the information of Authority members and the local community, treasurers will probably increasingly seek to conform to the standards generally accepted by their peers employed in other industries and other branches of the public services.

External audit

The external audit of the NHS is discussed in Chapter 7.

EXAMINATION QUESTIONS

6.1 Explain the key features of financial resource allocation within the National Health Service, and consider the possible advantages and disadvantages of this system from the viewpoints of (a) Parliament, (b) Regional Health Authorities and (c) the operational level of the health services.

6.2 Discuss the implications of the consultative document *Patients First* with particular reference to the role of the Finance function in the National Health Service. (CIPFA. Policy Making in the Public Sector. November 1980)

6.3 Critically describe the methods by which the government allocates resources to . . . health authorities through RAWP. (CIPFA. Policy Making in the Public Sector. November 1978)

6.4 In the case of . . . Health Authorities . . . , explain the principal arrangements which exist for the coordination of their work with that of local authorities. Could the arrangements be improved? (CIPFA. Policy Making in the Public Sector. November 1979)

6.5 Discuss the advantages and disadvantages of joint financing arrangements between local authorities and health authorities. (CIPFA. Policy Making in the Public Sector. November 1980)

6.6 'The government is currently encouraging the 'privatization' of as many public sector services as possible. Discuss the policy-making implications of privatization for a public sector organization of your choice.' Please answer in respect of the NHS. (CIPFA. Policy Making in the Public Sector. November 1981)

6.7 'In a public sector organization of your choice what machinery would usually be employed by senior management to ensure that the financial effects are properly taken into account when policies are being developed? Could it be improved?' Please answer in respect of the NHS. (CIPFA. Policy Making in the Public Sector. November 1978)

6.8 The present method by which Health Authorities obtain

their capital money has been criticized.

(i) Outline the method by which Regional . . . Health Authorities and Health Districts obtain their capital money and how cash limit controls are operated.

The National Health Service obtains its capital monies by direct allocation from the Department of Health and Social Security. The sum allocated is seldom adequate to meet all requirements. The allocations are made direct to Regional Health Authorities which then reallocate them to constituent . . . Health Districts. Capital monies are subject to cash limits control. Overspendings have to be carried forward and underspendings in excess of 10% are lost.

(ii) Discuss the advantages and disadvantages of the above system and comment on the implications if Regional . . . Health Authorities and Health Districts were to be allowed to raise loans and borrow in the money market.

(CIPFA. Accounting and Audit in the Public Sector. November 1980)

6.9 Health authority treasurers have to keep careful records of cash receipts and payments for reporting their performance to their cash limits. But they operate their budgetary control systems and prepare their final accounts on an income and expenditure basis, and it is understood that most treasurers would not want to abandon this arrangement in favour of a single system of accounting and budgeting based on cash flows. What reasons do you think treasurers would give for their viewpoint, and how far would you support or reject the reasons you identify?

6.10 'Describe the purposes and discuss the relevance of UK Statements of Standard Accounting Practice on the reporting of a public sector organization of your choice.' Please answer in respect of the NHS. (CIPFA. Accounting and Audit in the Public Sector. November 1978)

6.11 'Explain the main points of SSAP2, Disclosure of Accounting Policies, in particular the four fundamental accounting concepts. Discuss its application to a public sector organization of your choice.' Please answer the question in respect of the NHS. (CIPFA. Public Sector Accounting. November 1981)

6.12 Examine the case for and against the introduction of depreciation accounting in the National Health Service, given the particular manner in which its capital funding is presently arranged.

6.13 'District Health Authorities should be established for the smallest geographical areas within which it is possible to carry out the integrated planning, provision and development of primary care and other community health services.' (DHSS Circular HC(80)8 – LAC(80)3) Comment on the implications of this circular for the policy and resource planning processes in the new District Health Authorities. (CIPFA. Policy Making in the Public Sector. November 1981)

6.14 Discuss the advantages and disadvantages which you think will result from the restructuring of the UK National Health Service which took place in 1982. (Certified Accountants. Level 2, Paper 2.5D. June 1983)

6.15 Describe and discuss the main criteria selected by the Resource Allocation Working Party in 1975 for the allocation of resources to Regional Health Authorities in the National Health Service. (Certified Accountants. Level 2, Paper 2.5D. December 1983)

6.16 Discuss the implications for policy making in the National Health Service of the introduction of Unit Management Teams. (CIPFA. Policy Making in the Public Sector. December 1982) In answering this question you are recommended to take account of the recommendations on General Management included in the Griffiths Inquiry Report of 1983.

6.17 'Outline and discuss the function of performance indicators in the policy process of a public sector organization of your choice.' Please answer this question in respect of the NHS. (CIPFA. Policy Making in the Public Sector. December 1983)

BIBLIOGRAPHY

Ashford, J.R. *et al.*, (1981) 'A case study from the field of health care: modelling hospital costs', *Journal of Operational Research*, 32, No. 10, 851-64.

Association of Health Service Treasurers (AHST) *Budgetary Arrangements and Responsibilities in the NHS Following HC(80)8* (1981); *Financial Arrangements in the Restructured National Health Service* (February 1981); *Standard Accounting Practices for the National Health Service*, Final Report (February 1982); *Report of the Capital and Asset Accounting Working Party* (December 1984).

Bevan, G., Copeman, H., Perrin, J., and Rosser, R. (1980) *Health Care: Priorities and Management*, London, Croom Helm.

Bland, G. (1981) *Unit Budgets: a Critical Review*, Research and

Publications Sub-group of the Accounting Panel of the Chartered Institute of Public Finance and Accountancy.

Butts, M., Irvine, D. and Whitt, C. (1981) *From Principles to Practice (A commentary on health service planning and resource allocation in England from 1970 to 1980)*, London, Nuffield Provincial Hospitals Trust.

Carter, J., (1983) *Recent Developments in Financial Information for Management in Health Services*, Warwick Papers in Industry, Business and Administration, No. 10, Warwick University.

Chapman, L. (1979) *Your Disobedient Servant*, Penguin.

CIPFA (1980) *Health*, Vol. 30 of the Financial Information Service, (with looseleaf updates).

CIPFA, jointly with Association of Health Service Treasurers (1982) *Local Accountability* (the need and scope for health authority published annual financial reports).

Copeman, H.A. (1978) *Departmental Control and Financial Information*, Warwick University, Centre for Industrial, Economic and Business Research, Technical Paper for the Royal Commission on the NHS.

Davies, C. (1983) *Underused and Surplus Property in the National Health Service*, DHSS.

DHSS (1972) *Management Arrangements for the Reorganised National Health Service* (Grey Book), HMSO.

DHSS (1976) *Sharing Resources for Health in England*, Report of the Resource Allocation Working Party (the RAWP Report), HMSO.

DHSS (1976) *The National Health Service Planning System* (Blue Book).

DHSS (1979) *Patients First*, a consultative paper on the structure and management of the NHS, HMSO.

DHSS (1980) *Health Services Development: Structure and Management*, DHSS Circular HC(80)8.

DHSS (1980) *Hospital Services: the Future Pattern of Hospital Provision in England*.

DHSS (1980) *Report of the Advisory Group on Resource Allocation*.

DHSS (1981) *Care in Action*, a handbook of policies and priorities for the health and personal social services in England, HMSO.

DHSS (1982) *The NHS Planning System*, DHSS Circular HC(82)6.

DHSS (1983) National Summary of Performance Indicators for 1981 (and also more detailed volumes separately for each of the fourteen regions).

DHSS (1983) *Health Care and Its Costs*.

DHSS (1984) *The Health Service in England Annual Report 1984*, HMSO.

DHSS (1985) *Health Services Management Budgeting* (HN(85)3).

Drummond, M.J. (1980) *Principles of Economic Appraisal in Health*

Care, London, Oxford University Press.

Griffiths, R. (1983) *NHS Management Inquiry Report*, DHSS. (Also see HC(84)13, DHSS).

Guillebaud Report (1956) *Report of the Committee of Enquiry into the Cost of the National Health Service*, Cmnd. 9663, HMSO.

Hillman, R. (1984) *Specialty Costing in the National Health Service*, AHST/CIPFA.

Holland, W.W., et al (1980) *The RAWP Project*, Social Medicine and Health Services Research Unit, St. Thomas' Hospital and Medical School, London.

House of Commons Committee of Public Accounts (1981) 17th Report, *Financial Control and Accountability in the National Health Service*, HMSO.

Jones, T. and Prowle, M. (1984) *Health Service Finance* (2nd Edition), London, Certified Accountants Educational Trust.

Klein, R. and Buxton, M. (1978) *Allocating Health Resources, a Commentary on the Report of the Resource Allocation Working Party*, Royal Commission on the National Health Service, Research Paper No. 3, HMSO.

Kogan, M. et al (1978) *The Working of the NHS*, Royal Commission on the National Health Service, Research Paper No. 1.

Lapsley, I. (1981) 'A case for depreciation accounting in UK health authorities, *Accounting and Business Research*, Winter 1981, 21-9.

Lapsley, I. and Prowle, M.J. (1978a) *Audit in the National Health Service: a Conceptual Pespective*, Warwick University, Centre for Industrial, Economic and Business Research, Technical Paper for the Royal Commission on the NHS.

Lapsley, I. and Prowle, M.J. (1978b) *The Effectiveness of Functional Budgetary Control in the National Health Service; an Empirical Investigation*, Warwick University, Centre for Industrial, Economic and Business Research, Technical Paper for the Royal Commission on the NHS.

Le Quesne Report (1977) *Report of the Working Party on Resource Allocation in the NHS*, University of London.

Levitt, R. and Wall, A. (1984) *The Reorganised National Health Service* (3rd edition) London, Croom Helm. This is the definitive textbook on the NHS following the 1974 and 1982 reorganizations.

McKeown, T. (1976) *The Role of Medicine: Dream, Mirage or Nemesis*, London Nuffield Provincial Hospitals Trust.

Magee, C.C. (1981) 'The Potential for Specialty Costing in the NHS', *Public Finance and Accountancy*, 41-4.

Magee, C.C. and Osmolski, R.J. (1978) *A Comprehensive System of Management Information for Financial Planning, Decision Making and Control in the Hospital Service*, Warwick University, Centre for Industrial, Economic and Business Research, Technical Paper for the Royal Commission on the NHS.

Maxwell, R.J. (1981) *Health and Wealth*, Lexington Books (D.C. Heath). For international comparisons and policy discussion.

NHS/DHSS Steering Group on Health Services Information (Chairman, Mrs. E. Korner), (1984) *Sixth Report* (on the collection and use of financial information), HMSO.

Office of Health Economics, *Compendium of Health Statistics*, London, Office of Health Economics (new editions are published every few years).

Owen, A.J. (1978) *Health Authority Capital Budgeting: The State of the Art in Theory and Practice*, Warwick University, Centre for Industrial Economic and Business Research, Technical Paper for the Royal Commission on the NHS.

Perrin, J. (1978) *Capital Maintenance and Allocation in the Health Service*, Warwick University, Centre for Industrial, Economic and Business Research, Technical Paper for the Royal Commission on the NHS.

Perrin, J. *et al.* (1978) *The Management of Financial Resources in the National Health Service*, Royal Commission on the National Health Service, Research Paper No. 2, HMSO.

Perrin, J. *et al.* (1982) 'Depreciation accounting', in a series of four articles relevant to the NHS, *Public Finance and Accountancy*, May 1982.

Perrin, J. (1984) 'Accounting for Public Sector Assets', in *Issues in Public Sector Accounting*, Eds. A. Hopwood and C. Tomkins. Deddington, Philip Allan.

Rigden, M.S. (1983) *Health Service Finance and Accounting*, London, Heinemann.

Royal Commission on the National Health Service (1979) *Report*, Cmnd. 7615, HMSO. (See also Copeman, 1978; Klein and Buxton, 1978; Kogan et al., 1978; Lapsley and Prowle, 1978a and b; Magee and Osmolski, 1978; Owen, 1978; Perrin, 1978; Perrin et al., 1978.)

Salmon, P. (1983) *Report of the DHSS/NHS Audit Working Group*, DHSS.

Solomons, D. (1965) *Divisional Performance: Measurement and Control*, Richard D. Irwin.

Thornton Baker Associates (1984) *Competitive Tendering in the Provision of Domestic, Catering and Laundry Services*, Nuffield Provincial Hospitals Trust.

Wickings, I. (1983) *Effective Unit Management*, London, King Edward's Hospital Fund for London.

Wickings, I., Coles, J., Flux, R., and Howard, L. (1983) 'Review of clinical budgeting and costing experiments', *British Medical*

Journal, Vol. 286, 12 February.
Winyard, G.F.A. (1981) 'RAWP – New Injustice for Old?', *British Medical Journal*, Vol. 283, 3 October.

Essential reading

CIPFA-FIS Vol. 30 (*Health*) and Jones & Prowle (see bibliography) provide good detail on financial practice and statutory requirements for the NHS. Bevan et al and the Royal Commission Research Paper No. 2 cover wider issues from financial and planning perspectives. The only periodical with extensive coverage of NHS accounting and financial topics is *Public Finance and Accountancy*, published by the Chartered Institute of Public Finance and Accountancy.

GLOSSARY

Carry-forward An amount of funding allocation, or budget, unspent at year-end and which is allowed to be carried forward for spending in the next year, additional to the next year's regular funding.
RAWP RAWP stands for Resource Allocation Working Party, but the abbreviation is used commonly to signify the philosophy and process of allocating NHS (financial) resources so as in time to raise all authorities to an equal standard of resources as determined on a weighted-population basis.
Reserves In trading accounts 'reserves' usually signifies an element of past profits or capital contributions retained for investment in the assets of the enterprise. In the NHS, in contrast, 'reserves' usually denotes a small fraction of the revenue funding allocation which is being held back during the early part of a budget year, either to meet the gradual rise of inflation, or else to meet the cash needs of some specific commitment that commences only later in the year.
SIFT SIFT stands for Service Increment for Teaching. It is an increment to the funding allocation that regional health authorities receive on RAWP target criteria.
Specialty The term 'specialty' is used for specialized branches of (usually) hospital medicine (e.g. cardiology or neurology). Each specialty is normally headed by one or more 'consultants' with supporting junior doctors who between them manage an allocation of beds, ward space, operating theatre time, etc.

Top-slicing The deduction from any funding allocation, as a first charge, of funds needed by the funding body for its own operations, or for any reserves or priority schemes it supports, prior to the distribution of all remaining funds to lower tiers by criteria it may determine (e.g. RAWP).

Virement The process of transferring financial allocations from one budget or budget heading to another. Virement can arise between the budgets of a single budget holder, between budget holders, or between revenue and capital budget allocations at the level of the health authority as a whole. The amount of the latter type of virement is regulated within limits specified by the DHSS from time to time, as administered by RHAs to balance out the funds within the NHS as a whole, nationally.

7

External audit

AUDIT OF CENTRAL GOVERNMENT

7.1 INTRODUCTION

This chapter discusses the external audit of public sector bodies, its nature and its objectives. Comparisons will be made with the audit of companies and other organizations in the private sector. There will be discussion of recent developments in public sector audit and of the differing views which have emerged about its proper scope and organization. There will be no attempt to give instruction in detailed audit techniques: for that a specialized professional training is necessary.

It has already been shown that the public sector in the UK comprises a variety of organizations; but the main divisions of the sector into central government, local authorities, and nationalized industries and other public corporations will be followed in examining the role of audit. Before examining the three main areas, it is necessary to be clear about the essential nature of an external audit. What is it? What is it for?

The clues to the answers to these questions lie in the words 'external' and 'independent'. In the UK public sector, an external audit is intended first, to provide an assurance as to the reliability of the published accounts of the audited body. Second, it is intended to provide a further assurance as to the regularity (see Section 7.3) of the underlying transactions. Third, in the central and local government sectors but not the nationalized industries it aims to provide an assessment of the efficiency with which the body performs its functions. The auditor provides these assurances and assessments from the standpoint of someone outside the body in question and independent of it. His examinations and reports are expected to be honest, impartial, dispassionate, indeed fearless; as well, it is to be hoped, as expert and thorough. The independence of the external auditor is crucial if his reports are to have credibility and authority. How such independence may be secured is discussed below.

This brief definition of external audit leads immediately to two further questions. First, to whom are these assurances about financial or other matters, provided by this independent character, to be addressed? Second, what is the relationship between external and internal auditors? An answer to the second question can conveniently wait. The answer to the first depends on the constitutional position of the audited body: to whom is it answerable for its actions? A government department is answerable through its Minister and Accounting Officer (see Section 7.9) directly to Parliament. A nationalized industry is answerable to the responsible Minister – the electricity or gas industry to the Secretary of State for Energy, for example – and through him to Parliament on its general performance, but not on its day-to-day operations. A local authority is constitutionally independent of Parliament but can do only what Parliament empowers it to do. While Parliament acts on behalf of national electors and taxpayers and is distinct from the Executive – i.e. the central government – local authorities act on behalf of local electors and ratepayers in both a representative and an executive capacity. It follows that the external auditor of a government department reports to Parliament, the auditor of a nationalized industry to the Secretary of State, and the auditor of local authorities to the authority itself. In doing so, however, they always have in mind the interests of the general public, particularly their interests as the providers of the funds to pay for public services, and all these audit reports are normally publicly available.

The public audit services of most advanced countries set out to provide, in very broad terms, a financial audit of accounts and an efficiency or value for money audit of activities. The first of these centres on the adequacy of the systems for controlling the receipt and payment of public funds, the second on the way the resources purchased with those funds – manpower, capital equipment, buildings, supplies and so on – are allocated and utilized.

The term audit is sometimes applied to a different type of external check; for example a 'social audit', advocated by some people, would attempt to establish how far public institutions, and indeed large private corporations, had contributed to social, community or similar goals. We are not here concerned with these wider remits as such, though social considerations often play a part in public expenditure decisions and must be recognized and allowed for by the auditor. The critical examination of financial and resource management is a convenient general description of much of his activity.

7.2 AUDIT OF CENTRAL GOVERNMENT: THE STATUTORY BASIS

The law which for many years governed the external audit of central government, and still provides the basic authority for some of it, was the Exchequer and Audit Departments Act of 1866, as modified, in significant but not fundamental respects, by the 1921 Act. The 1866 Act brought together, under the newly created office of the Comptroller and Auditor General, the duties formerly discharged separately by the Comptroller General of the Exchequer, whose origins went back for several centuries, and Commissioners of Audit. It was part of the 19th century reforms intended to give Parliament an effective and unified control over the use of public revenues. At that time the largest spenders of those revenues were the Army and the Navy, and what was then called the Office of Works and Public Building. The Act provided for the appointment, by the Crown, of the Comptroller and Auditor General (whose full title is Comptroller General of the Receipt and Issue of Her Majesty's Exchequer and Auditor General of Public Accounts), but it did not give a separate statutory existence to his department, the Exchequer and Audit Department. It provided instead (as amended in 1921) that the C&AG, as he is always called for short, might appoint staff who would assist him in carrying out his statutory responsibilities for the examination, certification and reporting on government departments' accounts. The C&AG thus took personal responsibility for all the work of his officers, and until quite recently signed personally the audit certificate and report on virtually every account which the department audits. This contrasts with the arrangements in private auditing firms, where each partner manages the audit of his own accounts; or in local government where each district or commercial auditor is responsible by law for auditing and reporting on particular local authorities' accounts.

The C&AG has always been appointed from outside his Department, almost invariably with the wide experience of public expenditure and finance provided by service in the Treasury, and has not himself been a professional auditor or accountant. Appointment of someone with the latter kind of background would be possible, but since public audit is by no means confined to the financial audit of accounts and demands a close knowledge of the operations of Parliament and of the departments of State, it is clearly desirable that the person in charge should be familiar with public finance and with the problems of managing large departments and securing the best use of very large sums of public money.

The independence of the C&AG, and thus of all his staff, is secured by his appointment by the Queen, on the advice of the Prime Minister, by the payment of his salary directly from the Consolidated Fund, not from annual Votes, and by his freedom from dismissal except on a motion passed by both Houses of Parliament. He does not answer to any Minister of the Government, and indeed, although he works on behalf of Parliament, makes most of his reports to Parliament, and is now under the National Audit Act 1983 (see below) an officer of the House of Commons, he cannot be instructed by the House, or by any of its Committees, to undertake particular investigations. Thus within the broad statutory framework governing his audit he decides himself how to lay out the resources of his staff, how to conduct his audit work, and whether to report.

The audit of government departments can be divided into two sectors: the financial, more strictly the certification, audit, and the value for money audit. The basis for the certification audit was laid down in the 1866 Act, which established the arrangements by which the Executive – the government – should account for the public revenues they raised and the public funds they spent. Much of the Act dealt with accounting procedures and responsibilities, but its main provisions, which still apply, can be simply summarized. Departments were required to prepare annually 'appropriation accounts' showing how the sums voted by Parliament for specific purposes and services had been spent, what balances remained at the end of the year to be surrendered to the Exchequer, and occasionally – what was regarded for many years as a rather serious misdemeanour – how much on a particular vote or votes had been spent in excess of Parliamentary authority. As already noted, the C&AG had to examine and certify these accounts and report thereon to Parliament. If the Treasury failed to present to Parliament by the due date any report by the C&AG, then the C&AG himself was empowered to do so. This power has never had to be invoked.

Moving forward over 50 years, the Exchequer and Audit Departments Act of 1921 modified and updated the 1866 Act in three significant respects. First, provided that the C&AG was satisfied that the departments had themselves properly examined and confirmed the correctness of the vouchers supporting expenditure, he was allowed to dispense with the 100% audit of their transactions which appeared to be required by the original Act for the civil departments, though it must be highly doubtful whether for many years before 1921 anything of this order had been achieved, or even attempted. Instead he was given discretion to have regard to the departments' own examination in deciding the extent of his check of transactions. Though not specifically mentioned in the Act, the concept of a 'test audit' was thus established. The way in which test audits should be carried out, to give a reasonable degree of assurance about the particular accounting systems to which they are applied, is an important aspect of audit techniques. It has led into the systems-based audit and the use of statistical sampling where large numbers of transactions are involved, and its application is having to be rethought with the rapid extension of computerized accounting systems and auditing software.

Second, the 1921 Act provided for the preparation and audit in suitable cases of trading, manufacturing or production accounts as well as the appropriation accounts. The latter are purely cash accounts (as explained in Chapter 2). Trading accounts are prepared on a similar basis to private sector commercial accounts, with balance sheets, sources and application of funds statements, and are fully accrued.

The third innovation in 1921 was to require the C&AG to examine the revenue departments' accounts (Inland Revenue, Customs and Excise) as well as those of the spending departments. But there was, and is, an important difference. The C&AG is expected to satisfy himself, and to assure Parliament and the public, about the regularity of the appropriation accounts. In his audit of the Revenue Departments, however, he is required to satisfy himself only that the departments had established satisfactory procedures for the assessment and collection of all revenue due. He was not required to certify that all revenue which should have been collected had been; still less that individual taxpayers had been correctly assessed for tax. That would indeed have been an impossible task. This approach appears to be an early formulation of a 'systems-based audit', antedating by several decades the general adoption of that technique in both commercial and public audit work.

No further change in the law governing the C&AG's work occurred for another 60 years. But it was progressively developed on a non-statutory basis, particularly in the value for money field, with the active encouragement of Parliament through the Public Accounts Committee (see below), and the acquiescence of government departments. Then in the late 1970s and early 1980s an upsurge of Parliamentary interest in the public audit system coinciding with a new approach by the C&AG to his role and the responsibilities of his department led to a wide ranging debate and to the National Audit Act of 1983. The main strands in that debate are discussed below, but it is convenient to conclude this section with a summary of the main provisions of the 1983 Act.

The Act provided that:

(a) The C&AG should continue to be appointed by Her Majesty on a motion for an address by the House of Commons made by the Prime Minister, whose advice now however had to be tendered in agreement with the Chairman of the Committee of Public Accounts. The Chairman, who had previously been consulted informally, was thus given a statutory role in the appointment, recognizing the close interest of Parliament in the person, as well as the office.

(b) The C&AG should be an officer of the House of Commons; but – subject of course to his statutory duties – he should have 'complete discretion in the discharge of his functions' including in particular whether and how to carry out a 3E type examination under the Act (see (e) below). In taking such decisions however he was required to 'take into account any proposals made by the Committee of Public Accounts'. So was resolved the argument whether the C&AG should be subject to the directions of the PAC or, as some Members of Parliament would have liked, also of other Select Committees.

(c) A Public Accounts Commission should be set up, to include the Leader of the House and the Chairman of the PAC, with the functions of

(i) examining and presenting to the House of Commons the financial estimates for the National Audit Office, modified or not, for which purpose the Commission was to have regard to any advice given by the PAC and the Treasury;

(ii) appointing the Accounting Officer for the National Audit Office;

(iii) appointing an auditor for the National Audit Office, who would have power to carry out economy, efficiency and effectiveness examinations of its use of resources.

(d) A National Audit Office should be set up, headed by the C&AG and consisting of such staff appointed by him as he considered necessary 'for assisting him in the discharge of his functions'; their remuneration and other conditions of service also to be decided by him, thus ending the Treasury's powers in these respects.

(e) The C&AG should have a discretionary power to carry out examinations of the economy, efficiency and effectiveness with which government departments and other bodies subject to his audit or inspection used their resources, without however being entitled to question the merits of their policy *objectives*, and to report to the House the results of such examinations. (Author's italics).

(f) The C&AG should have power to carry out 3 Es examinations in any body (except the nationalized industries and certain other public authorities) whose members were appointed by the Crown and which he had reasonable cause to believe was funded as to more than half its income from public funds: the resolution of the argument as to whether the C&AG should have the right 'to follow public money wherever it goes'.

The Act also repealed a provision of the 1866 Act relating to the appropriation accounts, to allow for flexibility in the year of account, to facilitate speeding up of certification and presentation; and it removed or amended certain powers by which the Treasury could require the C&AG to carry out particular investigations.

7.3 THE OBJECTIVES OF THE FINANCIAL AUDIT

The financial audit of government departments is intended to give an assurance that in all material respects:

(a) their accounts properly present the transactions to which they relate;

(b) they have spent the money voted to them only for the purposes intended by Parliament, as described in the Estimates and Supplementary Estimates presented at the beginning of each financial year and subsequently; and

(c) that the expenditure conforms to the authority governing it, i.e. has met the requirements of 'regularity'.

In even plainer words, this means that the money provided by Parliament has been spent as intended, that no significant unlawful, improper or irregular payments have been made, and that the figures are satisfactory.

These simple-sounding objectives conceal some complex problems for the C&AG and his staff. Although the basic form of the appropriation accounts is simple – cash spent in the year compared with cash voted – the figures in the final accounts run into billions of pounds for all the major departments, and they represent and summarize not only very large numbers of transactions, but very complex purchasing, construction, contracting and staffing operations. The building of hospitals, the design and development of advanced military equipment, the installation of large computer systems, the payment of many millions of social security benefits each week, are just a few of these highly diverse activities. It is therefore a major technical audit task to check that the accounting and financial control systems underlying the figures in the accounts are reliable and efficient. This work is necessarily done on a selective basis and increasingly utilizes techniques, such as sampling and the evaluation and testing of systems, similar to those applied by commercial auditors in the audit of large private sector concerns.

To check that government spending conforms with the specific terms of statutes, for example that financial assistance given by the Department of Industry to private firms is in accordance with the Industry Act or other governing legislation, does not in practice raise many difficult problems, or usually take much time. This is partly because legislation governing spending is normally drawn up in fairly broad terms, so that difficult questions of interpretation seldom arise, and partly because government officials in the UK do not set out to misapply funds outside the specific conditions set by Parliament.

Conformity with the statutes is clearly an essential part of 'regularity'. But the audit of regularity extends a good way beyond this. Detailed rules and regulations are often drawn up, under the authority of the governing Acts themselves, to set out the exact conditions and criteria which have to be met if people or companies are to be entitled to various types of state payments. The largest, but by no means the only, services of this kind are social security, and agricultural and industrial assistance schemes. Some social security benefits are payable only if the applicant has made sufficient national insurance contributions. To be entitled to unemployment benefit, a person has to be 'genuinely seeking work'. To qualify for a hill farming subsidy, a farmer may have to maintain his sheep for sufficient periods above certain altitudes. To qualify for an industrial grant, a company may have to build a factory within particular areas and to equip it for specified industrial purposes. These rules and regulations can be voluminous, complex and open in some cases to arguments about interpretation. They may take the form of 'subordinate legislation', for example a statutory instrument which has to be laid before, and in some cases approved by, Parliament. They may simply be departmental rules, sometimes approved by the Treasury, sometimes not, which the responsible Minister is entitled to lay down by administrative action.

Very large sums of public money are disbursed under systems of this kind. As a matter of just and efficient administration people should get what they are entitled to, and not more. It is the duty of the National Audit Office, as part of their regularity audit, to check that departments are applying such rules correctly. They will do so selectively, and with regard, as in all their work, for the relative importance, or materiality, of the various areas of expenditure. They may find that some rules are prone to cause errors because they are overcomplicated or unclear. They may find that officials have made payments which, through an honest but excessive exercise of their initiative, bend the rules unduly. They may even come to the view that a scheme, let us say for paying farmers to drain or fence certain types of land, is so complex that it takes too much manpower to administer and might with advantage be replaced by a simpler one.

With the exception of the last, all these illustrations relate to the concept of regularity of expenditure. Similar examples can be found in other government programmes, for example the rules governing the distribution of funds to promote the arts, or sport, or research. Such functions as these are often entrusted to special bodies or councils, subject to rules and guidance by their parent department: the Arts Council, under the Department of Education and Science; the Medical Research Council under the Department of Health and Social Security, and so on. In such cases as these the rules to which they have to work will be relatively simple, unlike those governing social security schemes, which run into many volumes. But they are further aspects of the way in which regularity, in matters of government spending, is defined.

It is to these features of the accounts – accuracy of the figures, legality and regularity of the transactions – that the C&AG's certificate to Parliament exclusively relates. It is sometimes called the 'attest' function of an audit. It gives independent assurance, within approved standards, that the audited body has properly presented its financial transactions in its accounts and has conformed to the rules governing them. In principle this kind of audit can be, and is, applied to a wide range of bodies, from international organizations, such as the Food and Agriculture Organization or the World Health Organization of the United Nations, to the local cricket club, as well as to government departments.

The essential point with which to close this part of the discussion is that the financial or certification audit, constitutionally important as it is, has limited objectives in the assessment of operational efficiency. It is true that the analysis of government activities and expenditure which is a necessary part of a well conducted financial audit may well lead into wider studies. It is also the case that an evaluation of financial control and information systems is likely to be of value not only for certification purposes but to judge a department's progress in the development of effective internal management systems. But other operational audit techniques, conveniently subsumed in the term 'value for money audit', need to be developed. Before discussing them, it is first necessary to make a brief digression into the field of commercial accounting and audit.

7.4 COMMERCIAL AND GOVERNMENT ACCOUNTING

Government spends money and uses large resources of manpower to provide a wide variety of services to the community: defence, health, support for industry and agriculture, social security, and many others. For the most part these services are not paid for directly by those who benefit from them. Some charges, such as those for medical prescriptions, or for use of the Severn bridge or Dartford tunnel, are made; but the former covers only a small part of the cost and most of the services are not provided with a commercial motive – to make a profit.

It is true that a relatively small part of the activities of government departments or closely related bodies is commercial in its nature and aims. The Royal Mint, as well as manufacturing the coin of the realm, which is 'sold' to the Treasury under rather special arrangements, also manufactures and sells coins and medals for overseas customers and is expected to cover its costs and charge market prices for this business. Her Majesty's Stationery Office publishes and sells many official documents and reports, if not at a profit at any rate with the intention of recovering the cost. The national museums run shops for their prints, replicas and so on where they aim to break even or do better. The special accounts for these activities are themselves commercial in style; they present their results in essentially the same way as an industrial or trading company, and they are audited accordingly. But in the scale of government activities as a whole, this kind of activity is relatively small.

Commercial accounts are intended to show the results of trading operations over the year; and the financial state of the business, more specifically its net book value at the end of each year. To do so both income and expenditure have to be assessed as accurately as possible, which is a more complex task than simply logging up cash payments and receipts. Income has to take account of sums due in respect of various activities and attributable to the year in question; expenditure has to include amounts representing the proportion of the firm's assets, stocks and work in progress used up in producing the year's income; provisions against future loss or liabilities have to be assessed – and so on. When to these calculations it is necessary to add an assessment of the effect of inflation on the firm's profit and asset valuations, through the application of current cost accounting, the production and audit of the accounts of any sizeable commercial concern is a considerable exercise, involving acts of judgement as well as of record and classification.

This brief sketch of commercial accounting is intended only as background to two points. First, as mentioned above, there are some government activities which can and should be presented and accounted for in this way. They include not only the production and sale of a range of goods, from coins and medals to prints of mediaeval manuscripts, but also, for example, the manufacture of military equipment for the country's own forces, or the provision of office supplies to departments, where it is thought desirable to work out the 'full cost' on some appropriate type of commercial accounting, to assist control and to promote the right decisions.

The second point is a wider and crucial one. The making of profit or loss, and the increase or decrease each year in the value of a business, are critical tests of its success or failure. They measure the extent to which it achieves its essential objectives. There may be others. A firm which contributes to social progress or cultural achievement, which makes its staff happy in their work, or sponsors a tennis tournament, may earn applause for doing so. Its far-sighted directors may well judge that there are also likely to be financial benefits. But if it consistently fails in the primary task of profit making, it is unlikely to survive, short of Government rescue, for long.

7.5 VALUE FOR MONEY AUDIT

None of this applies, clearly, to government department:
providing or promoting the large communal services of defence
education, health, law and order, and so on. Their efficiency
their performance, their success has to be judged by quite
different tests, and by quite different methods. This is the field in
which the public audit services seek to apply the concepts now
broadly known as value for money or efficiency auditing. They do
not displace the audit of accuracy in accounting or of propriety
and regularity of transactions described earlier. They complemen
and extend it, and require different techniques. To what exten
they can be satisfactorily applied by staff trained and experienced
in financial audit is an issue of current discussion and some
controversy. Good financial auditors have also produced usefu
value for money reports on a wide range of financial managemen
matters. Such work can also be satisfactorily done by people
without professional accountancy or audit training if they have
the right aptitudes and approach.

The prime responsibility for achieving value for money of
efficiency is the management's, and not the public auditor's
Senior civil servants, and ultimately their Ministers, are respons
ible and are held accountable for all their actions in running and
managing their departments. But the C&AG and his staff play
their same independent role in assessing and where necessary
criticizing the performance of the bodies they audit in these
respects as they do in what may be described as the more forma
financial audit field. They thus promote two distinct objectives
accountability of the executive government to Parliament and, it is
hoped, its efficiency and effectiveness.

The terms 'value for money' and 'efficiency audit' are not term:
of art, still less precise definitions. Value for money audit ha:
been commonly used in the UK as a convenient description of the
evolving interests and work of E&AD over many decades, with it:
origin sometimes pinpointed at the year 1888 when there was ar
interesting confrontation between the C&AG and the Army
Council over a little matter of contracts for Army ribbon, from
which the former emerged the winner. The argument was
whether the C&AG was within his rights in extending his
examination of Army expenditure beyond the accepted matters of
conformity with Parliamentary authorization into the area of
economy in contracts. The C&AG owed his success largely to the
support of the Public Accounts Committee of the House of
Commons, established in 1861, whose present role is described
below. Over the succeeding century the C&AG has developed the

application of value for money audit into many aspects of the financial management of government departments, with a marked acceleration in scale and coverage from the early 1950s, as the great post-war surge in government activity and the corresponding expenditure programmes gathered weight.

Traditionally this work focussed on 'the elimination of waste and extravagance'. Within recent years the wider role of national audit offices has been more closely analysed and defined in a way which now has widespread international recognition. The General Accounting Office of the USA is usually credited with formulating, and publicizing, the three-fold division into economy, efficiency and effectiveness audit.

In this context economy is taken to mean the achievement of a given result with the least expenditure of money, manpower or other resources, while efficiency imports the idea of converting resources into a desired product in the most advantageous ratio. But this is sometimes a rather subtle distinction, and the more important divide is between the pursuit and audit of economy and efficiency on the one hand and of effectiveness on the other, because the latter brings into account the goals or objectives which the activity in question is intended to meet.

The examination of effectiveness in government and other public sector programmes and policies raises issues which are often intractable and sometimes controversial. The development or purchase of nuclear weapons is intended to contribute to the goal of national security. The extension of comprehensive education is intended to promote educational and social aims. The introduction of the family income supplement was hoped to secure a minimum standard of living for the families of low-paid workers in employment. Subsidies for defined forms of industrial investment aimed to encourage the development of particular parts of the country, and reduce unemployment. The transformation of the old employment exchanges into job centres and their siting in the High Street had a similar aim. These cases and a great many more raise the questions:

(a) Should the auditor be involved in effectiveness at all?
(b) If so, does this not bring him to question policy decisions?
(c) Has he the necessary skills?

Parliament has now decided, in the National Audit Act and the Local Government Finance Act 1982, that the audit of both central and local government should cover effectiveness. In this respect, so far at least as central government operations are concerned, the United Kingdom has lined up with the legislatures of the United States, the Netherlands and Sweden among others, while the

243

Australians, for example, have decided otherwise.

The question of the involvement of the external auditor in policy questions is a sensitive one. It is for those running an organization, and answerable for its results, to take and defend policy decisions; for example, to develop a new civil aircraft, to build a new comprehensive school, or to broadcast news in English to various parts of the world. But the auditor may feel it necessary and justifiable:

(a) to question whether the goals which the policy decisions are meant to serve have been established;

(b) to examine whether managements have themselves established adequate procedures to assess the effectiveness of their policies;

(c) to quantify the costs of the decisions taken;

(d) to report on whether the goals have in fact been achieved;

(e) to suggest alternative ways in which the goals might have been more effectively met.

This is a formidable list of possibilities. Few national auditors regard the whole lot as within their remit; probably only the General Accounting Office of the USA covers (e). The Australian and Canadian Auditors General are required to stop at (c) and do not go on to (d) or (e). The C&AG would regard all except (e) as in principle within his remit. But he would be circumspect and realistic in deciding which particular government projects or programmes to examine in this way. He would have much in mind the degree of authority and cogency his report was likely to have; and the impact it was likely to make. He is not in business to study policy options, nor to write academic studies. His object, in this part of his value-for-money work, is to contribute to more effective decision-taking, and more efficient execution of policies, by reference to past and current experience, problems and mistakes.

Although it is useful to analyse value for money auditing as above, it is as well not to conceptualize too far. In the UK, at any rate, value for money audit has come to describe a wide variety of enquiries into central government operations, including the development and production of military equipment; the building of hospitals, factories and offices; the application of agricultural and industrial assistance; the design and installation of computer systems; charging policies for government services; use and disposal of land; control of civil service manpower. The C&AG's reports have concentrated on financial management in the broadest sense, including the management of contracts. They have also raised matters of organization, and more recently the control of civil service manpower. They have not, however, extended into the field of operational research or work study. Some people find difficulty in accepting that the 'value' in value for money can be judged by an auditor. As in so much intellectual discourse it depends what you mean by value. In the practice of public audit it is usually necessary to stop short of an assessment of ultimate value, and be content with more easily judged measures of performance. 'Output measurement' is notoriously difficult in many public services. It is nearly always necessary to be content with the 'intermediate objectives' which a project or service is intended to meet: school places provided, rather than educational advance secured; families given a minimum income, rather than guaranteed a particular standard of wellbeing. But to judge and report whether performance has measured up to plans, budgets, and intentions is certainly one main object of value for money audit.

Traditionally, most E&AD value for money reports had concentrated on individual examples of waste, contractual failings, inadequate planning, or other aspects of financial ineptitude. Such examinations were however by no means small in scale: the building of the Thames barrier, the refit of a warship, the construction of a motorway or hospital, and many other governmental operations cost many millions of pounds and require expert planning, contracting and financial control. Scope for shortcomings in one or more of the 3 Es was not lacking, either in major projects of this type or in smaller scale activities, ranging from university land holdings to the provision of meteorological information. Value for money audit was therefore nothing new to the C&AG and the E&AD, whose archives are full of such reports dating back many years.

Nevertheless it became clear in the later 1970s that further development of this work was necessary. In particular:

(a) A much greater degree of 'top down' planning and supervision was required, to ensure that resources were efficiently used and priorities established. Formerly, most value for money reports had emanated from the audit divisions, often though not exclusively as an offshoot of their financial audit work. This approach fostered and rewarded individual initiative, but could not ensure that the most significant areas were covered or avoid some misdirection of effort.

(b) Wider studies of departmental operations, including their systems for financial control and the provision and use of management information, needed to be made. Studies of individual projects could certainly carry implications for the adequacy of such systems, and lead to improvements, but they lacked the authority of broader based reports. The Financial Management Initiative in government departments, described in Chapter 2, will no doubt stimulate the NAO's interest in this area.

(c) Some subjects important for government efficiency and of interest to Parliament could only be effectively studied by investigating the practice of several government departments. Examples in recent years have been the organization and use of internal audit, the control of manpower, and investment appraisal.

(d) The E&AD needed to extend their links with the departments and bodies they audited, to spread awareness of their own evolving aims, ideas and methods and to make their decisions on what to investigate and how to do so better informed. By long standing tradition, E&AD's relationship with departments had been markedly at arm's length, with the overriding aim of safeguarding the C&AG's independence. Their role, as invigilators on behalf of Parliament, had been accepted and respected, but consultation on what they should investigate was neither offered nor expected. This attitude, which derives with great respectability from the preservation of the external public auditor's full freedom of action, is at variance with the practice both of private sector auditing firms and of newer institutions such as the Audit Commission (see below).

(e) New methods of value for money investigation, sometimes using skills additional to those of financial audit, and applied by specially constituted teams, needed to be tried and assessed.

To effect changes in these directions, to ensure high standards of financial audit, and to deal satisfactorily with staff recruitment, professional training, relations with other public audit bodies at home and abroad and with the private sector, the senior management of E&AD was expanded and strengthened, a central capability developed, and the methods of work of the whole office reviewed.

The new look to value for money work which emerged from these developments is well summarized in Table 7.1, an extract from the booklet published by the National Audit Office in 1983 explaining the C&AG's role and the responsibilities of the Office.

It is worth considering how value for money audit relates to the

Table 7.1
Main stages of a typical major audit investigation

Survey of main areas of expenditure and risk	1
Selection of area, programme or project for examination	2
Preliminary study to determine scope, objectives, time-scale, staffing of main exercise; and to prepare plans and work allocations	3
Main exercise carried out by auditor or audit team. Progress and results monitored as study proceeds	4
Results reviewed by senior staff; decisions taken on necessary action	5
Correspondence and discussion with audited body, leading up to draft report (if necessary)	6
Report approved by C&AG; sent to Accounting Officer for confirmation of fairness and accuracy	7
Considered by Committee of Public Accounts with evidence from audited bodies	8
Committee report published and presented to Parliament	9
Treasury Minute published in response to criticisms, comments and recommendations made; confirms remedial action taken or proposed	10
Consideration of Treasury Minute by Committee of Public Accounts, with further follow-up and report as necessary	11

The target time-scale for completion of stages 4-7 would normally not exceed 6-9 months, so as to maintain topicality and impact. Later stages might then occupy a further 39 months from the date of the Committee hearing, depending on the scale of the further examination and the nature of the Government's response to the matters raised. Source: National Audit Office (1983), by permission.

Rayner studies mentioned in Chapter 2, to assignments undertaken by management consultants, and to the efficiency studies of nationalized industries commissioned by the government from the Monopolies and Mergers Commission or private accounting/consultancy firms. There are similarities throughout:

(a) All such examinations proceed by rigorous assembly and analysis of evidence, both from documents and discussion.

(b) Every attempt is made to reach agreement with the body under examination on the factual adequacy and accuracy of material in the final report.

(c) Provisional conclusions are tested by the reactions of the body under examination and due weight given to objections or counter argument.

(d) The objective is a fair, balanced report, making whatever criticisms and recommendations for improvement are thought to be justified, on the sole responsibility of the examining body.

But there are also significant differences, both constitutional and methodological:

(a) The external auditor takes his own unfettered decisions as to what he will examine, when he will do so and whether he will make a public or other report. Consultancies are by invitation of the client, who decides – no doubt in discussion with the consultant – the scope of the enquiry and how it is to be conducted. The report is an internal one. Rayner Studies are also internal government exercises, not so far normally published. MMC enquiries, or those undertaken by consultants on the invitation of the central government, are external to the body under examination and normally published but are not self-initiated.

(b) Major MMC or consultancy efficiency studies have been wide ranging investigations into the operations of public bodies, leading to numerous conclusions and recommendations and not inconsiderable dispute. An internal consultancy report is usually more narrowly defined and is to some extent judged by the acceptability and practicability of its recommendations to the client, who will have spent money on the study in an endeavour to improve its efficiency and profitability. Most of the C&AG's investigations have also been concerned with specific aspects of financial management, with shorter reports designed for further examination by Parliament under the arrangements described below. It appears that local authority auditors and the Audit Commission will broadly follow this approach, though they will stress the comparative performance of local authorities and they have nothing comparable to the external influence of the Public Accounts Committee to strengthen their impact.

(c) The Rayner studies are carried out internally by particular departments, using selected members of their own staff who examine in considerable detail a specific aspect of administration or policy, questioning both its objectives and its methods. They are supported by the small central efficiency unit and enjoy strong ministerial backing.

There are two important parts of the central government sector where special audit features apply, namely the national health service and the universities.

7.6 NATIONAL HEALTH SERVICE

The National Health Service is under the full control of the Secretary of State for Social Services and his department, the Department of Health and Social Security (DHSS). Audit of the NHS is shared between the C&AG and the department. The accounts of the individual health authorities are audited by the 'statutory auditors'. They are civil servants of the DHSS, assigned to this special duty and trained for it; they make their reports to the Secretary of State. The C&AG is responsible for examining and certifying the summarized health authority accounts, which bring together the operations of all the individual authorities. But his staff have full access to the books and records of all the health authorities, as well as those of the DHSS, and the corresponding Scottish and Welsh Departments. He is therefore in a position to examine and report on all aspects of the financial control and management of the NHS and its constituent authorities. Reports on health service matters have featured largely in the C&AG's annual reports to Parliament. They have dealt for example with hospital planning and construction, computer developments, and cost control of drugs.

It was suggested during the 1980-81 review of the C&AG's role (see section 7.10) that it would be desirable to bring the statutory auditors into the E&AD under his direction, so that there would be a fully integrated audit service for the NHS. The PAC recommended in favour, but the Government preferred not to disturb the existing arrangements. In one or two cases, however, the audit of health authorities has been taken over by private accounting firms as part of the Government's policy (1982) of increasing their participation in the audit of public services.

7.7 THE UNIVERSITIES

Most of the funds provided to the universities, for both capital

249

and current expenditure, come from the Exchequer. They are distributed by the Secretary of State for Education and Science to individual universities on the advice of the University Grants Commission. The accounts of the universities themselves are audited by commercial auditors and until 1967 the C&AG had no access to their records or responsibility to report on their affairs. This reflected the view, since proved unfounded, that to involve him would be prejudicial to the universities' autonomy and a possible threat to academic freedom. After sustained pressure from the PAC the Government agreed in 1967 to allow the C&AG to inspect the universities' books and to report as he saw fit on their financial management. Since then the C&AG has made many such reports, and it has become generally accepted that the provision of large sums of public money justifies this extra measure of public accountability.

It should be noted that an 'inspection audit' of this kind provides the National Audit Office with the necessary information for examining and if necessary reporting on value for money matters affecting an organization, even though the financial audit is carried out by other auditors. The universities are the most important example of an inspection audit but there are many others in the central government area. As already noted, the 1983 Act authorizes the C&AG to conduct them in certain bodies receiving at least half their income from public funds.

7.8   INTERNAL AND EXTERNAL AUDIT

Most large organizations, in both the public and private sectors, have their own internal audit arrangements. The essential difference between internal and external audit is that the former is part of the management, is organized and directed, and reports, as senior management decides; whereas the latter is completely independent and, subject to the law, decides these matters for itself. Internal audit is intended to contribute to the probity and efficiency of the enterprise from within; external audit shares this objective, operating from outside, but also serves the further objective of external accountability. The scope of the work of internal audit staff may therefore be wide or narrow, varying from straightforward matters of internal financial control to a remit virtually as wide as that of the C&AG himself. The staff are nowadays likely to be led by, and to contain a growing proportion of, professionally qualified people. Some concern has been expressed in recent years about the quality of the approach and work of internal audit in both public and private bodies, and both central and local government are taking steps to raise its standards and improve its effectiveness. This is a matter of considerable interest to the external auditor; despite the significant constitutional difference in the two roles it is generally accepted that the measure of independence given to the internal auditor within the public authority or firm should justify the external auditor in relying substantially on his work where he is satisfied that it meets the necessary professional standards. Subject to this essential condition an agreed division of labour between internal and external audit is increasingly accepted as a sensible and economic arrangement.

7.9 REPORTING TO PARLIAMENT; THE ROLE OF THE PUBLIC ACCOUNTS COMMITTEE

An external auditor does not address his reports to the body he audits, except in the case of local authorites (see page 260 below). In the case of a company, the auditor reports to the shareholders, not to the directors. In the case of government departments, the C&AG reports to Parliament, not to Ministers. He and his staff may, and often do, bring to the notice of government departments various matters which appear to him to need action but do not merit a public report. But that is part of the normal constructive relationship which ought to exist between the two organizations.

By long tradition the reports of the C&AG are considered by the Committee of Public Accounts (PAC) of the House of Commons. The Committee's terms of reference empower them to examine any of the accounts which are laid before Parliament. It should be noted that this gives the committee a considerably wider remit than that of the C&AG. For example, all the annual reports and accounts of the nationalized industries and other public corporations are laid before Parliament, and could therefore be examined by the PAC, even though the C&AG is not the auditor of most of them. In practice, an understanding was reached that the PAC would leave the examination of the nationalized industries to the former Select Committee on Nationalized Industries – not so far (1985) replaced by any one comparable select committee since the recent changes in select committee structure (see Chapter 2).

The PAC does not nowadays spend much time on matters of financial irregularity or constitutional impropriety. There are not many of them, and most which do occur are not of sufficient seriousness to warrant intervention by the committee. A serious fraud case, fortunately rare in central government administration, might certainly engage their attention, as might a failure by a department to secure Parliamentary authority for expenditure. But most of the committee's work is based on the C&AG's value for money reports on financial management; and in deciding which matters merit a report the C&AG has much in mind the likely interest of the subject to the committee and the prospect of useful recommendations for improvement arising from their enquiries.

NAO staff have full access, not only to the accounts of departments, but to all papers and documents relevant to the departments' financial administration. They can thus form their own independent judgement of the merits or shortcomings of departmental action; they are not dependent on government officials to produce their version of events. In the preparation of draft reports care is taken to establish a solid basis of fact upon which the C&AG can take his decision whether to report or not. If he does decide to report he gives the departmental Accounting Officer concerned an opportunity to comment on the report whose accuracy as to fact is thereafter seldom challenged.

The method of the PAC's own examination is also of special significance. Again, by long tradition, when they decide to take evidence on matters raised in the C&AG's reports they summon the Accounting Officer, who is not a finance officer, however senior, but the permanent secretary or other official in charge of the whole department. He may be and usually is supported by senior colleagues, but he is the official witness. The duty of answering to the PAC for the regular and economical administration of his department is a duty which is taken very seriously. Though arduous and sometimes gruelling, the committee's examination of these senior witnesses sets out to be fair and constructive. The committee makes its own report to the House on the basis of its examination of the Accounting Officer and any other witnesses outside his department it may decide to call. It includes criticisms if thought justified, and any necessary recommendations for change or improvements. It may even, on rare occasions, commend good performance.

The next step is for the department to consider the committee's report and to prepare a reply. It is unusual for the committee's recommendations to be rejected, but by no means unheard of. The replies of all departments on whose activities the PAC has reported are agreed with the Treasury, and submitted as a Treasury minute to the House of Commons. This is in effect the response of the government to the PAC. A debate is arranged on the PAC's reports, and in the succeeding session of Parliament it is normal for the Accounting Officers to be examined further on any points in the Treasury minute on which the PAC remains unsatisfied.

There is no doubt that this is an effective and well tried system of accountability. The C&AG works closely with the PAC, though without being subject to their directions, and they with him. The Treasury is always represented at PAC hearings, and though themselves sometimes in the dock as well as the witness box its officials also seek to cooperate as far as possible with the Committee. The effect of the system is not confined to the particular matters on which the C&AG reports. The probability that any serious failure of financial control or inefficiency in administration will lead to a report by the C&AG and to a PAC investigation exercises a sharpening effect throughout departmental hierarchies.

7.10 PROPOSALS FOR CHANGE

In recent years there has been an upsurge of Parliamentary interest in the public audit, and no less than three select committees of Parliament have enquired into it and made recommendations for change: the former Expenditure Committee, the Procedure Committee, and the PAC itself. The system of audit was dealt with by the first two committees as one part of much wider remits, and all the main points raised by them were covered in the PAC's review of the role of the C&AG in the 1980-81 session of Parliament. Attention can therefore be concentrated on that review, which was the first of its kind since the C&AG and his department had been established well over a century ago. It was itself preceded by the government's decision, stimulated by the increased Parliamentary interest in matters of financial control and accountability, and perhaps by the C&AG's own views, to review the C&AG's role.

At the start of that process the government issued a consultative green paper. It summarized the C&AG's existing role, supported his development of a systems-based financial and regularity audit, encouraged him to extend his value for money work while stopping short of involvement in the merits of particular policy objectives, but it provisionally opposed any significant extension of the range of his activities to cover other parts of the public sector, as had been suggested by the C&AG

himself and generally supported by the other select committees.

Criticism of the existing audit system had concentrated on these points:

(a) Compared with other advanced national audit offices, E&AD did too much financial and regularity audit and not enough efficiency and effectiveness audit.

(b) The C&AG and the PAC examined past transactions instead of considering current policy options.

(c) The C&AG and his staff should be officers of Parliament, subject to directions from the House of Commons.

(d) The range of the C&AG's rights of access needed to be extended so that he could examine the use of public funds by all bodies receiving them, and should include access to books and records of the nationalized industries and other public corporations.

(e) The C&AG needed to take over responsibility for the local authority audit service in order to improve accountability to Parliament in respect of the very large central government subventions to local authorities through the rate support and other grants.

These criticisms and suggestions are fully explored in the government's green paper (Cmnd. 7845, March 1980), the PAC's first special report in session 1980-81 on the role of the C&AG (HC 115-1), and the government's response to that report giving their conclusions (Cmnd. 8323). A considerable volume of evidence, both written and oral, was given to the PAC by several interested bodies and persons, and published by the PAC in their report. A guide to these reports and evidence is included in the bibliography for this chapter. They provide, for the first time in over 100 years, a source of authoritative material and argument on the subject of the national audit office. A summary of the main issues follows.

Complaint (a) that the C&AG's work was largely restricted to financial and regularity audit was misconceived. He, the government, and the PAC continued to put much importance on the need for a sound financial and regularity audit supporting his certification of government accounts; but the criticism appeared to ignore the large volume and wide scope of his reports directed to value for money matters, extending over several past decades.

There is more substance to the 'stable door' criticism (b), though not nearly so much as may at first appear. It is of the essence of an audit that it investigates what has happened or is happening, and seeks to draw useful conclusions and recommendations for change from past experience, and no doubt in many cases past mistakes. In this sense it is concerned with the working out of existing decisions or policies, particularly their financial and economic consequences. It is not primarily concerned with suggesting alternatives, though in some cases this may be a clear implication of audit findings. In short, from an audit of past and present practice one hopes to secure future improvement.

The proposal that the C&AG and his staff should be House of Commons Staff, subject to Parliamentary direction, has now been rejected. Its constitutional attraction was apparent, since the C&AG reports to Parliament and work in many ways 'on their behalf'. It was opposed by the C&AG and the professional accountancy institutions, and was turned down by the Government. The main argument was that the C&AG should have full independence, within his statutory remit, to decide on his own enquiries and dispose his resources as he thought best. The C&AG stressed in his evidence that in so doing the wishes and suggestions of the PAC would be given full weight, and this has now been reflected in legislation.

The view that the national auditor should have powers to follow public money – or as the Procedure Committee more narrowly defined it, 'money provided by Parliament' – wherever it went, also has constitutional appeal. Money voted by Parliament finds it way through many different types of grant and assistance to individuals and companies. It had to be asked how practicable and acceptable it would have been to expect the audit staff to have rights of access to all their books and records. The issue has been resolved in the 1983 Act as described above.

The arguments for and against giving the C&AG access to the books and records of some or all of the nationalized industries and public corporations so that he could report on their operations are fully discussed in the evidence submitted to the PAC in the course of their review. The essential arguments in favour were:

(a) The industries' assets are acquired from public funds or on Exchequer credit and many of them have a monopolistic position conferred by Parliament.
(b) Examinations and reports by the C&AG would fill an important gap in the accountability of the industries.
(c) They would be a check on and stimulate their efficiency.

The arguments against were:

(a) The industries already operate under statutory provisions, report to Parliament and the public through their annual reports and accounts, and readily respond to requests to give written or oral evidence to select committees of Parliament, notably the former Select Committee on Nationalized Industries.

(b) The responsible Ministers have certain statutory powers of control, most significantly in relation to their investment programmes, and have in practice influenced other policies, particularly on prices and major closures. Ministers have to answer for these actions to Parliament.

(c) The government had indicated that it proposed to extend the use of enquiries by the Monopolies and Mergers Commission to provide an external check on efficiency, so that a further incursion by the C&AG was unnecessary. (This was subsequently carried out in the Competition Act 1980).

(d) The need to justify decisions to the C&AG's staff would inhibit speed and enterprise in decision-taking, responding to external audit enquiries would be expensive in staff time and money, and there would be difficulties about the confidentiality of some information, particularly where commercial partners were involved.

The sponsor departments added

(e) That if the C&AG were to be given access to the records of the industries with a view to reporting on value for money matters, the responsible departments would also need to seek more information to establish satisfactorily their own positions.

The C&AG argued that (a) and (b) did not adequately meet the point about a gap in accountability. There was in his view no effective substitute, from this point of view, for free access by his staff and his right to report to Parliament, independently of both Ministers and the industries, as he saw fit. As regards (c) the Monopolies and Mergers Commission had no such independent role; they would operate in this field only when so instructed by the government. On (d) the E&AD had long experience of handling confidential matters; and a body subject to his audit should continue to take whatever decisions they thought right – they did not have to be justified to him.

The PAC reported in favour of giving the C&AG this extended remit. The Government disagreed. In the debate on the National Audit Bill the advocates of change failed to carry the day, so that the nationalized industries and the local authorities remained outside the C&AG's purview. It may in consequence be suggested that the 1983 Act was of limited significance.

So far as the scope of the C&AG's audit within the public sector is concerned, this is true. But the Act gave statutory recognition to important changes in the approach and standing of the C&AG and his office. His complete independence of any constraint, actual or potential, by the executive government was assured by the substitution of direct Parliamentary controls on his budget for those of the Treasury. His establishment as an officer of Parliament, and the provision giving Parliament, through the Chairman of the PAC, a statutory voice in his appointment neatly recognized his close relationship with Parliament without subordinating to MPs his judgement in discharging his statutory duties and the use of his resources. His long standing commitment to value for money audit as a major part of his activities was endorsed and the 3 Es given statutory status. Moreover as explained below, he had already, in the Local Government Finance Act 1982, been given a role in the examination of relationships between central and local government, and certain rights in relation to the Audit Commission for Local Authorities to assist him to discharge it. The change of name, from Exchequer and Audit Department, with its undertones of Treasury connection, to National Audit Office was more than symbolic of the ending of a long historical phase. It expressed a new outlook and approach.

AUDIT OF LOCAL AUTHORITIES

England and Wales

For 140 years the external audit of local authorities was undertaken primarily by the District Audit Service, succeeded in 1983 by the Audit Commission for Local Authorities in England and Wales.

The district audit system dated from the Poor Law Amendment Act of 1844 which created the office of district auditor to examine the accounts of the local bodies that administered poor law relief. During the succeeding half century the duties of district auditors were gradually extended to cover the accounts of highway, public health and education bodies, as local administration was itself expanded under Acts of Parliament into these wider fields. By the end of the century the accounts of most local authorities in England and Wales were audited by district auditors.

District auditors were independent statutory officers answerable to the courts who took personal responsibility for the audit of the accounts of all the local authorities in their district. The number of districts varied over the years; in 1983 there were 13 covering over 450 local authorities and about 8000 local councils, down to parishes. District auditors and their staff, about 550 in total at that time, were formally civil servants, for whose appointment and numbers the Secretary of State for the Environment had statutory responsibility. But by reasons of their statutory office and long tradition they were not subject to control or direction by the Minister in the execution of their duties. Staff numbers apart, which was a subject of contention, they were treated as an independent professional service.

In addition to the district auditors themselves, the service also included the important post of Chief Inspector of Audit, with a small central staff reporting directly to him. Since district auditors and approved auditors had full personal and professional responsibility for their audit work the Chief Inspector had no power to direct them. But his responsibility to ensure that proper standards were being maintained gave him considerable influence as the de facto head of the service.

For some years local authorities had the right to choose whether to be audited by the district auditor or by an 'approved auditor', i.e. a professional accounting firm, whose appointment had to be approved by the Secretary of State. Before 1983 only a small minority of authorities had chosen professional firms.

In the later 1970s the central government, in particular the Treasury, were taking an increased interest in the audit and accountability of local authorities, as one aspect of central/local government financial relations and the drive for greater efficiency and cost consciousness in public bodies.

In 1976 the Layfield Committee on Local Government Finance (Report, Cmnd. 6453), recommended the appointment of 'an independent official with a similar status to that of the Comptroller and Auditor General' to head an expanded and strengthened local audit service, whose functions would include:

(a) the assignment of auditors to each local authority, who would no longer have any choice in the matter; and

(b) the making of regular reports on 'issues of general interest or public concern', which should be made available to the public.

The Committee also recommended the establishment of a 'higher institution' to which the head of audit's reports should be submitted: either a Parliamentary committee with terms of reference similar to those of the Public Accounts Committee, or a body with representation drawn largely from local government. Though this particular constitution was faulty, the Committee's analysis of the limitations of local authority audit were generally sound, and the later decision to set up the Audit Commission with a Controller of Audit as its chief executive fulfilled some of their proposals. Meanwhile as an interim development the Secretary of State for the Environment set up an Advisory Committee on Local Government Audit (in England and Wales) headed by an independent chairman and including other independent members as well as experienced local councillors, and the C&AG. The Committee, which was advised by the Chief Inspector, was intended to give greater weight to the work of the local government audit service and to propose ways in which it could be usefully developed.

At the same time the C&AG had himself been considering the local authority audit arrangements in relation to his own responsibilities and future role. He put forward a proposal to merge the E&AD and the local government audit service, arguing that:

(a) the nature and objectives of the work of the two services were basically similar;

(b) local government provides important services such as education, housing and personal social services under statutory arrangements, and guidance from central government, and for which the taxpayer provides over half the funds;

(c) Parliament therefore has a major interest in the arrangements whereby central government departments influence and to some extent control these expenditures;

(d) bringing together the two audit services under one head would be the best way of achieving an integrated examination of the provision and control of services, respecting the right of *individual* local authorities to remain free of accountability to Parliament.

In opposition to those views the local authority associations and other local authority interests argued that the proposal would lead to an unjustified and unconstitutional incursion of central government and Parliament into the affairs of local authorities, who were solely responsible to their own electors.

The Government believed 'that the interests of all parties concerned, including local electorates, will best be served by the establishment of an Audit Commission for Local Authorities in England and Wales' (Cmnd. 8323, paragraph 16). They attached particular importance to the value for money content of local authority audit, and agreed that it was desirable for cooperation on technical matters to be developed between the District Audit

Service and E&AD.

The establishment of the new Audit Commission was provided for in the Local Government Finance Act 1982. Its provisions cover the following main points.

(a) Members of the Commission are appointed by the Secretary of State, who has power to give the Commission directions, but not directions relating to particular audits.

(b) The Commission appoint their own staff, subject to
  (i) approval by the Secretary of State of the appointment of the Commission's chief officer, the Controller of Audit;
  (ii) the requirement that an offer of employment had to be made to members of the District Audit Service.

(c) The Commission appoint auditors to local authorities and other local public bodies, either from their own staff or from members of professionally qualified firms; but not to water authorities, for whom audit by commercial firms is now prescribed, as for the nationalized industries.

(d) The Commission is to fix fees for audits.

(e) The Commission is required to produce an audit code of practice, embodying what appears to them to be the best professional practice with respect to standards, procedures and techniques; this code, in accordance with an amendment accepted by the government, to be approved by Parliament.

(f) Auditors will have comparable responsibilities as formerly with regard to financial and regularity audit, and as to illegality or wilful misconduct.

(g) Auditors are required to satisfy themselves that proper arrangements are made by the audited body 'for securing economy, efficiency and effectiveness in its use of resources'.

(h) Auditors are required to report to the body concerned, or publicly, on the same lines as previously applied.

(i) 'Any persons interested' may inspect the accounts and related documents, and a local government elector may object in respect of matters of legality, wilful misconduct or otherwise in the public interest.

The main aims of this important statutory change in audit arrangements for local authorities were to increase the weight and effectiveness of the audit, particularly in the pursuit of value for money; to establish its independence of the government more clearly; and to involve private auditing firms in the work to a substantially greater extent. The power of the Secretary of State to give the Commission directives may be thought to conflict with their independence. It is justified by the government on the grounds that Parliament, which provides substantial funds to local authorities and regulates their activities, would expect the government to have such a power in reserve.

The Commission came formally into existence and started operations in April 1983. Its first Chairman was an experienced businessman and among its other fifteen members were senior local councillors and former officers, the former Chief Inspector, the director of the Chartered Institute of Public Finance and Accountancy, and independent businessmen and academics. Its staff was recruited from the District Audit Service, other public bodies and the private sector. Its first controller was an experienced management consultant.

This new body, launched at a time of exceptional tension between central government and local authorities in constitutional, political, and financial relationships, faced three main tasks:

(a) The establish itself as competent, fair but forceful and independent of both central and local government;

(b) To create an effective and unified approach to wide ranging audit operations in a large number of disparate authorities; and

(c) To establish cooperation between its own operational staff and the substantially increased numbers of commercial accountants who would now enter an unfamiliar field.

This was a formidable programme. Immediately, the Commission had to appoint auditors for the 456 major authorities without direct experience of the capabilities of district auditors or competing commercial firms. This was achieved through an intensive series of presentations and consultations. In the first year 70% of the audits were awarded to the directly employed District Audit Service and 30% to major commercial firms, a proportionate distribution which left the private sector somewhat short of the share which the government had envisaged, but which was in any case a matter for the Commission's judgement.

The Commission also set out to establish both a professional and philosophical framework within which its audits would be directed and supervised. Elements in this framework were countrywide comparative analyses of local authority functions, staffing patterns and expenditure programmes; suggested principles of organization, management structures, accountability and motivation of staff; and comprehensive guides for the conduct of both the regularity audit and value for money studies.

In producing and disseminating this substantial collection of material the Commission was at pains to stress its intention to help local authorities to help themselves, to improve their use of resources, and to disprove the view that it had been established as an instrument of central government to help curb and cut local expenditure. To state what should be obvious, it was not their role to determine local government policy, nor to set spending levels or service priorities. But it could consider the consequences of policies being pursued by authorities and comment on their financial and other effects.

The Code of Local Government Audit Practice, prepared following consultation with the Local Authority Associations and the professional accountancy bodies and approved by Parliament, sets out in some detail how the audit is to be conducted. Within these guidelines however the auditor is expected to do his job independently of both the Commission and the local authority. The Code covers both the regularity audit and the value for money or 3 Es audit. It remains a primary objective to check that public money is spent only as authorized by law, to expose improper or fraudulent practices, and to ensure that the financial statements give an accurate and complete picture of an authority's expenditure, revenue and financial position. In these respects the auditor is required to apply best professional practice in terms of standards, procedures and techniques.

The importance of sound financial accounting systems for efficiency, clarity and public accountability should not be under-rated. Linked, as they should be, with the production of financial management information for councillors and staff they provide an essential basis for policy decisions, monitoring of service operations, and day to day control. But emphasis has increasingly been laid on the adequacy of council management structures, the machinery for taking and implementing policy decisions, and the effective use by local authorities of the very large sums of public money and skilled manpower for which they are responsible; in other words on value for money in its widest definition.

For many years a value for money audit had been applied to the affairs of local authorities, though its extent had been limited by the staff resources which the government had been willing to sanction. In recent years the Chief Inspector had promoted the examination of selected areas of service expenditure across a range of local authorities, including the financing of polytechnics, staffing ratios in primary and secondary schools and in colleges of further education, the operation of bonus pay schemes and the costs of child care. Studies of this kind are now being actively pursued by the Audit Commission in all areas of local government activity.

In approaching this part of their task the Commission has provided its auditors with local authority 'profiles', summarizing comparative statistics and thus drawing attention to issues which at first sight may merit investigation; it has identified specific services for their particular attention; and it has itself commissioned and funded special studies under sections 26 and 27 of the Act. The areas examined by auditors in 1984 included colleges of further education, police civilianization, school meals and refuse collection, leisure centres and purchasing, as well as overall arrangements for securing economy, efficiency and effectiveness. Special studies included housing management and maintenance, services for children in care, non-teaching costs in schools, and vehicle fleet management. One purpose of these studies is to provide material for future 'flavours' on which all auditors can draw for the specific work in the value for money field they decide to undertake.

The studies the Commission is also required to 'undertake or promote' under Section 27 of the Local Government Finance Act are also of significance. They are to be designed

> . . . to enable it to prepare reports as to the impact —
> (a) of the operation of any particular statutory provision . . . ; or
> (b) of any directions or guidance given by a Minister of the Crown (whether pursuant to any such provision or otherwise), on economy, efficiency and effectiveness in the provision of local authority services and of other services provided by bodies whose accounts are required to be audited in accordance with this Part of this Act, or on the financial management of such bodies.

Moreover —

> (2) The Commission shall publish . . . . its report of the results of any study under this section, and shall send a copy of any such report to the Comptroller and Auditor General.

And —

> (3) Where the Comptroller and Auditor General has received a copy of any such report he may require the Commission to furnish him with any information obtained by it in connection with the preparation of the report . . . ; but no information shall be requested by the Comptroller and Auditor General under this section in respect of any particular body.
> (4) The Comptroller and Auditor General shall from time to time lay before the House of Commons a report of any matters which, in his opinion, arise out of any studies of the Commission under this section and ought to be drawn to the attention of that House.

This section reflects the fact that local authorities are subject to the controls and guidance exercised by departments of the central government. The nature of those controls, and the way they are administered, can affect the efficiency with which the authorities discharge their statutory responsibilities. This is a matter which concerns not only the authorities themselves and the Audit Commission, but Parliament, who decide what services are to be provided locally, and also the central government which provides most of the money to finance them. The Comptroller and Auditor General, on behalf of Parliament, is in the best position to examine and assess the relationships between Whitehall departments – the Department of the Environment, the Department of Education and Science, the Department of Health and Social Security and others – and the local authorities. He has direct access to the books and records of the central departments, and under Section 27 he is empowered to examine also the findings and supporting evidence of the Commission on these matters, and to report thereon. But he is precluded from examining the affairs of any individual local authority, since he is not their auditor; nor does Parliament have any right to examine directly the way the individual authorities manage their resources. Nevertheless, those reports of the Commission which are made publicly available may influence the views of Parliament on the use by local authorities of public funds, and on the central controls imposed from time to time.

The broad ambit of the local government audit service is thus nowadays similar to that of the National Audit Office, though the structure of local authority accounts and the system of reporting show important differences from those applicable to central government. Four points require specific mention:

(a) The right of members of the public, as local government electors, to inspect, question and object to the accounts and to inspect the auditor's report. Any objection is heard by the auditor taking the views of the local authority into account, and if he upholds it, he may take action as in (b) or (c) below. There are no such rights in respect of the accounts of central government.

(b) If it appears to the auditor that any item of account is contrary to law he may apply to the court for a declaration accordingly, except where the item is sanctioned by the Secretary of State. If the court makes the declaration it may order any person, normally a councillor or official of the local authority, responsible for incurring or authorizing the unlawful expenditure, to repay it in whole or in part. Where the amount involved exceeds £2000 and the person responsible is a councillor there is provision for the court to disqualify him from local government office.

(c) Where money has not been brought to account or a loss has been incurred through wilful misconduct the auditor must certify the amount as being due from that person and, subject to rights of appeal to the courts by the person(s) affected by the auditor's certificate, the amount then becomes recoverable. Disqualification from membership again ensues in the case of a wilful misconduct certificate where the sum involved is over £2000 and the person involved is a member.

(d) A local elector may make an objection on any matter about which he considers the auditor should make a report in the public interest. In these cases the final decision is taken by the auditor, as he is the only arbiter of whether or not such a report should be made.

The provisions as at (b) and (c) above replaced since 1972 the former powers of district auditors themselves to disallow items of expenditure, and to surcharge those responsible. It is thus a misconception to attribute now to the auditor himself the power to disallow expenditure or to exact repayment from those responsible. These powers are exercised only by the courts.

The Audit Commission has set out to combine strong 'top down' direction and assistance for its auditors with recognition of their full independence in forming their opinions and framing their reports. It has adopted a much more public style than the District Audit Service, which like the former Exchequer and Audit Department operated in a low key with the minimum of publicity. It has sought to involve the local authorities in its broad objectives but unlike the departments of central government they have no long tradition of acquiescing in value for money studies of their operations, still less in public reports thereon. Some authorities continue to regard such studies as an infringement of their right to determine policy and an attempt to secure cuts in the provision of public services. These arguments will no doubt continue, but it is a safe prediction that an extended 3Es audit of publicly accountable non-commercial bodies is here to stay.

Scotland

The District Audit Service described above operated in England and Wales but not in Scotland, where different arrangements for the external audit of local authorities had developed. Prior to the

Local Government (Scotland) Act 1973, which reorganized the pattern of Scottish local government, the local councils and associated public boards were audited individually by private accounting firms, appointed by the councils themselves. The 1973 Act provided for the creation of an independent Commission for Local Authority Accounts in Scotland, consisting of not more than twelve or less than nine members, appointed by the Secretary of State for Scotland after consultation with local authority associations and other appropriate organizations.

The Commission's main duties are:

(a) to secure the audit of the local authority accounts by appointing 'such officers and agents as they may determine to carry out the audits';
(b) to consider all audit reports and to investigate all matters raised therein;
(c) to make recommendations accordingly to the Secretary of State;
(d) to advise the Secretary of State on any matter relating to the accounting of local authorities which he may refer to them for advice;
(e) to appoint a Controller of Audit.

There is no provision, as in England and Wales, for the C&AG to be involved in certain matters concerning relationships between central and local government: this aspect of external audit had not become so prominent in Parliamentary discussion at that time.

The Controller of Audit, who is responsible for coordinating, guiding and supervising the conduct of the audit, has statutory status and specific functions. He is *required* to make to the Commission such reports as they may require with respect to local authority accounts. He *may* make a report to the Commission on any matters arising out of the accounts so that they may be considered by the local authority or brought to the attention of the public. And he is *required* to report to the Commission on various types of illegal or improper accounting, or loss caused by negligence or misconduct.

The other main feature of the Scottish local audit arrangements was the appointment by the Commission, on the advice of the Controller, of their own permanent audit staff who now share with private accounting firms responsibility for the individual audits, in the proportion of about 60% (private) to 40% (permanent staff). In this respect therefore the arrangements for local authority audit in Scotland are now similar to those in England and Wales, though they have developed by different routes. But the Controller of Audit has a more independent position in Scotland, standing, as it were, between the individual auditors and the Commission rather than acting simply as the Commission's chief executive. The difference finds expression in the form of the Scottish Commission's annual report, which is divided into a report by the Commission and a report by the Controller. All individual audit reports, whether they take the form of formal qualification, a report to members or a report to officers, have to be copied to the Controller who himself then decides whether to report to the Commission.

The professional scope of the audit in Scotland is similar to that more recently enunciated in the Local Government Finance Act 1982, covering matters of efficiency in addition to the formal financial audit. Professional standards have been promulgated and a system of audit reviews by the Controller's senior staff instituted to monitor adherence to them. But the Commission has drawn attention in successive annual reports to the inability of their auditors, through shortage of suitable staff resources, to carry out as much value for money work as they think necessary, and this remains a problem. It will be interesting to see the extent and manner of the cross fertilization of local authority audit methods and approaches north and south of the border.

EXAMINATION QUESTIONS

7.1 Describe briefly the role of the Comptroller and Auditor General as the external auditor of central government. What are his relations with Parliament?

7.2 What are the main similarities and differences between external audit in the public and private sector? What special experience would you expect private accounting firms to bring to the audit of public bodies?

7.3 What do you understand by value for money audit? Explain, with examples, what is meant by the examination of economy, efficiency and effectiveness in public sector operations.

7.4 What are the arguments for and against an external value for money audit of nationalized industries and other public corporations of a commercial type? Do these arguments apply equally to such government trading fund bodies as the Stationery Office and the Royal Mint?

7.5 In what way do local authorities differ from central government departments? How far do these differences support the view that external audit of local authorities should not come under the C&AG?

7.6 If you were appointed Controller of the Audit Commission for Local Authorities in England and Wales what would your plan of action be?

BIBLIOGRAPHY

Audit of central government and departmental bodies

Until recently very little has been published on the audit of central government. There is, however, an extensive range of reports by the C&AG and the PAC, covering several decades and many subjects. The National Audit Office (Audit House, Victoria Embankment, London EC4Y 0DS) would recommend particular reports, to illustrate general or particular interests.

During 1980-81 an extensive and authoritative discussion on the role of the C&AG and related topics, covering central government, local authorities and nationalized industries took place. This began with the issue of a Government green paper, *The Role of the Comptroller and Auditor General* (Cmnd. 7845) in March 1980 and led to a major report by the PAC in February 1981, *First Special Report from the Committee of Public Accounts, Session 1980-81*. The Government's response to this report was published in July 1981 (Cmnd. 8323). Among the papers submitted to the Committee and published as vol. III of their Report (Appendices to the minutes of evidence), attention is specially drawn to the following:

Memoranda by the C&AG: Appendices XIV, XVI, XXXIX, XLI, XLII.

Memoranda by the Chief Inspector of Local Government Audit: Appendices IX and XLVII.

Memoranda by the Consultative Committee of Accountancy Bodies: Appendices XX and XL.

Memorandum from the Chairman of the National Enterprise Board: Appendix XXI.

Memorandum from the Nationalised Industries Chairmen's Group: Appendix XXV.

Memorandum from the Advisory Committee on Local Government Audit: Appendix XXVI.

Memorandum by the Local Authority Associations: Appendix XXXVI.

Memorandum by the District Auditors' Society: Appendix XXXVII.

Letter from the Second Permanent Secretary, HM Treasury: Appendix XLVIII.

See also: Vilma Flegmann (1980) *Called to Account: The Public Accounts Committee of the House of Commons, Sessions 1956-66 to 1977-78*, Gower 1980. This book examines the role of the PAC in the Parliamentary control of expenditure, considers the way the committee works, its relations with the C&AG and his department, the Treasury and other government departments. It includes a summary of all PAC inquiries during the period examined. Mrs. Flegmann is an economist at the Bath University Centre for Fiscal Studies.

Audit of local government

Local Government Act 1972.
Local Government Finance Act 1982.
Audit Commission Code of Practice 1983 (HMSO).
Audit Commission Report and Accounts (annually – HMSO).
Audit Commission Studies 1983, e.g.
   The Impact on Local Authorities of the Grant Distribution System.
   Improving Vehicle Fleet Management in Local Government.
   Aspects of Non-Teaching Costs in Secondary Schools.
Commission for Local Authority Accounts in Scotland: annual reports.

8

An overview

This book is neither a primer on bookkeeping for the public sector nor a detailed treatise containing all the statutory and other professional requirements expected of financial officers in any particular branch of the public sector. The former is dealt with in other books with a different kind of purpose, the latter is beyond the capability of any single book. The book is intended rather to be a guide and summary of the accounting and financial practices and issues to be found within the public sector and was written because of the authors' wish to make a contribution towards greater understanding of these practices. It is also intended to be a contribution and stimulus towards improvement in public sector financial management and control, and towards a greater interchange of ideas and skills, not only among current practitioners but also the students who will be their heirs. It will hopefully also be of use for those academics who increasingly find that they need to know more about the public sector's accounting practices in their teaching and in their personal research.

The non-commercial part of the public sector used to be an island (indeed almost a group of separate islands) of distinctive accounting and financial practice, somewhat isolated from the rest of the profession. That has been changing. But there remains a pressing need for the development of more effective bridges between the public and private sectors. Both sectors have much to learn from each other in this field. Certainly neither has as yet attained the full contribution to financial reporting envisaged in 1975 by the Accounting Standards Committee in *The Corporate Report*. Bridge building could take place as a result of cooperation among professional institutes in supporting the work of the Accounting Standards Committee to develop a programme of accounting standards of the widest general applicability within all sectors of the economy. It could also come about through the encouragement of job mobility, so that accounting, finance and audit specialists seeking experience and promotion move freely between the public and private sectors. An illustration of the benefits is that many of the leading Treasurers currently working in the NHS are people who entered it from local authorities, nationalized industries or the private sector as a result of the additional professional posts created by the 1974 reorganization.

This final chapter steps aside a little from the discussion of financial practice in the individual branches of the public sector discussed in earlier chapters, and seeks to provide a degree of overview and to deal with matters of general relevance.

8.1 ACCOUNTING PRINCIPLES AND PRACTICES

The private sector has relatively homogenous objectives and a common statutory framework of accountability. Thus there can be generally accepted accounting principles which cover most aspects of individual organizations' accounts, however great their variety. But in the four main branches of the public sector considered in this book – central government, local authorities, nationalized industries and the NHS – there are large variations in the style and nature of external reports and in the accounting concepts that underpin them. These mirror the tremendous diversity of structures, financial arrangements and operational objectives. The nationalized industries are undoubtedly a 'special' part of the public sector since, although they are constituted under separate statutes and with distinctive features reflecting public policy, they can operate for the most part as if they were commercial organizations and can more easily fit the model of conforming to best commercial accounting practice. In the rest of the public sector, however, there is no comparable set of standards.

Taking the sectors in turn, central government presents a very different picture when dealing with external or internal reporting. In external reporting, the large majority of activities and expenditure are not subject to the conventional accounting principles and practices prescribed by the accountancy profession. The number (and influences) of professionally qualified accountants within central government is still relatively small, despite recent initiatives to recruit more. The formal financial accounts of central government have been developed within the civil service over 100 years or more to meet the needs of Ministers and permanent secretaries, to satisfy themselves and Parliament that public money was spent as intended, and with probity. The system therefore has an underlying logic, as Chapter 2 showed, but was not originally devised to ease the analysis of operational performance for professional or economic assessments, or for readily comprehensible presentation to a wider public. For certain parts of central government matters have been 'clarified' by separating the finances of self-contained parts of central government's operations of a quasi-commercial character into trading funds. These are then accounted for in a commercial format. For the bulk of the appropriation accounts, however, considerable further improvements could still be made in their structure and degree of clarity, as well as in their relationship with other central government reports, without challenging their essential framework.

Internally, however, different considerations and aims apply. It is accepted that the formal annual accounts should, as far as practicable, link with departmental organization and responsibilities. But civil servants as line managers cannot work successfully without a properly devised system of management accounting and control which provides information on which decisions can be taken in far more detail than is available in the annual accounts. The Financial Management Initiative is in part directed towards this and there is certainly scope here for the contribution of professional accountants to improvements in the existing systems.

In the NHS, as previously indicated, there is a use of accounting principles and practices which represents a position somewhere between central government's strong concern for cash accounting and control and the trend of the accounting profession to view accounting data as background information from which to distil more concise and analytical forms of reporting. The NHS, although financed on a cashflow basis, does use accrual principles in its income and expenditure reporting, albeit as yet without fixed asset valuation and full balance sheet reporting, and therefore without depreciation accounting. In the NHS and other central government organizations where devolved management is allowed, where managerial objectives are better served by departure from simple expenditure accounting and where professional accounting leadership of their finance functions is encouraged, there may well be steady pressure for the adoption of accounting principles and practices broadly consistent with the rest of the accountancy profession.

There has certainly been a great deal of effort over many years to develop an adequate framework for local authority accounts, and an interesting feature of recent years is how, in relevant parts of local authorities' activities, there have been moves to adopt accounting standards which were designed for commercial organizations. The differences in terminology and presentation between local authority and company accounts have tended to mask underlying similarities. Of course, there are differences in the area of capital accounting, though these are being reduced, not least because of the experience that local authorities have gained from applying commercial accounting principles to their Direct Labour Organizaitons (DLOs). The importance of the DLO legislation and of improved annual reports has clearly been a factor in stimulating improvements in local authority accounting. But above all it has been the active programme of research and analysis by CIPFA and its Accounting Panel that has enabled so much development to take place. The local authority experience has clearly indicated that, where there is a sound underlying basis, substantial progress can be made towards the public sector using accounting principles and standards which are the normal currency of private sector accountants and commercial organizations.

Diversity in accounting practices can cause considerable problems in the cases where privatization of some services or the outright sale of public sector assets are being considered. Privatization is a policy issue in which there may sometimes be trade-offs between effectiveness and politics. However these trade-offs are decided, professional accountants and their advisers have the duty to try as best they can to assess the costs and performance of public services fairly, so that the fullest financial and economic information is available for decision-makers. For example, the public should not lose financially through public assets being sold off at less than their economic value. Nor should services be contracted out at rates that look attractive only because proper and realistic opportunity-cost analyses have not been carried out and reported.

Given that the search for alternatives is an essential element of the search for value for money, the existence of alternative forms of service provision such as contracting-out should in principle provide a useful benchmark against which to measure services as currently provided. One problem facing those advising on such alternatives is how far it is possible to evaluate the alternatives on strictly comparable terms. There is also the problem that the costs and benefits can rarely be reduced to purely financial terms. Issues such as the quality of services provided and the degree of effective control available to the public authority also have to be taken into account.

8.2 ACCOUNTING FOR CAPITAL

The method of funding and accounting for capital expenditure is possibly the most prominent example of divergence of practice between the non-commercial public sector and the private sector.

To take the NHS as an example, once it has received its capital allocation and invested this (mainly in bricks and mortar) it is treated as a 'sunk cost' in economic terms or in effect as a 100% first year write-off in accounting terms. No permanent fixed asset accounts are created. No depreciation is calculated, deducted or reported. No current cost accounting or other inflation adjustments to capital value are calculated. Indeed no conventional balance sheet is prepared in which the foregoing accounting measurements could be disclosed.

It can be argued that in practice this departure from 'normal' accounting conventions does not matter, since the NHS does not trade or declare profits, and a 'return' on its capital assets cannot be calculated anyway. Moreover, each NHS region has its own planning methods for assessing the state of the capital stock of each of its health districts as a basis for determining relative degrees of need and priority in the allocation of major capital funds. And if there are proposals to sell off surplus land or buildings, accounting book values are largely irrelevant to the decision. It is the balance between the value-in-use to the health authority on the one hand, and the negotiable market value to private buyers on the other which provides the financial guidance on whether or not the assets should be sold.

The above considerations demonstrate that there is no clear case that health authorities need conventional fixed asset and depreciation accounting as a general principle or standard, or specifically to guide decisions either on capital outlays on buildings or on the disposal of major assets. But the case is not so clear as regards the lack of information on the original costs, depreciation charges, and current values of plant, equipment, fittings and furnishings in use in the NHS. Without such information it is unlikely that planned maintenance and replacement policies will be optimal. Moreover the lack of depreciation costs in the accounts and in the internal budgets and costings of the NHS may give managers a misleading view of the true relative costs of different activities. This could result in some internal misallocation of resources. This is not, of course, to suggest that financial cost-effectiveness is the only basis on which health authorities or other public bodies will determine issues concerning privatization or affecting the allocation of major resources. Nevertheless, as discussed in detail in Chapter 6, NHS treasurers are increasingly arguing for the adoption of capital asset accounting methods which may include depreciation charges for plant and equipment and notional lease charges for land and buildings.

There are methods other than depreciation accounting, for charging capital costs into the annual accounts and into the budgets and accounts of individual departments or services within the management accounting arrangements of the organization. Local authorities do not use depreciation accounting for most of their fixed assets. Instead, they use loan-charge accounting. By this method the accounts typically are charged annually with an amount that comprises the combined aggregate cost of the interest paid and the capital repayment in servicing the borrowed capital used for the major capital investments of the authority. The arrangements may be technically compared to a conventional mortgage. In the early years the bulk of the charges are needed to meet the interest, and the small residue is applied to reduce the principal. As the years progress and the principal gradually falls, so the proportion of interest falls and the proportion of capital repayments rises. Although not a depreciation charge related to the reducing value of assets in use, or processed through the same accounts, the actual effect of the loan charges on service accounts is essentially the same as if annuity-basis depreciation plus interest on unrecovered capital was charged to operational accounts in a commercial-type accounting system.

Of course, in practice annuity-basis depreciation is rarely charged to operational accounts in commercial organizations. Probably the main reason is that depreciation calculated on this basis, with its relatively low depreciation charges in the early years of asset use, does not fairly reflect the pace of exhaustion of the physical or 'market' capacity of the asset. Nor is it sufficiently prudent or conservative in writing off that part of the original cost of an asset which is exposed to risk during its working life. But in the context of 'negligible risk' in which most public service organizations operate, the loan-charge method is probably a reasonable method of allocating capital charges which have to be met year by year over known periods from annual income. Such calculations will help to indicate the 'full cost' of providing services such as education but it will not provide the basis for pricing policy (council house rents for example).

8.3 EXTERNAL REPORTING

Improving the basis of accounting is one element in improving public sector external financial reporting, but not the only one. Within the public sector there have been criticisms both of the form and content of external reports and also of the systems by which they are generated and used. This topic runs deep into the whole question of accountability in the public sector.

Accountability is of course the basis on which public sector external reports are produced. Yet there are a number of uncertainties and ambiguities after the need for accountability has been established. For example external reports are certainly used as public relations documents throughout the public sector. This is entirely understandable bearing in mind that public sector bodies are bound to be involved in lobbying for resources and for policies, and that an external financial report is a useful vehicle for such activity. But there must then be an implicit conflict between the idea that a document is designed to give an account of stewardship of public funds and the idea that it is a vehicle for political pressure. This does not mean that there is cheating on the figures themselves, but it is likely that the dual roles will give rise to a conflict about the way the facts are presented and interpreted. Such a conflict is not peculiar to the public sector – it is quite usual in the private sector to have the Chairman explaining in the same sentence of an Annual Report that although the organization has done very well indeed and the shareholders can feel confident in the management, there will not be enough for wage rises.

Public sector external reports are also often used for reference purposes, as a means of communicating to staff and, in the case of central government some of the documents are even used as the basis of internal control. But there is a problem throughout the public sector in deciding who exactly the potential readers are and what they require. The constitutional position of elected bodies is usually clear enough, but the fact is that many elected members of such bodies, including many Members of Parliament, are not financially trained. A further conflict therefore often arises in external reporting about the level at which external reports should be pitched. On the one hand there are some elected representatives who are highly trained financially and expert in the field. On the other there are those (usually the majority) who are interested laymen and women without financial knowledge. The problem of addressing both audiences is solved in some cases by providing more than one document, in others by providing information aimed at different types of reader in the same document. But often both sets of readers are left unsatisfied because the same document is aimed at the wrong level for each audience. A further difficulty in resolving this problem is that there is usually no easy way of finding what users want and how their information needs can best be met.

Taking various parts of the public sector in turn, there are those who have said that local government suffers from a surfeit of accountability as explained in detail in earlier chapters. Certainly the multiplicity of documents provides a benchmark against which other parts of the public sector can be compared. First there are the **Financial Accounts**, which are more often now prepared in line with generally accepted accounting principles and standards. Then there is the mandatory, increasingly comprehensible and in some cases first-class **Annual Report**, which includes performance indicators. Then there is the **Ratepayers Leaflet**, published before the financial year, which gives key aspects of the budget. During the course of the year, reports on the progress of local authority spending are typically presented in open committee. Finally, before the audit is completed, 'interested persons' may inspect the detailed accounts and put questions to the auditor.

The National Health Service is organizationally similar in one main respect to local authorities in that it has a large number of diverse units, each with a specific controlling body (the health authority) which has a measure of discretion as to how its allocated resources for capital and current expenditure are to be applied. There are also major differences. The NHS is operationally unified and responsible to the Secretary of State, and unlike local authorities it has no significant autonomous source of finance. But there are sufficient similarities to ask whether there is a practical reason (other than administrative effort) why each health authority should not be required to publish comprehensible financial accounts and an Annual Report of the kind that a growing number of authorities already produce voluntarily. Further, health authorities are not dissimilar from local authorities in open reporting during the year. But if local authorities have to open their accounts to inspection and allow questions of the auditor, there are those who have said that these obligations are equally valid for the health service. According to this argument, the fact that the health authorities are locally organized and managed might make them well suited to local monitoring.

The position of central government ought to be much simpler, since Parliament is the main 'customer' for the financial information, with the Press, pressure groups and other interested parties interpreting the information for the general public. Yet although the sheer volume of information is impressive, the users have made it clear that they do not feel well served and the reports need to be much clearer to achieve the objectives of financial reporting. Thus, while the voluminous detailed estimates and appropriation accounts meet existing constitutional needs, they have almost no audience. Their whole role needs to be examined in the context of the need to make general improvements in the financial documents provided to Parliament. Such improvements have already taken place in some documents, such as the Public Expenditure White Papers. But even this document remains hard to follow for the non-expert. A more logical way to present information of this kind might be through annual reports by all government departments. These could be the basis of the examination of expenditure proposals by Parliamentary Select Committees and could contain information on expenditure plans and actuals, as well as on performance. This could be provided in a readable and interesting way, with no loss of accuracy but a great gain in comprehensibility and therefore public appeal.

Finally the position of the nationalized industries is probably the simplest of all the public sector bodies. This is because both the industries and the government have been keen for many years to try and ensure that the industries are as close as possible to private sector practice. Their annual reports are generally of high quality by the standards of either the public or the private sectors and in most cases much more informative. Yet they too suffer from the ambiguities discussed at the beginning of this section and many of the problems in external reporting stem from the difficulty of reconciling the views of those who believe that they are private sector companies which happen to be publicly owned, with those who believe that they are in the public sector for a purpose related to national priorities.

8.4 BUDGETARY CONTROL

Budgetary control within the nationalized industries is essentially similar to private industry although the process is made more difficult, the industries have argued on numerous occasions, by regular and usually unwelcome interventions by central government. Indeed many of the issues in the field of budgetary control are common to all types of organization – decisions about priorities, how much flexibility should be allowed, how control should be organized and so on.

By contrast, in the non-commercial public sector, many of the senior professionals believe very strongly that the important services it provides are under-supplied with resources in relation to public need and are not relevant for scrutiny by normal criteria of performance assessment. In a commercial organization a part of that organization might be given a specific workload to complete and be expected to complete it at minimum cost. This can also apply in the provision of the more routine of public services, but in other cases, including the NHS, the idea of providing anything less than the best possible level of service is unattractive. It is presumed that cost minimization conflicts with this goal. But is is more difficult to monitor and control the best possible level of services for given expenditures than it is to monitor and control the minimization of cost for the completion of an assigned volume of tasks. There is also the related problem that some public services, notably local and health authorities, are dominated by the professional rather than by the managerial ethos, with the presumption that only peer-review by members of the same profession provides an appropriate and acceptable evaluation of performance. These attitudes were fostered during a long period of sustained growth in the public service in the post-war period. Currently, with the curtailment of growth in public services, indeed with some absolute reductions, there is some evidence not only of acceptance that expenditure must be contained, but also that efficiency must be improved to maintain existing services, and to provide resources to develop new services of high priority. Thus the problem for the budgetary control process is not so much that of containing expenditure within prescribed limits, but of finding activities of low benefit relative to cost on which savings can be made and diverted to activities with high benefit relative to cost. All this involves difficult judgements and finance staff on their own clearly cannot achieve it. Rather their task is to help create a climate of opinion favouring efficiency and the continuing attempt to maximize the benefit achieved from a given input of resources. They must also supply relevant and timely information on costs and resource uses to assist the identification of opportunities for efficiency improvements, and for savings. Finally, it may be necessary to build incentives into the system, so that managers who take action to improve efficiency or make savings can obtain recognition or indeed the opportunity to use some part of the savings they have achieved on other activities under their control. This may require a change of attitude all round, with finance staff pressing for close personal interaction with other managers and professions to help maximize their contribution to the organization.

8.5 NON-FINANCIAL PERFORMANCE

The difficulty of establishing a 'bottom line' (a euphemism for profit) for public sector bodies is acknowledged to be one of the major problems in establishing how well an organization has performed. Measuring the resoruces put into an organization has always seemed easier than measuring how effectively those resources have been used. One of the areas to which attention has been increasingly drawn across the whole of the public sector has been the provision of non-financial performance indicators to try to give indications about how well an organization has performed, and whether the trends are going the right way. For nationalized industries, these measures have been part of the control framework since 1978. For local authorities and health authorities, a mass of indicators is now available to enable comparisons to be made from one area of the country to another. In the case of central government, performance indicators now have such a high status that Treasury Ministers have taken pains to point out how many of them are available in the main government economic documents.

These indicators are undoubtedly a useful addition to what has been available hitherto. But they need to be used with some caution. There is a tendency, for example, to compile so many indicators that it becomes impossible to use what is available. There is also the danger that the indicators are not an accurate reflection of what they are supposed to measure. Numbers of patients treated per day is not necessarily a good indication of the quality of health care any more than a reduction in the number of social workers per head of population is an indication of improved productivity. And the measures need to be interpreted with great care. A trend shown by a particular indicator need not be good or bad in itself and has to be taken in context. Trade-offs in particular need to be taken into account when interpreting the data. Thus it may be desirable to increase productivity, but if this is at the expense of quality, the two need to be considered together to make sure that the trade-offs have been properly worked out.

8.6 AUDIT

It may be that there is less difference between the public and private sectors in the financial audit function than there is in respect of the accounting and financial control functions. Many non-commercial public sector bodies including the universities, an increasing proportion of local authorities and several health authorities are now audited by private sector firms.

The professional skills and techniques of the auditor of financial statements and accounts are broadly similar and transferable between the public and private sectors, and between profit-making and non-profit organizations. But there are also important differences. For profit-making organizations the dominant objectives of the audit must be to validate the fairness of the profit figure, and the truth and fairness of the valuations in the balance sheet. This assists owners and lenders, as well as their professional advisers, to assess the value, prospects and riskiness of their debt or investment. But the non-trading parts of the public sector do not use their assets to produce goods or services for sale, and do not therefore generate profits from their activities. Instead, typically, they expend all their allocated funds on providing services. It is a reasonable concern of Parliament and the public that public expenditure should be made only for duly authorized purposes and should conform to high standards of probity. It follows that public audit must pay careful attention to those requirements.

Beyond this, however, there is growing parliamentary and public concern to make the best use of resources which are scarce in relation to needs by improving efficiency or productivity. In recent years this has provided increased emphasis on the value for money dimension of public sector auditing. Private sector audits do not include this value for money dimension since a simpler criterion of success in meeting commercial objectives is readily available and the statutory framework within which private sector audit is conducted has, accordingly, limited responsibilities. Private sector auditing firms normally concentrate their evaluations of efficiency in their management consultancy departments, which operate not as auditors but at the invitation of clients. But where the firms are appointed as auditors to public authorities, they are having to extend their activities into the value for money field as an integral part of the audit operation.

Two matters of controversy are, firstly, how far the public sector audit services should be integrated, and how far led or coordinated by the National Audit Office, and secondly, to what extent private sector auditors should be allowed to expand their share of the conduct of external audits of public sector organizations. Both these issues have strong political undertones.

8.7 THE ROLE OF ACCOUNTANTS IN THE PUBLIC SECTOR

Within all branches of the public sector apart from central government, there is a clearly identifiable finance function embracing both accounting and financial advice, with senior staffing dominated by qualified accountants. The Civil Service is quite different since there are few professional accountants in senior finance posts in government departments. Indeed the Treasury employs fewer professionally qualified accountants than the finance department of a typical local authority. This might not be a matter for comment if the Treasury performed only its pivotal roles in public finance and macro-economic planning. But it also performs a role in relation to the internal control of central government's own expenditure, as well as public expenditure planning in relation to the economy. It also has responsibility for the form and content of the Government's own external and internal financial reports.

The problem of inadequate accountancy expertise in central government was addressed as long ago as 1968 by the Fulton Committee. Although the post of Accounting Advisor to the Government has been created since then and the number of secondments from commercial firms has increased considerably, there is less contribution to the decision-making process at the highest level of administration than the nature and complexity of the problems of present-day government indicates is desirable. While in part this may be due to the difficulties of attracting suitable candidates, there is also the difficulty of the sheer inertia of the system to overcome in appreciating what accountants have to offer to administrators.

There is, nevertheless, much which can be done to enhance the quality and effectiveness of the role of accounting and finance professionals in the operational branches of the public services as a whole. While the role of financial specialists is broadly recognized, the actual contribution that accounting and finance skills can make is as yet not fully so. This may in part be due to inadequate staffing and/or grading levels for trained accountants. But it may also be because the public sector has too often failed to offer the high-quality training, timely career recognition and participation in challenging tasks of policy formulation that has been available in many parts of the private sector.

The faults may not always lie with the employers, however. Perhaps too many public sector accountants have been content for too long to concentrate on carrying out their statutory or formal activities, without developing to the full the additional services they could provide, or by ensuring that they and their staff broaden their knowledge and understanding of their organizations by active involvement with staff in the operational departments. It is only through such deep involvement that accountants can understand the full range of information needs of managers and of governing authorities. Only then can they most effectively deploy their functional and analytical skills.

EXAMINATION QUESTIONS

Note: In preparing answers to these questions it may be found helpful to refer back to earlier chapters and the publications included in their bibliographies.

8.1 Are there any reasons of substance for concern at the present degree of difference in the detailed practices of accounting and external reporting followed in the commercial sector as compared to the non-commercial public sector? Illustrate your arguments

8.2 Study the SSAPs published by the Accounting Standards Committee and explain, with reasons, why you think each Accounting Standard is, or is not, relevant to one branch of the Public Sector with which you are familiar.

8.3 One argument for depreciation accounting is that it allows financial reports to disclose how far an organization has maintained intact its net investment in capital resources (after CCA or other appropriate adjustment for change in the purchasing power of money). Are there good reasons why this argument is less relevant to local authorities or the NHS than it is to the nationalized industries and water authorities which do compute and report depreciation? Explore this and explain your viewpoint fully.

8.4 Do the external reporting practices of other branches of the public sector, or indeed of the private sector, suggest to you any improvements that could be made to the external reporting practices of local authorities? Support suggestions with a reasoned case.

8.5 What differences would you expect to find between the budget-setting and budgetary-control practices of a typical nationalized industry as compared to a health authority? Suggest likely causes and the degree of justification for the differences identified.

8.6 For a branch of the public sector with which you are familiar, specify, explain and justify any additions to the current roles and activities of finance staff that you think would improve the quality of management and/or accountability in the organization concerned.

8.7 'Accountability is unthinkable without good accounting.' Discuss.

Abbreviations

See Glossaries for definitions where relevant

ACC	Association of County Councils
ADC	Association of District Councils
ALA	Association of London Authorities
AMA	Association of Metropolitan Authorities
ASC	Accounting Standards Committee
C&AG	Comptroller and Auditor General
CAA	Civil Aviation Authority
CASPE	Clinical Accountability, Service Planning and Evaluation
CCA	Current Cost Accounting
CCLGF	Consultative Council on Local Government Finance
CEC	Central Establishment Charges
CIPFA	Chartered Institute of Public Finance and Accountancy
CLF	Consolidated Loans Fund
COSLA	Confederation of Scottish Local Authorities
DGH	District General Hospital
DHA	District Health Authority
DLO	Direct Labour Organization
DOE	Department of the Environment
EFL	External Financing Limit
E&AD	Exchequer and Audit Department
FIS	Financial Information Service
FMI	Financial Management Initiative
FSBR	Financial Statement and Budget Report
GAS	Government Accounting Service
GDP	Gross Domestic Product
GLC	Greater London Council
GRE	Grant Related Expenditure
GREA	Grant Related Expenditure Assessment
GRF	General Rate Fund
GRP	Grant Related Poundage
HIP	Housing Investment Programme

HRA	Housing Revenue Account
ICAEW	Institute of Chartered Accountants in England and Wales
IMTA	Institute of Municipal Treasurers and Accountants
INLOGOV	Institute of Local Government Studies (University of Birmingham)
LAMSAC	Local Authorities Management Services and Computer Committee
LBC	London Borough Council
MINIS	Management Information for Ministers
MMC	Monopolies and Mergers Commission
MPO	Management and Personnel Office
NAO	National Audit Office
NICG	Nationalized Industries Chairmen's Group
OSG	Official Steering Group
PAC	Public Accounts Committee
PDC	Public Dividend Capital
PESC	Public Expenditure Survey Committee
PPBS	Planning, Programming, Budgeting Systems
PRP	Penny Rate Product
PSBR	Public Sector Borrowing Requirement
PWLB	Public Works Loan Board
RAWP	Resource Allocation Working Party
RCCD	Revenue Consequences of Clinical Developments
RCCS	Revenue Consequences of Capital Schemes
RCCO	Revenue Contribution to Capital Outlay
RCMA	Revenue Consequences of Medical Appointments
RHA	Regional Health Authority
RRR	Required Rate of Return
RSG	Rate Support Grant
RV	Rateable Value
SCNI	Select Committee on Nationalized Industries
SCT	Society of County Treasurers
SIFT	Service Increment for Teaching
SMR	Standard Mortality Ratio
SOLACE	Society of Local Authority Chief Executives
SSAP	Statement of Standard Accounting Practice
SSRC	Social Science Research Council
TPP	Transportation Policy and Programme
TSG	Transport Supplementary Grant
ZBB	Zero Base Budgeting

Index